Smaragdus of Saint-Mihiel
The Crown of Monks

CISTERCIAN STUDIES SERIES NUMBER TWO HUNDRED FORTY-FIVE

Smaragdus of Saint-Mihiel

The Crown of Monks

Diadema monachorum

Introduced and
Translated
by
David Barry, OSB

α

Cistercian Publications
www.cistercianpublications.org

LITURGICAL PRESS
Collegeville, Minnesota
www.litpress.org

A Cistercian Publications title published by Liturgical Press

Cistercian Publications
Editorial Offices
Abbey of Gethsemani
3642 Monks Road
Trappist, Kentucky 40051
www.cistercianpublications.org

Translated from Smaragdi Abbatis, *Diadema Monachorum*; Smaragdi, *Opera Omnia,* PL 102, ed. J.-P. Migne (Petit-Montrouge: Migne, 1851), colls. 593–690.

1   2   3   4   5   6   7   8   9

Library of Congress Cataloging-in-Publication Data

Smaragdus, Abbot of St. Mihiel, fl. 809–819.
    [Diadema monachorum. English]
    The crown of monks / Smaragdus of Saint-Mihiel ; introduced and translated by David Barry, OSB.
        pages cm. — (Cistercian studies series ; NUMBER 245)
    Includes bibliographical references.
    ISBN 978-0-87907-245-2
    1. Monastic and religious life—Early works to 1800.   2. Benedict, Saint, Abbot of Monte Cassino. Regula.   I. Barry, David, OSB, translator. II. Title.

BX2435.S5713   2013
248.8'942—dc23   2012046257

Dedication

Revera Deum quaerentibus
Nihil amori Christi praeponentibus
Vitam aeternam omni concupiscentia spiritali desiderantibus
Hoc opusculum interpres dedicat.

Contents

Introduction to Smaragdus's Crown of Monks

Through his writing, and perhaps especially through his most widely read book of advice to monastics—the *Crown of Monks*, presented here in English translation—Smaragdus remained influential through several centuries following his death. Smaragdus (born ca. 760, died ca. 830) became Abbot of Saint-Mihiel in the early ninth century and was a monk and abbot of considerable standing in the church of his time. A supporter of Charlemagne and of his son and successor Louis the Pious, Smaragdus was active in the reform of the church during their short-lived empire. He even wrote a *speculum* or *fürstenspiegel*, a "mirror for princes" known as the *Via regia*, for Louis when he was still ruling in Aquitaine. Smaragdus collaborated with Saint Benedict of Aniane in the reform of monastic life in the Carolingian empire, taking part in the Council of Aachen (816–817) and drawing heavily from Benedict's hugely important *Concordia regularum*[1] in writing his own *magnum opus*, his *Expositio in regulam S. Benedicti*[2] (*Commentary on the Rule of Saint Benedict*), to help monasteries and monks facing their new situation of being required to base their monastic observance solely on the Rule of Benedict. Readers of this book may know of Smaragdus's *Commentary on the Rule of Saint Benedict*, published in 2007 in the

---

[1] PL 103:713–1380.

[2] PL 102:689–932; *Smaragdi Abbatis Expositio in Regulam S. Benedicti*, ed. Alfredus Spannagel and Pius Engelbert, Corpus Consuetudinum Monasticarum 8 (Siegburg: Verlag Franz Schmitt, 1974).

same Cistercian Studies Series as this work.[3] Further details about
the life and influence of Smaragdus can be found in the three in-
troductory essays contained in that volume. But, like Benedict, it is
perhaps through his writings that we find Smaragdus most surely.

Smaragdus's *Diadema monachorum* (*Crown of Monks*) preceded his
commentary and, together, they established him as one of the most
significant interpreters of Benedict in his day. *Diadema* made him a
key voice on the spiritual and ascetical practices of monastic life for
succeeding generations. The translation here is made from the Migne
text in PL 102. A prominent European publisher of critical editions
of patristic and medieval writings advertised a forthcoming critical
edition of the *Diadema* in the late 1980s, but the advertisement was
discontinued in the 1990s, and the edition did not reappear.

Previous scholarship on Smaragdus manuscripts also indicates
his importance to monastic thought. The late Dom Willibrord Witters, monk of the Abbey of La Pierre-qui-Vire in France, made a
detailed study of the diffusion of Smaragdus's writings in the Middle
Ages, bringing the research in this area up to the mid-1970s. At that
stage the total of Smaragdus manuscripts each containing one of his
works was some two hundred fourteen, with another forty-three
listed in medieval library catalogues. Witters gave the number of
manuscripts and catalogue listings for each of Smaragdus's works
century by century and showed how the larger numbers of both
coincided with reform movements in monastic life (Benedictines and
Cistercians) and religious life (Premonstratensians and Augustinians)
that occurred in the ninth-to-tenth, twelfth, and fifteenth centuries,
with fifty-three, forty-five, and thirty-three manuscripts, respectively.
The most copied of the works was the *Diadema monachorum*, which
scored one hundred fourteen manuscripts and eighteen listings in
library catalogues. The provenance and date of thirty-three of these
manuscripts was not ascertained at the time of Witters' article. The
curve of the remainder is not quite the inverse of that of the total-
ity of the manuscripts: ninth–tenth centuries (6), eleventh century

---

[3] Smaragdus of Saint-Mihiel, *Commentary on the Rule of Saint Benedict*, trans.
David Barry, CS 212 (Kalamazoo, MI: Cistercian, 2007).

(12), twelfth century (44, and 10 listings in catalogs), and fifteenth century (16). Witters also mentions something that deserves to be more widely known, at least in the world aware of the significance of manuscript tradition. Up to the time of his article, there was only one known case of a manuscript containing several of Smaragdus's works, which is known as *Vaticanus Reginensis lat.* 190. It belonged to the great French Jesuit patrologist Dénis Pétau (1583–1652), and then to Queen Christine of Sweden (1626–1689), from whom apparently it passed into the Vatican Library. It was used by Dom Luc d'Achery for his edition of the *Via regia,* published in Paris in a collection of ancient writers in 1661 and reproduced in Migne's PL 102; *Reginensis lat.* 190 was also used by Lucas Holste for the *editio princeps,* published in 1662, of Smaragdus's *De processione spiritus sancti.* This very important manuscript went missing from the Vatican in 1797. One wonders in what collection it lies buried, if still extant, waiting to be rediscovered—and perhaps by a researcher in the twenty-first century.[4]

THE *DIADEMA MONACHORUM* AND *FLORILEGIA*

The *Diadema monachorum* is the first of Smaragdus's two extant works directed specifically to monks. He intended it as a daily resource for monastic communities. In the prologue to the *Diadema,* Smaragdus writes that it was already customary in monasteries observing the Rule of Benedict to have a morning community gathering (chapter) at which the Rule was read. And it was also customary to have an evening chapter, as laid down in the Rule, for the time between the evening meal and Compline, or on fast days between Vespers and Compline. Smaragdus suggests that *his* book, conveniently divided into one hundred chapters, be read at this evening chapter as meeting the requirements spelled out by Benedict for reading at this time (see RB 42).

---

[4] Willibord Witters, "Smaragde au moyen age: La diffusion de ses écrits d'après la tradition manuscrite," *Etudes Ligériennes d'histoire et d'archéologie médiévale* (1975): 361–76. Dom Willibrord gave a photocopy of the article to the writer when the latter visited La Pierre-qui-Vire in 1988.

The prologue also clearly states Smaragdus's aim and method. He sought to provide reading material for well-established monks such that will arouse them "to a keener and loftier yearning for the heavenly country," and for weak monks, "to strengthen and instill fear . . . leading them to amendment and a life more in keeping with the Rule" (of Saint Benedict). His method is to cull that material (he speaks of it poetically as gathering flowers from their garden) from the conferences and lives of the (Desert) Fathers and from the writings of various doctors. Each of these sources draws heavily on the Scriptures.

The practice of gathering selected excerpts from one or more writers relating to one or more topics had become, by Smaragdus's time, its own literary genre known as *florilegium*. It seems to be almost as ancient as writing itself, with the collections being called anything from an *alphabetum* to a *viridarium*.[5] Writers on the subject of *florilegia* distinguish three main types: profane, religious, and mixed. Of the religious type in Christian literature, there are *florilegia* that are Biblical, patristic, and Biblical-patristic, and one of the subtypes is the monastic *florilegium*, the *Crown of Monks* being one of the best examples in the Latin series. Readers who need to know more about *florilegia* should refer to helpful work by H. M. Rochais.[6]

SMARAGDUS'S SOURCES: CHURCH DOCTORS AND FATHERS

Smaragdus's two main individual authorities are Saint Gregory the Great (540–604) and Saint Isidore of Seville (ca. 560–636). He draws on each of them more often than any other source. He quotes most often from Gregory's *Moralia in Job* and his *Regula pastoralis* and also refers frequently to the *Homilies on Ezechiel, Homilies on the*

---

[5] Rochais' article in the DS (see n. 6 below) gives a short list of thirty-eight different terms by which *florilegia* were designated in the catalogs; the *New Catholic Encyclopedia* (NCE) article expands the list to sixty-four (see n. 6).

[6] Henri M. Rochais, "Florilèges spirituels latins," *Dictionnaire de spiritualité* 5:435–60. Henri M. Rochais, "Florilegia," *New Catholic Encyclopedia* 5, 2nd ed. (Washington, DC: Catholic University of America, 2003), 780–82. This last article is almost identical with the same writer's similarly titled article in the first edition of the NCE from 1967.

Gospels, and *Dialogues II*. Gregory wrote the basic text of the *Moralia* while acting as the Roman Church's *apocrisiarius* in Constantinople (579–85/86), but he did not complete editing it for publication until sometime after 596, when he was fully occupied in his work as Bishop of Rome. The *Moralia* was sent first to bishops in Spain. The dedicatory letter placed at the beginning is addressed to Saint Leander, Bishop of Seville, Isidore's brother and predecessor in that see. Leander was one of the ecclesiastics who, while visiting Constantinople, pressed Gregory to undertake the work in the first place. The other four works of Gregory that feature in the *Crown of Monks* date from Gregory's time as Pope (590–604). In the *Regula pastoralis* 2.6, Gregory specifically refers to the *Moralia* more than once as a place where he has already mentioned something he says again in the *Regula pastoralis*. In fact, this turns out to be a feature of the *Regula pastoralis*—that Gregory not infrequently quotes his earlier work.

For the most part, Gregory's writings reached Smaragdus by way of another Spanish churchman who belongs to the end of Isidore's century, one Taio, Bishop of Zaragoza (+ ca. 683). This meditation becomes obvious when the references to Taio's *florilegium*, five books of *Sententiae*, are listed. In most instances, Smaragdus in any one chapter quotes from one chapter in Taio, but Taio's quotations are taken from the range of Gregory's works referred to earlier. There are only a few quotations from Gregory in Smaragdus that do not appear in Taio.

The second main authority whom Smaragdus quotes is Saint Isidore of Seville, who in 600 succeeded his brother Leander in that see. The overwhelming majority of quotations from Isidore come from his *Sententiae*, which is another *florilegium* drawn from Pope Gregory's writings, chiefly the *Moralia*, with some excerpts from Saint Augustine. Isidore's *Differentiae* and his *Etymologiae* are also occasionally quoted by Smaragdus. Taken together, Gregory and his work (made available by Taio and Isidore) support Smaragdus's pastoral and practical emphasis.

Saint Bede the Venerable is another of Smaragdus's sources, mainly through his commentaries on the four gospels and on the Catholic Epistles. There are a few quotations from other teachers and doctors of the church: Saint Cyprian, Saint Jerome, Saint Augustine, Saint John Chrysostom in a Latin translation of his sermons, Saint

Ephrem the Syrian in a Latin translation of his work on the Beatitudes, Cassiodorus's *Commentary on the Psalms*, Pseudo-Maximus, and Saint Caesarius of Arles. Lesser known writers quoted in the *Crown of Monks* are Pope Gregory's notary, Paterius, then Primasius of Hadrumetum in Africa, and Paul the Deacon. Finally, Smaragdus quotes from his earlier works, the *Via regia* and his *Collectiones in epistolas et evangelia,* also known as the *Liber comitis.* I am assuming that the *Via regia* was written before the *Diadema*, a position based on the research of H. H. Anton[7] and accepted by modern scholars such as Fidel Rädle,[8] Pius Engelbert,[9] and Jasmijn Bovendeert.[10] Efforts to track down sources for all the material proved unsuccessful. After a sustained period of attention to Smaragdus's sources, I am inclined to agree with the tentative hypothesis proposed by Spannagel with regard to Smaragdus's *Commentary on the Rule*—a hypothesis with which Rädle concurs as regards the present work—that there may well be another *florilegium* between Smaragdus and most of the lesser or less-frequently quoted authors featured in the second half of the *Crown of Monks.*[11] It does not seem feasible for a monastery of that period to have in its library sets of complete works of the writers quoted, or even separate copies of all the individual works quoted. And history tells us that there were a number of *florilegia* in existence by Smaragdus's time.

I also venture the opinion that some writing—at least of the material in the *Crown of Monks* not traced to other sources—might be Smaragdus's own. Almost the whole of chapter 97 could well be

---

[7] H. H. Anton, *Fürstenspiegel und Herscherethos in der Karolingerzeit* (Bonner Historische Forschungen 32, 1968). Bibliographical details cited from Rädle's *Studien*, 68 and 234; see following footnote.

[8] Fidel Rädle, *Studien zu Smaragd von Saint-Mihiel*, Medium Aevum: Philologische Studien 29 (Munich: W. Fink, 1974).

[9] Spannagel and Engelbert, *Smaragdi abbatis expositio*, XXVI, note 22. The introduction is by Engelbert.

[10] Jasmijn Bovendeert, "Royal or monastic identity? Smaragdus' *Via Regia* and *Diadema Monachorum* Reconsidered," *Texts and Identities in the Early Middle Ages*, ed. Richard Corradini and others (Vienna: Austrian Academy of Sciences, 2006), 239–51.

[11] Rädle, *Studien* 75; see also 194 on the same page.

Smaragdus's own contribution to the collection of excerpts from other writers.

SMARAGDUS'S SOURCES: THE DESERT FATHERS AND MOTHERS

The fourth-century Egyptian desert provided pithy advice for later monastics, including Smaragdus. It is not Cassian's *Conferences* as generally understood, but the *Sayings*, the *Verba seniorum* that Smaragdus mines for the other important portion of his material. These *Sayings* feature in the *Lives of the Fathers*, the *Vitae patrum*, eight of which are reproduced in PL 73, four of these being almost entirely taken up with the *Verba seniorum*; and in the *Apophthegmata patrum* that are published as an appendix to Palladius's *Lausiac History* in PG 65. Smaragdus quotes from the *Sayings* in fifty-one of his one hundred chapters. Occasionally he places the quotation at the beginning of the chapter, but he regularly places one or several at the end. All told, Smaragdus quotes over one hundred twenty sayings ranging in length from one line to a few dozen.

From which of the several collections of sayings did Smaragdus quote? A lot more comparative study would be needed before one could give a confident answer to that question. One of the indicators is the number of unidentified "old men" the sayings are attributed to. This seems to be characteristic of the following four series of *Verba seniorum*:

1. Book 3 of the *Vitae patrum* or *Verba seniorum* (PL 73:739–810) with 220 entries and tentatively attributed to Rufinus

2. Book 5 of the *Vitae patrum* or *Verba seniorum* (PL 73:855–988) by an unknown Greek author, translated by the deacon Pelagius, with a total of 653 entries arranged according to subject matter in 18 books, hence the title "Systematic Collection"

3. Book 6 of the *Vitae patrum* or *Verba seniorum* (PL 73:991–1022) with a total of 89 entries divided in 4 books, continuing the *Systematic Collection*, also by an unknown Greek author, and translated by the subdeacon John (see Ward, 213)

4. Book 7 of the *Vitae patrum* or *Verba seniorum* (PL 73:1025–1062) with a total of 162 entries in 44 chapters, continuing

the *Systematic Collection*, also by an unknown Greek author, translated by the deacon Paschasius

The *Alphabetical Collection*, best represented in the *Apophthegmata patrum* (PG 65:71–440), features 129 *abbas* and 3 *ammas*, with 946 apophthegms attributed to them. Poemen "the Shepherd" was not an uncommon name in the desert. The person or persons bearing that name are the most prolific, the number of apophthegms under that name being 187. Benedicta Ward's translation, *The Sayings of the Desert Fathers*, adds fifty-five sayings from J.-C. Guy's study[12] to the total, of which twenty-two are attributed to Poemen, bringing the total of Poemen sayings to 209.

Many of the sayings are repeated in the different collections, sometimes verbatim, or with only minor variations, additions, or omissions attributed to a different elder or left anonymous. Where I have been able to trace them I have given references to the various collections in PL 73 and PG 65 where a saying appears, mentioning the name of the father given in the Greek text when it is anonymous in the Latin texts used by Smaragdus, and mentioning whether there are noteworthy differences between his text and those of his presumed sources.

THE *CROWN OF MONKS'* TEACHING: BRIEF OVERVIEW

Perhaps the secret of the *Crown of Monks'* popularity in the Middle Ages is the quality of the material that Smaragdus excerpted from his sources and his skill in selecting and arranging it for his monastic audience to listen to at the time of day intended, just before Compline. With his twin purpose in mind—(1) to arouse the strong "to a keener and loftier yearning for the heavenly country" and (2) "to strengthen and instill fear" into weak monks, in the hope of "leading them to amendment and a life more in keeping with the Rule"—Smaragdus addressed in succession topics of perennial

---

[12] J.-C. Guy, *Les Apophthegmata des Pères du Désert* (Bellfontaine: Begrolles, 1966); *The Sayings of the Desert Fathers: The Alphabetic Collection,* trans. Benedicta Ward, CS 59 (Kalamazoo, MI: Cistercian Publications, 1975, 1981).

significance to monks. The chapter headings bear this out: prayer, psalmody, reading, love of God and neighbor, observance of the commandments, confession, compunction, fear of God, the love of Christ, the desire for heaven, the virtues of prudence, simplicity, patience, humility, obedience, ascetical practices such as fasting, abstinence, reserve in speech, bearing with temptations and with divine corrections, returning to sin after (shedding) tears, on knowing our Lord Jesus Christ, on prayer without ceasing, on the battle of the virtues, on circumcising the vices, on the fact that virtues spring from virtues and vices from vices, on the grace of God, the grace of tears, on the love and grace of God, on the impulse of the Spirit and the impulse of the flesh, and so on.

Further insight into Smaragdus's general theological and spiritual leaning can be gained from some statistics derived from the *Diadema*. He mentions God four hundred sixty-two times, the (Holy) Spirit thirty-three times, the Father forty-one (these include God the Father eight times and the Creator and Father once). Christ is mentioned one hundred seventy-two times, which includes Christ Jesus ten and the Lord Jesus Christ ten times. The name "Jesus" is mentioned alone only when quoting Saint Paul, "Son of God" four times, and "Son of Man" twice. Hell rates three mentions, punishment twenty-four, four of these referring to eternal or everlasting punishment. Heaven, on the other hand, scores one hundred four mentions, either alone or in combinations such as heavenly joys (three), heavenly contemplation (four), heavenly things (seven), heavenly homeland (five), heavenly country (two), heavenly beatitude (three). These numbers show that Smaragdus is more concerned to focus our attention on God, Christ, the Holy Spirit, and heaven than he is to confront us with hell and eternal punishment.

Finally, grace looms large in Smaragdus's theology, and the word occurs more than eighty times in the *Diadema*. We are saved by grace, helped by grace in dealing with temptation, enlightened by grace, given the grace of tears and compunction, of prayer and contemplation, and we are given a foretaste of glory by grace.

It need hardly be said that not all matters of concern to monastic people in the twenty-first century are immediately addressed by Smaragdus: the role of monasteries, monks, and nuns in the modern church and world; community, ecumenical, and interfaith dialogue; navigating the world of work, business, economics, and politics; emotional and personal development to promote psychosocial and psychosexual maturity; and witnessing to Christ in a de-Christianized, indifferent, hedonistic, and perhaps positively antagonistic and secularist society, to name a few such modern concerns. But what one will find in the *Crown of Monks* is rich matter for *lectio*, prayer, meditation, and contemplation, forming monastic minds and hearts for facing whatever challenges come our way, linking us with the formative years of the monastic tradition and pointing us where the tradition points us—inwards, onwards, and upwards to the final goal, the kingdom of heaven.

Translator's Preface
and Acknowledgments

David Barry

I gratefully acknowledge the encouragement of our late abbot, Dom Placid Spearritt (+2008), and of our present abbot, Dom John Herbert, and the members of my monastic community to complete this translation. In accessing critical editions of Smaragdus's source texts, I have been helped by the librarian of the Veech Library at the Catholic Institute, Sydney, the librarians of the Reid Library, University of Western Australia, and our own monastery librarian, Sue Johnson. Father Ian Edmonds helped greatly with the proofreading (as he did, unacknowledged, with my translation of Smaragdus's *Commentary*), and Tony James with the exacting task of checking the numerous references. Doctor Katharine Massam, Professor of Church History at the United Faculty of Theology, Melbourne, was most helpful with suggestions for improving and completing the introduction. Father Mark Scott, OCSO, executive editor at Cistercian Publications, has helped significantly with advice on editorial matters and his consistent encouragement. And finally, Hans Christoffersen, publisher at Liturgical Press, and his staff have lived up to their mission, vision, and heritage. Thank you, all.

I was encouraged to see this work through to completion by favorable reviews of my translation of Smaragdus's *Commentary* in *Cistercian Studies Quarterly* 43.4 (2008) by Edith Scholl, OCSO, and *American Benedictine Review* 60.3 (September 2009) by Colleen

Maura McGrane, OSB, the latter with some constructive and helpful criticisms. Thank you, both.

Feast of Saint Mechtild, November 19, 2010

Unless otherwise indicated, the ellipses used in this work mark places where Smaragdus omits phrases or sentences from the writing he is quoting.

Abbreviations of Works Cited

ACW   Ancient Christian Writers series. Westminster, Maryland: Newman; New York: Paulist, 1946–

ANF   Ante-Nicene Fathers. 10 vols. 1866; Grand Rapids, MI: Eerdmans, 1951.

CCM   Corpus consuetudinum monasticarum. Ed. Kassius Hallinger, et al. Siegburg, Germany: F. Schmitt, 1963–

CCSL   Corpus Christianorum Series Latina. Turnhout, Belgium: Brepols, 1953–

Clavis   *Clavis Patrum Latinorum.* Eds. Eligius Dekkers and Aemilius Gaar. Steenbruge: Saint Peter's Abbey, 1951.

CS   Cistercian Studies series. Spencer, MA; Washington, DC; Kalamazoo, MI, 1966–

CSEL   Corpus Scriptorum Ecclesiasticorum Latinorum. Vienna, 1866–

DSp   *Dictionnaire de spiritualité.* Paris: Beauchesne, 1937–1995.

FCh   Fathers of the Church series. Washington, DC: Catholic University of America, 1948–

LXX   Septuagint

NPNF   Nicene and Post-Nicene Library of the Fathers. Series 1 & 2, 14 vols. each. 1886; Grand Rapids, MI: Eerdmans, 1956, 1979.

PG   J.-P. Migne, *Patrologiae Cursus Completus, Series Graeca,* 162 vols. Paris, 1857–66.

PL   J.-P. Migne, *Patrologiae Cursus Completus, Series Latina,* 221 vols. Paris, 1844–65.

PLS   *Patrologiae Cursus Completus, Series Latina, Supplementum.* Ed.
         A. Hamman. Paris 1958–

RB   *Regula monachorum sancti Benedicti; Rule of Saint Benedict.*

RBas   *Regula Basilii.* See Basil in bibliography.

Sayings See Ward in bibliography.

Wisdom See Ward in bibliography.

Authors and Works Cited

Ambrosiaster
    In Gal   *In epistolam ad Galatas*
    In Phil   *In epistolam ad Philippenses*
Auctor incertus
        Sermones suppositii 108.
    In Eph 5:1   *In epistolam ad Ephesios.*
    In ep Pauli   *In epistolas Pauli.*
Augustine   Saint Augustine, Bishop of Hippo (354–430).
    En in ps   *Ennarationes in psalmos.*
    Tr ev Jo   *Tractatus in evangelium Joannis.*
    Serm   *Sermones* (Sermons).
Basil   Saint Basil of Caesarea (ca. 329–379).
    RBas   *Regula Basilii* (Basil, *Parvum Asceticon*).
Bede   Saint Bede the Venerable (673–735).
    In Jac   *Super epistolam Jacobi* (Commentary on James).
    In 1 Pt   *Super epistolam primam Petri* (Commentary on 1 Peter).
    In 2 Pt   *Super epistolam secundam Petri* (Commentary on 2 Peter).
    In 1 Jo   *Super epistolam primam Johannis* (Commentary on 1 John).
    In Mt   *In Matthaei evangelium expositio* (Commentary on the Gospel of Matthew).

In Mc	*In Marci evangelium expositio* (Commentary on the Gospel of Mark).
In Lc	*In Lucae evangelium expositio* (Commentary on the Gospel of Luke).
In Jo	*In Joannis evangelium expositio* (Commentary on the Gospel of John).
Caesarius	Saint Caesarius of Arles (ca. 469–542).
Serm	*Sermones.*
Cassian	John Cassian (ca. 360–ca. 435).
Inst	*Instituta patrum* (The Institutes). Eng.: NPNF ser. 2, 11.
Cassiodorus	Cassiodorus (ca. 485–ca. 585).
Ex ps	*Expositio psalmorum.*
Cyprian	Saint Cyprian of Carthage (ca. 200–258).
Dom orat.	*De dominica oratione* (On the Lord's prayer). Eng.: ANF 5.
De pat	*De bono patientiae* (On Patience). Eng.: ANF 5.
De mort	*De mortalitate* (On Mortality). Eng.: ANF 5.
Defensor	Defensor of Ligugé (seventh–eighth centuries).
Scint	*Liber scintillarum.*
Ephrem	Saint Ephrem the Syrian (ca. 306–373).
	De beatitudine animae.
Evagrius	Evagrius of Pontus (345–399).
Gregory	Saint Gregory the Great (540–604).
Dial	*Dialogorum libri IV* (Dialogues).
Hom ev	*Homiliae in evangelia* (Homilies on the Gospels).
In Hiez	*Homiliae in Hiezechihelem* (Homilies on Ezekiel).
Mor	*Moralia* (Morals on the Book of Job). Eng.: in Library of the Fathers, 3 vols. Oxford, 1843–1850.
Past	*Regula pastoralis* (Pastoral care). Eng.: NPNF ser. 2, 12.
Isidore	Saint Isidore, Bishop of Seville (ca. 560–636).

Etym	*Etymologiae* (Etymologies).
Diff	*Differentiae.*
Sent	*Sententiae* (Sentences).
Synon	*Synonoma.*
Jerome	Saint Jerome (340–420).
Ep	*Epistolae.*
In Mt	*In Matthaeum.*
In Gal	*In Galatas.*
In Eph	*In Ephesios.*
Johannes Chrysostomus	Saint John Chrysostom (Latinus).
Hom	*Homily 7 On Joseph sold by his brothers.*
Iulianus Pomerius	Iulianus Pomerius (fifth–sixth centuries).
Vita cont	*De vita contemplativa*
Pseudo-Maximus	(fifth century?).
Hom	*Homily 1, 7 & 8 On the Fast of Lent.*
Paterius	Paterius, Bishop of Brescia (former notary of Gregory the Great—sixth–seventh centuries).
Expositio	*Liber de expositione veteris ac novi testamenti de diversis libris S. Gregorii Magni concinnatus.*
Paulus Diaconus	Paul the Deacon (ca. 730–799).
Hom	*Homily 54* (ex Origine).
Pelagius	Pelagius (ca. 354–after 418).
In Eph	*In epistolam ad Ephesios* (On Ephesians).
Primasius	Primasius of Hadrumetum (sixth century).
In ep Pauli	*In epistolas Pauli.*
Pseudo-Macarius	
Ep ad mon	*Epistola ad monachos* (compiled eighth century—see *Clavis*, 1843).

Smaragdus   Smaragdus of Saint-Mihiel (ca. 760–ca. 830).

    Collect   *Collectiones in epistolas et evangelia (Expositio
                 Libri comitis).*

    Commentary   *Commentary on the Rule of Saint Benedict.*

    Via reg   *Via regia* (The Royal Way).

Taio   Taio, Bishop of Saragossa (bishop 651, died 683).

    Sent   *Sententiarum libri quinque.*

The Crown of Monks

PROLOGUE

This modest little book is the result of our work. In it, with Christ's help, we have collected the sayings of many orthodox fathers, gathering the choicest and sweetest-smelling flowers while coursing through their flourishing meadows. From their flower-strewn field, full as it is of the Lord's blessings, we have collected the things we ascertained as necessary for monks, and have endeavored to bring them together in this little book. The things we have in mind are such as may win the hearts of mature monks, arousing them to a keener and loftier yearning for the heavenly country. And they are also such as may both strengthen and instill fear into the hearts of weak monks, leading them to amendment and a life more in keeping with the Rule.

It is written in the Rule of Saint Benedict: *As soon as the brethren have risen from the evening meal, let all be seated in one place, and let one brother read the Conferences or Lives of the Fathers, or at least something that may edify the hearers* [RB 42.3]. That is why we have brought together in this little book a limited amount from the conferences of the fathers, from the accounts of their lives and their institutions, and a large amount from various doctors, and have formed the whole into a hundred chapters. Monks have the custom of reading the Rule of Saint Benedict each day at the morning chapter meeting; we would like this book to be read at their evening chapter meeting.

We read in the same Rule of Saint Benedict that whatever good work we begin we should beseech God with earnest prayer to bring it to perfection [see RB Prol. 4]. For this reason we consider in the first chapter of this book the duty of prayer.

CHAPTER 1

On Prayer

The remedy for those who are hot with the enticements of the vices is this: every time they are stung by any vice let them apply themselves to prayer, because frequent prayer extinguishes the attack of the vices. The mind must do this intently and perseveringly, ever asking and knocking, until with the very strength of our intent we overcome the importunate suggestions of fleshly desires that din at the door of our senses. And we must keep up the fight until we overcome by our persistence. Negligent prayers cannot obtain what they ask even from a mere human being. When people pray they call the Holy Spirit to themselves; and when the Spirit comes, straightway the demons' temptations, that immerse themselves deep in human minds, being unable to endure his presence, take flight.

Prayer is a matter of the heart, not of the lips. God does not pay attention to the words of the one praying, but he looks at the person's heart. Now if the heart prays quietly and the voice is silent, even if it escapes the notice of human beings it cannot remain hidden from God, who is present to the conscience. It is better to pray with the heart in silence without the sound of the voice than to use only words without a stretching out of the mind.[1]

It is not our words that speak in God's most secret ears, but our desires. For if we ask for eternal life with our mouth but do not long for it with the heart, even though we call out aloud we are silent. But if we long for it from the heart, then even though we are silent with

---

[1] Isidore, Sent 3.7.1–4; CCSL 111:220–21; PL 83:671B–72B. At the end Isidore has *sine intuitu mentis*, "without the gaze of the mind"; Smaragdus has *sine intentu mentis*.

our mouth, we cry out loud while keeping quiet. That is why in the desert the people make a great noise with their voices, and Moses remains silent from the noise of words; and yet though silent, he is heard by the ear of the divine kindness. To him God says, *Why do you call out to me?* [Exod 14:15]. So the secret cry is within, in desire. It does not reach human ears, but it fills the hearing of the Creator.[2]

One must never pray without groaning, for the remembrance of sins engenders mourning. For when we pray we bring to mind our fault, and then we know more truly that we are guilty. And so when we stand before God we ought to groan and weep as we remember how grave are the crimes we have committed, and how horrible are the punishments of hell that we fear. The mind should keep itself after prayer in the condition it is in when it offers itself in prayer. For prayer brings no profit if we again commit what we are now asking pardon for. Those who do not repeat by sin what in prayer they ask to have washed away, doubtless receive in their prayers the desired effect. . . . For we truly pray when we do not think of anything else. . . . Our belief is that we really obtain the divine gifts we ask for when our prayer involves a simple loving presence.[3]

When we stand to pray . . . we must keep watch and apply ourselves wholeheartedly to our prayers, so that every fleshly and worldly thought departs. The mind must not have any other thought than what it is praying for. For this reason the priest . . . prepares the brothers' and sisters' minds by saying, "Lift up your hearts," so that when the people respond, "We lift them up to the Lord," they may be warned that they must not have any other thought than the Lord.[4]

One who is being subjected to injury ought not to cease praying for those who are inflicting the injury; otherwise, according to God's sentence, one sins by not praying for one's enemies [see Matt 5:44]. Just as a remedy applied to a wound brings no healing if the iron weapon is still lodged in it, so prayer is of no benefit if resentment is still in the mind or hatred remains in the heart.[5]

[2] Gregory, Mor 22.17; CCSL 143B:1122–23; PL 76:238C.
[3] Isidore, Sent 3.7.5–6, 8b, 10b; CCSL 111:221–22; PL 83:673A–74A.
[4] Cyprian, Dom orat 31; PL 4:557B.
[5] Isidore, Sent 3.7.13–14; CCSL 111:223; PL 83:674B.

The sacrifice that consists of prayer is more willingly accepted when, in the sight of the merciful judge, it is seasoned with love of neighbor. People really enhance this sacrifice if they offer it even for their adversaries [see Rom 12:20].[6]

So great must be the love for God of the one praying, that there is no lack of hope of obtaining the prayer's result. We pray in vain if we do not have hopeful trust. Let everyone, then, says the apostle James, *ask in faith, without doubting* [Jas 1:6].[7] The Lord also says, *Everything whatsoever you ask for in prayer with faith, you will receive* [Matt 21:22].

A certain old man once came to Mount Sinai, and when he was leaving a brother met him on the way, and with groans said to the old man, "We are sorely tried, Abba, on account of the drought; we do not get rain." The old man said to him, "Why do you not pray and ask it of God?" He answered, "We do pray and earnestly beseech God, and yet it does not rain." The old man said, "I think it is because you do not pray with sufficient attention. Do you wish to know if it is so? Come, let us stand together in prayer." And stretching out his hands to heaven he prayed, and immediately the rain came down. When the brother saw this he was struck with fear. He fell down and worshipped the old man.[8]

For the Lord also said to the disciples, *Have faith. Truly I tell you, if anyone says to this mountain, "Be taken up and thrown into the sea," and does not hesitate at heart, what that person says will be done* [Mark 11:23].

We read that this was done by the prayers of the blessed Father Gregory of Neo-Caesarea. . . . Wishing to build a church in a suitable

[6] Taio, Sent 3.22; PL 80:878BC, quoting Gregory, Mor 35.11; CCSL 143B:1787; PL 76:761AB.

[7] Isidore, Sent 3.7.15 (Smaragdus omits the last part of the quotation from the Letter of James); CCSL 111:223; PL 83:674B–75A.

[8] PL 73:943A (14); see also PG 65:311 [312]D–[313] 314A; *Sayings*, 133 [158], 2. In the Alphabetical Collection the old man is named as Abba Xoius. This indicates that Smaragdus was using one or more of the Systematic Collections preserved in Latin. In the PG 65 references, the bracketed column number refers to the Greek text, the unbracketed refers to the accompanying Latin translation. For *Sayings* the first number gives the page in the first edition, the bracketed number gives that of the second edition.

place, when he saw that the place was narrower than required . . . he came by night to the spot and on bended knees prayed the Lord[9] to make the mountain longer in keeping with the faith of the petitioner. When it was morning, he came back and found that the mountain had left as much space as was needed for the builders of the church.[10]

And Saint Scholastica placed her hands and head on the table and prayed that it might rain; and at once rain came down from heaven upon those present.[11]

Accordingly the prayers of the righteous[12] receive a favorable hearing rather slowly, so that they may accumulate greater rewards by the delay. Prayer is more suitably poured out in private places, with God the only witness. . . . Nor does an elaborate speech do anything to win God's favor . . . but the pure[13] and sincere intention of the prayer.[14]

Certain persons asked Abba Macarius, "How ought we to pray?" And the old man said to them, "There is no need to speak much in prayer, but to stretch out one's hands frequently and say, Lord, as you will, and as you know, have mercy on me."[15]

Hence blessed Benedict says, "We should know that it is not for our much speaking but for our purity of heart and compunction of tears that we are heard. And therefore prayer must be short and pure, unless it happens to be prolonged under the influence of an inspiration of divine grace. In community, however, prayer is to be made quite short" [RB 20.3-5].[16]

---

[9] Bede has *admonuit Dominum promissionis suae*, "he reminded the Lord of his promise"; Smaragdus's text reads simply *oravit Dominum*.

[10] Bede, In Mc 11:22–23; CCSL 120:580–81; PL 92:247D–48A.

[11] See Gregory, Dial 2.33.

[12] Isidore (Sent 3.7.23a) has *quorundam orationes*, "some [certain] people's prayers"; Smaragdus's text reads *justorum exaudiuntur orationes.*

[13] Isidore (Sent 3.7.29b) has *sed pura sinceraque orationis intentio*, "but the pure and sincere intention of the prayer"; Smaragdus's text reads: *sed plura sinceraque orationis intentio.* I have translated according to Isidore.

[14] Isidore, Sent 3.7.23a, 27, 29b; CCSL 111:226–27; PL 83:677A–78A.

[15] PL 73:942CD (10a); 806B (207a); see also PG 65:[269] 270C; *Sayings,* 111 [131], 19.

[16] Smaragdus's first chapter, *On Prayer*, is much longer than the chapter with the same title in the *Via regia.*

CHAPTER 2

On the Discipline of Psalmody

We ought to make every effort to obey the one who admonishes us through the prophet, saying, *Sing psalms wisely* [Ps 46(47):7], that is, let us not seek what strikes the ear but what gives light to the heart. And what we sing with the tongue let us carry out in what we do. Those persons sing wisely who understand what is being sung in the psalms. For none act wisely who do not understand what they are doing. Just as with all foods it is by the sense of taste that we distinguish the savor, so likewise for the words of Holy Scripture prudence and understanding fulfill this role. So if people apply their soul to each word of the psalmody, as the sense of taste is applied in distinguishing the savor of various foods, they have fulfilled the saying, *Sing psalms wisely* [Ps 46(47):7].[1]

It is good to pray always with the heart, and it is good to glorify God by spiritual hymns with the sound of the voice as well. To sing only with the voice without the heart's attention is nothing. But as the apostle says, *Admonish one another, and with thanksgiving in your hearts sing psalms, hymns and spiritual songs to God* [Col 3:16].[2] This means, singing psalms with the heart and not only with the voice. Elsewhere he says, *I will sing psalms with the spirit, and I will sing psalms with the mind also* [1 Cor 14:15].

---

[1] See RBas 279; PG 31:1279 [1280] A; and RBas 110; CSEL 86:137.

[2] Smaragdus here quotes Colossians 3:16, whereas Isidore's text (Sent 3.7.30) quotes four words from Ephesians 5:1—*cantantes in cordibus vestris,* "singing in your hearts."

As we are guided aright by prayers, so we find delight in our study of the psalms. For singing psalms is useful for consoling sad hearts, making minds more grateful, delighting the fastidious, arousing the sluggish and inviting sinners to lament. Though the hearts of carnal people may be ever so hard, as soon as the sweet tone of a psalm is heard it bends their mind to a loving reverence. Although it is not the modulation of the voice that should move the Christian so much as the divine words that are said there, somehow a greater compunction of heart is born from the singer's modulation. For there are many who, deeply touched by the sweetness of the chant, bewail their faults and are moved even to tears by the very charm and delightfulness of sung psalmody. Only in the present life is prayer poured forth as a remedy for sins, but the frequent singing of the psalms points the way to the perpetual praise of God unto eternal glory, as it is written: *Happy are those who live in your house; forever they will praise you* [Ps 83(84):4]. Whoever performs the service of this work faithfully and with an attentive mind is in some way joined to the angels.[3]

[And so in another place the same psalmist says,] *In the presence of the angels I will sing psalms to you* [Ps 137(138):1]. Here is shown the power of psalmody; those who with a pure heart sing psalms among their fellow humans also seem to be singing on high with the angels.[4] And so the apostle says, *Admonish one another with psalms, hymns and spiritual songs, singing in your hearts* [Col 3:16].[5]

Therefore we must sing, and sing psalms, and praise the Lord more with the mind than with the voice. This precisely is what *singing in your hearts* means.[6] For when the voice of the psalmody expresses the intention of the heart, through it the way to the heart is made ready for almighty God, for him to infuse the mysteries of prophecy or the grace of compunction into the attentive mind. And so it is written: *A sacrifice of praise will honor me, and there is the way by*

---

[3] Isidore, Sent 3.7.30–33; CCSL 111:227–28; PL 83:678AB–79A.

[4] Cassiodorus, Ex. ps. 137[138]:1; CCSL 98:1237; PL 70:980A; ACW:53, 367.

[5] Smaragdus's wording of Colossians 3:16 here differs slightly from his quotation earlier in this chapter.

[6] Jerome, In Eph 5:19; PL 26:528C.

which I will show them the salvation of God [Ps 49(50):23]. . . . And also: *Sing to the Lord, sing psalms to his name; make a road for him who goes up on the west; the Lord is his name* [Ps 67(68):4]. For he who trod down death by rising went up on the west. When we are singing to him we are making a road, so that he may come to our heart and set us on fire with the grace of his love.[7]

---

[7] Gregory, In Hiez 1.1.15; CCSL 142:12–13; PL 76:793AB.

CHAPTER 3

On Reading

We are made clean by prayer and instructed by reading. Both are good if both can be done; if not, it is better to pray than to read. One who wishes to be always with God must frequently pray and frequently read. For when we pray, we speak with God; but when we read, God speaks with us. All progress comes from reading and meditation. For what we do not know we learn by reading; and what we have learned we preserve by means of meditation. The reading of the Holy Scriptures confers this twofold gift: it instructs the mind's understanding, and it brings the one who is withdrawn from the world's vanities to the love of God. . . . Application to reading has two elements: the first is, how the Scriptures may be understood; the second, how to use and value what they say. It is reasonable for humans to be eager to understand what they read, and then to be able to bring to light what they have learned. . . . God's law contains both reward and punishment for those who read it. The reward is for those who keep his law by living well; the punishment is for those who despise his law by their evil living.[1]

Sacred Scripture calls its readers' minds to the heavenly homeland, and changes their hearts from earthly desires to embrace things above; it exercises them by its more obscure sayings, entices little ones with its humble form of words . . . and by the habit of reading takes away any distaste from the reader. Those it assists with its humble words it lifts up by sublime ones. Sacred Scripture in some

[1] Isidore, Sent 3.8.1–4a, 5, 7; CCSL 111:229–30; PL 83:679A–80A.

10

way grows with its readers: it becomes familiar to its unskilled readers, and yet the learned always find new things there.[2]

God says to the prophet Ezekiel, *O mortal, eat whatever you find*
[Ezek 3:1]. For whatever is found in Sacred Scripture is to be eaten.
Its less important parts make for simplicity of life, while its more
important parts build up a discerning understanding.[3]

By reading the precepts of Sacred Scripture, we who were lying
dead in our faults are brought back to life. And so the psalmist says
to Almighty God, *I will never forget your words, for in them you have
given me life* [Ps 118(119):93]. . . . In the darkness of the present life
Holy Scripture has become light for our journey. Thus Peter says,
You do well to be attentive to this as to a lamp shining in a murky place
[2 Pet 1:19].[4]

When readers find the message of Sacred Scripture uninteresting,
the sense of the divine word does not arouse their minds or shine
forth in their thoughts with any intellectual grasp of its light. But if
they search for well-ordered ways of right living, and find through
the heart's step how they may position themselves to do a good work,
the profit they derive from the sacred message is in proportion to the
progress they have made in its company. What generally happens is
that if those inflamed by the grace of heavenly contemplation devote
their whole attention to heavenly things, they come to realize that
the words of Sacred Scripture are indeed mystical. For the wonderful
and unutterable power of the sacred message is recognized when the
reader's mind is penetrated with heavenly love.[5]

---

[2] Taio, Sent 3.40; PL 80:896CD, quoting Gregory, Mor 20.1; CCSL 143A:1003;
PL 76:135BC.

[3] Taio, Sent 3.40; PL 80:896D, quoting Gregory, In Hiez 1.10,2; CCSL 142:145;
PL 76:886CD.

[4] Taio, Sent 3.40; PL 80:897A, quoting Gregory, In Hiez 1.7,16.17; CCSL
142:93; PL 76:848BC.

[5] Taio, Sent 3.40; PL 80:897AB, quoting Gregory, In Hiez 1.7.8; CCSL 142:87–88;
PL 76:843D–44AB. In the third sentence, Taio has changed Gregory's second person
singular to the third person singular, and *mystica* replaces *coelestia*, "heavenly."

CHAPTER 4

On Love of God and of Neighbor

Charity consists in the love of God and of neighbor. We preserve the love of God in ourselves when we are not separated from charity towards our neighbor. Those who cut themselves off from association with their brothers and sisters are deprived of a share in divine charity. Nor can anyone love God who is known to err in love of neighbor. Christ is both God and man. So anyone who hates another does not love the whole Christ.[1]

Although some may seem to be sharers [in Christ] by their faith and holy works, yet because they are deprived of the charity of fraternal love, they do not grow in virtue. For as the apostle says, *If I hand over my body so as to burn, but do not have love, it profits me nothing* [1 Cor 13:3]. Without the love of charity, despite believing rightly, one cannot arrive at beatitude. The reason is that, so great is the power of charity, without it not even prophecy and martyrdom are believed to count for anything. No prize weighs as much as charity. Charity holds first place among the virtues. And so the apostle calls charity *the bond of perfection* [Col 3:14], because all the virtues are bound together with it as bond.[2]

Obedience consists first of all in charity. This charity comprises two precepts: that God is to be loved, and the neighbor as well. And

[1] Isidore, Sent 2.3.7; CCSL 111:98; PL 83:603B.
[2] Isidore, Sent 2.3.1–3; CCSL 111:96–97; PL 83:602CD–3A.

right behavior is made perfect by the fulfillment of the Ten Commandments, so that when people begin to do good they no longer
do evil.[3]

There are two precepts of charity, namely, love of God and
love of neighbor, [and through these precepts the sayings of Sacred
Scripture cause us to live, because we grasp the love of God and of
neighbor in the divine words].

Through love of God love of neighbor is begotten, and through
love of neighbor love of God is nourished. One who does not bother
to love God is clearly unable to love neighbor. We progress more
fully in love of God if we are bound beforehand in the bosom of
that same love by charity towards our neighbor. Therefore because
love of God gives rise to love of neighbor, the Lord when about to
say through the law: *You shall love your neighbor,* prefaced it by saying,
You shall love the Lord your God [Matt 22:37-39; Luke 10:27; Deut
6:5]. His purpose was first to establish firmly in the soil of our heart
the root of his love so that afterwards brotherly love might sprout
forth through the branches. . . . Love of God grows together with
love of neighbor, as John bears witness when he upbraids [certain
people] and says, *How can those who do not love their brother or sister
whom they see, love God whom they do not see?* [1 John 4:20]. This
divine love is born of fear but it changes into genuine affection as
it grows [see 1 John 4:18].

Almighty God often makes known how far someone is from
charity for God and neighbor, or what progress someone has made
in it. Arranging everything in a wonderful order, some he presses
down through scourges, and others he supports by successes. And
when for a while he forsakes certain ones, he reveals the evil that
lies hidden in the hearts of others. Generally in fact it is the very
ones who court us when we are happy who assail us when we suffer misfortune.[4]

We make our journey on earth without stubbing our foot if we
love God and neighbor with our whole mind. For we do not really

[3] Taio, Sent 1.32; PL 80:761CD.
[4] Taio, Sent 1.32; PL 80:761D–62AB, quoting Gregory, Mor 7.24; CCSL
143:352–53; PL 75:780CD–81AC.

love God if our neighbor is excluded, nor do we really love our neighbor if God is not included. We read of the Holy Spirit being given twice to the disciples: first, by the Lord while he was dwelling on earth [see John 20:22-23], afterwards by the Lord presiding in heaven [see Acts 2:1-4]. The Spirit is given on earth so that we may love our neighbor, but he is given from heaven so that we may love God. Now why was he first given on earth and afterwards from heaven, unless we are clearly being given to understand that, according to John's word: *How can those who do not love their brother or sister whom they see, love God whom they do not see?* [1 John 4:20]. Let us then love and embrace our neighbor who is near at hand to us, so that we may be able to arrive at the love of him who is above us. When the mind reflects deeply on the neighbor let it also ponder on what it may exhibit to God, so that it may deserve to rejoice perfectly in God with the neighbor. For we will then come to the happiness of the numerous assembly above, concerning which we have received the pledge of the Holy Spirit, if we make for that end with total love, namely love of God and of neighbor.[5]

Every commandment is concerned with love alone, and all are one precept. Whatever is commanded is solidly based only when based on charity. . . . So the Lord's precepts are many and they are one: many by difference of work, one in the root that is love. How one is to possess love of God and of neighbor, he himself makes known when in very many sayings in his Scripture he commands us to love our friends in him and our enemies for his sake.[6]

So let us, dearly beloved, love our Lord God as he commanded, that is, let us love him with our whole heart, our whole soul and our whole strength [see Deut 6:5; Matt 22:37-39; Luke 10:27], because he first loved us [see 1 John 4:10]. For thus John, who reclined on that source of love at the supper, says in his letter, Brothers, let us love the Lord, because he first loved us [see 1 John 4:19]. For human frailty could not love the Lord unless he first loved our na-

---

[5] Taio, Sent 1.32; PL 80:762BC, quoting Gregory, Hom ev 30,10; CCSL 141:267–68; PL 76:1227ABC; see CS 123:247.

[6] Taio, Sent 2.29; PL 80:818D, quoting Gregory, Hom ev 27,1; CCSL 141:229–30; PL 76:1205AB; see CS 123:212.

ture. For he loved us before we came to be, and so it was in order that we might be that he created and quickened us, nourished and guarded us; he led us to the bath of rebirth, renewed us, governed us and brought us to the age of understanding. All this he did for us mercifully and through the excess of his love. Therefore, dearly beloved, let us open the eyes of our heart and know that we are so much loved by our Lord Jesus Christ that we may have no doubt his blood was shed for us.

Let us hang our heart on the love of our Creator. Let us love him, and not just a little or in part, but with our whole heart, our whole soul and our whole mind [see Deut 6:5; Matt 22:37; Luke 10:27]; let us not put the love of anything before the love of our Lord Jesus Christ. For he says, *One who loves father or mother more than me is not worthy of me* [Matt 10:37]. For truly, if we love God with our whole heart, we must not prefer the love of parents or friends or children to love of him.

But if we love the Lord, we must of necessity love our neighbor as ourselves, for *on these two commandments hang the whole law and the prophets* [Matt 22:40; see Rom 13:10]. Therefore one who does not love God and neighbor does not fulfill the law and the prophets. For it is written: *This is the commandment we have from God: those who love God must love their brothers and sisters also* [1 John 4:21]. *By this shall all know that you are my disciples, if you have love one for another* [John 13:35]. And: *Dearly beloved, let us love one another, because love is from God; everyone who loves brother or sister is born of God and knows God* [1 John 4:7]. *If we love one another,*[7] *God dwells in us, and his love is perfected in us* [1 John 4:12]. Blessed, therefore, is the love that is charity, which embraces, loves and cherishes everyone. Truly blessed is that which nourishes virtues and wipes out sins. It quells anger, shuts off hatred, expels avarice, checks quarrelling, and routs all vices at the same time. *It endures all things, believes all things, hopes all things* [1 Cor 13:7]. Amidst reproaches it is secure, amidst angry outbursts it remains calm, amidst hatred it is kind, and it is firm in the truth;

---

[7] Smaragdus's text in PL 102 here has *Si diligas invicem*, which I am treating as an obvious mistake for *Si diligamus invicem*.

it is not torn apart by vicious assailants, stolen by robbers, burnt by fire or divided by heresy. It stands indivisible, remains impregnable and beyond explanation, perseveres unshaken, rejoices unspoiled. It is the bond of all the virtues, the glue of souls, the harmony of minds and the fellowship of the elect. It powerfully strengthens the mind to prevent it from being broken by adversities; it also carefully tempers it to prevent it from being lifted up by prosperity. Lest it be overcome by anger, this love suppresses anger with reason.

This is truly [as I see] a most noble and excellent virtue. Therefore, brethren, let us hold on to it with all our might, so that it may be with us and abide with us. May it rise with us, journey with us, rejoice with us and feast in our company. For it is fitting for such a royal virtue to be continually present in the gathering of the brothers and sisters.[8]

---

[8] A long passage from his *Via regia* 1; PL 102:935A–937A. Adapted to his different readership for use here and quoted by Smaragdus in his later *Commentary on the Rule of Saint Benedict*, 4.21; see CS 212:186–87.

CHAPTER 5

On the Observance
of God's Commandments

After the practice of love, let us see what the very author of love orders us to observe. For he says, *If you love me, keep my commandments. And I will ask the Father, and he will give you another Advocate, to dwell with you forever* [John 14:15-16]. Let us then direct our attention, friends, to how much our Lord Jesus Christ loves us, who requires from us love for him with a promise, and says that the Holy Spirit will remain with us forever if we follow up love for him with keeping his commandments. He bestows on us all good things, and to will what is good and do it is the first thing he gives us. We are highly esteemed by him so that we may highly esteem him; we are loved by him so that we may love him. We are known so that we may know; we are helped so that we may work, and by working be enriched with the virtues. So if the love of God and of neighbor delights us, the result is that we do what he has ordered, for our love is measured by what we do.

One who does not faithfully fulfill God's commandments cannot sincerely love him. For he says, *Any who love me will keep my word, and my Father will love them, and we will come to them and make our home with them. Those who do not love me do not keep my words* [John 14:23]. John the Apostle, filled with the love of God, also says, *By this we can be sure that we know him, if we keep his commandments. Whoever says, "I have come to know him," but does not keep his commandments, is a liar, and the truth is not in such a one; but whoever does keep his word, truly in this person the love of God has been perfected* [1 John 2:3-5].

17

Job also says of himself, *My foot has followed God's steps; I have kept his way and have not turned aside. I have not departed from the commandments of his lips, and I have hidden in my bosom the words of his mouth* [Job 23:11-12]. . . . And admonishing the Israelite people the Lord himself says about love of him and the observance of his commandments: *And now, Israel, hear the statutes and ordinances that I am teaching you today to observe, so that you may do them and live* [Deut 4:1] *in them. Observe and be careful lest you ever forget the Lord your God, and neglect to keep his commandments, his ordinances, and his statutes, which I am commanding you today* [Deut 8:11]. *And now, O Israel, what does the Lord your God ask of you? Only to fear the Lord your God, to walk in his ways, to love him, to serve him with all your heart and with all your soul, and to keep his commandments and his decrees that I am commanding you today, so that it may be well with you* [Deut 10:12-13]. *If you will only hear* . . . *and observe all his commandments* . . . *the Lord will set you higher than all the nations that live on the earth* . . . *Blessed shall you be in the city, and blessed in the field. Blessed shall be the fruit of your womb, and the fruit of your ground* . . . *The Lord will send a blessing upon your barns, and upon all the works of your hands* [Deut 28:1, 3, 8].[1]

And so John the Apostle says, *By this we know that we love God's children, when we love God and keep his commandments. For the love of God consists in this, that we keep his commandments; and his commandments are not burdensome* [1 John 5:2-3]. The Lord himself also says this: *Any who love me will keep my word* [John 14:23]. So the proof of love lies in its being manifested in work. For we truly love God if we observe his commandments and firmly keep ourselves from self-will. Clearly, those who pour themselves out through unlawful desires do not love God; in their own will they contradict God.[2]

---

[1] Smaragdus, Via reg 2, adapted to a monastic audience; PL 102:937C–38C.
[2] Bede, In 1 Jo 5:2-3; CCSL 121:319–20; PL 93:113AB (see CS 82:214–15) quoting Gregory, Hom ev 30,1; CCSL 141:267; PL 76:1220C; see CS 123:236–37.

CHAPTER 6

On Fear

I t is written: *The fear of the Lord is the beginning of wisdom* [Ps 110(111):10]. *The fear of the Lord is glory and boasting, and gladness and a crown of exultation. The fear of the Lord will delight the heart, and will give gladness and joy and length of days* [Sir 1:11-12]. *Fear the Lord, and turn away from evil* [Prov 3:7], *because for those who fear the Lord it will be well at the end; on the day of their death they will be blessed . . . To fear the Lord is the fullness of wisdom* [Sir 1:13, 20].[1] What begets wisdom is the fear of the Lord; it is riches, and life and glory.

The fear of the Lord drives out sin [Sir 1:27]. Fear represses vice, and makes a person cautious and careful. *For a person who is without fear cannot be justified* [Sir 1:28]. Where there is no fear there is dissolute living. Where there is no fear there is gross profanity.[2] Where there is no fear crimes abound.[3]

Those who fear the Lord do not disbelieve his word, and those who love him will keep his ways. . . . Those who fear the Lord will prepare their hearts [Sir 2:18, 20], *and in his presence will sanctify their souls. Those who fear the Lord will keep his commandments, and will have patience until his inspection* [Sir 2:18, 20-21]. The fear of the Lord means not to despise the righteous poor, and not to extol the unrighteous rich. For David says, *Serve the Lord with fear, and make exultation for him with*

---

[1] A string of scriptural quotations to illustrate what fear of God means and entails.

[2] Isidore (Synon 2.26) has *ibi perditio mortis est*, "there is death's perdition"; Smaragdus has *ibi sceleratio est.*

[3] See Isidore, Synon 2.26; PL 83:851B. Some phrases are direct from Isidore.

trembling [Ps 2:11]. And, *Fear the Lord, all you his holy ones, for those who fear him want for nothing* [Ps 33(34):9]. And, *Happy are all who fear the Lord, who walk in his ways* [Ps 127(128):1]. Moses also says, *After the Lord your God you must walk, him you must fear, his precepts keep, and him obey* [Deut 13:5 LXX]. The apostle also says, *With fear and trembling work out your own salvation* [Phil 2:12]. Again Solomon says, *The fear of the Lord is the crown of wisdom, making peace complete, and the enjoyment of health* [Sir 1:20]. *Both are gifts of God* [Sir 1:23]. *You who fear the Lord, wait for his mercy; do not turn aside from him, or else you will fall. You who fear the Lord, trust in him, and your reward will not be made empty* [Sir 2:7-8]. *You who fear the Lord, love him; and your hearts will be enlightened* [Sir 2:10]. Blessed is the one who is given the fear of the Lord as a possession. *The fear of the Lord is like a paradise of blessing, and they covered a person beyond all glory* [Sir 40:28].[4]

And in praise of fear Solomon furthermore says, *The fear of the Lord adds days* [Prov 10:27]. Let us therefore, brothers, fear the Lord, but with that fear *which, being holy, lasts forever* [Ps 18(19):9]; with that chaste fear which to the days of this time will add eternal days for us, perpetual days, immortal and everlasting days. In fact, it will add one day that is without evening or ending, a day full of happiness and joy, brim full of unfailing light, supported by the company of angels, a day uninterrupted by night, unobscured by darkness, a day unclouded, that summer's heat does not make unbearable, nor winter's cold render sluggish; it will be one unending day that we will have together with the saints, in common with the angels, an eternal day with both. May it bestow on us, with all happiness and joy, fellowship with the angels; may it make us companions of the patriarchs, count us among the number of the prophets, and make us in boundless joy companions of the apostles.[5]

[And because the apostle John says in Scripture:] *There is no fear in love, but perfect love casts out fear; for fear has punishment, and whoever*

---

[4] Another string of scriptural quotations to illustrate what fear of God means and entails.

[5] Smaragdus, Via reg 3; PL 102:940AB; quoted with adjustments to his monastic readers, and used in his *Commentary*, Prol. 12; CS 212:77–78.

fears is not perfect in love [1 John 4:18], we must with discretion and care understand two kinds of fear.

For fear is of two kinds. The one kind makes humans fear God so that they may not be cast into Gehenna. The other kind is the fear that introduced charity; but it comes in such a way that it may depart. For if you still fear God because of punishments, you do not yet love him whom you thus fear. You do not desire good things, but are on your guard against evil things. But because you are on your guard against evil things you are correcting yourself and are beginning to desire good things. When you begin to desire good things, holy fear will be in you, a fear that you may lose the good things, and not that you may be cast into Gehenna, but that the Lord's presence may leave you, whom you embrace and long to enjoy forever.[6]

A certain brother asked an old man, "How does the fear of the Lord come into the soul?" The old man said, "If a person has humility and poverty, and does not judge the other—that is how the fear of the Lord comes into him."[7]

A certain old man said, "Fear and humility, dire need of food, and beating of the breast, let these abide in you."[8]

And another old man said, "*And what you hate, do not do to anyone else* [Tob 4:15]. If you hate anyone to speak ill of you, do not speak ill of anyone. If you hate anyone to slander you, do not slander anyone. If you hate anyone to hold you in contempt or inflict injuries on you, do not do any of these things to anyone. For one who is able to keep this word, it is enough for salvation."[9]

A certain old man said, "This is the life of the monk: Work, obedience, meditation, not to judge, not to speak against others, not to murmur. For it is written: *You who love the Lord, hate evil* [Ps 96(97):10]. The life of the monk is this: not to associate with the

---

[6] Bede, In 1 Jo 4:18; CCSL 121:318; PL 93:112A; see CS 82:211–12. Bede is here largely quoting from Saint Augustine's In 1 Jo 9:5.

[7] PL 73:857B (19); see 1045B (2); *Wisdom*, 2, 5; PG 65:171 [172]C (5); *Sayings*, 53 [62], 5. The unnamed old man in this and the next saying is Abba Euprepius, according to the Greek text.

[8] PL 73:857B (20); see also 1045B (3); PG 65:171 [172]D (6); *Sayings*, 53 [62], 6.

[9] PL 73:857BC (21); see also 791D–92A (153) and 1039BC (2); *Wisdom*, 35, 121.

unjust, not to look upon what is evil, not to act out of curiosity, not to listen to foolish things, not to seize what belongs to another, but rather to hand over one's own belongings; not to be proud of heart or malicious in thought, not to stuff one's stomach, but to do everything with discretion. It is in all these things that one is a monk."[10]

Abba James said, "As a lamp lights up a dark bedroom, so the fear of God, if it comes into someone's heart, enlightens that person and teaches all the virtues and the commandments of God."[11]

Certain of the fathers asked Abba Macarius the Egyptian, "How and when do you eat and when fast, as your body is so dry?" And the old man told them, "As wood in a man's hand dries out when it is used for turning bushes in a fire, so the fear of God consumes a man's bones if he has his mind fixed on the fear of God."[12]

---

[10] PL 73:857CD (22).
[11] PL 73:861C (7); see also PG 65:231 [232]C; *Sayings*, 89 [104], 3.
[12] PL 73:861CD (8); see PG 65:267 [268]C (12); *Sayings*, 110 [130], 12.

CHAPTER 7

On the Wisdom That Is Christ

he fear of the Lord is the crown of wisdom [as Scripture says], *and to fear the Lord is the beginning of wisdom; and the fullness of wisdom and the root of wisdom is the fear of the Lord* [Sir 1:18a, 14, 16, 20 in that order]. Let us, then, dearly beloved, fear the Lord and prepare our souls to receive wisdom, so that living wisely, [reverently and justly, we may merit to possess with wisdom itself an eternal kingdom]. For so it is written: Those who keep her will be justified by her [see Wis 6:11], *and she will easily be seen by those who love her, and found by those who seek her* [Wis 6:12]. For it is written: *The desire for wisdom leads to perpetual kingdoms* [Wis 6:20]. . . . For this reason Solomon says,[1]

I prayed, and understanding was given me; I called on God, and the spirit of wisdom came to me. . . . I chose to have her rather than light. . . . I loved her more than health and all beauty . . . because her light cannot be extinguished. All good things came to me together with her, and through her hands a reputation beyond measure. I rejoiced in them all, because this wisdom goes ahead of me . . . for she is an unfailing treasure for humans; those who made use of it became sharers in friendship with God. . . . There is in her a spirit that is intelligent, holy, unique, manifold, subtle, mobile, clear, undefiled, distinct, agreeable, loving the good, keen, irresistible, beneficent, humane, steadfast, sure, possessing all power, overseeing all things, and receiving all spirits, intelligible. . . . For wisdom is more mobile than all things mobile. . . . For she is a breath of the power of God, and a pure outflow of

---

[1] Smaragdus, Via reg 4; PL 102:941D–42C.

23

*the glory of Almighty God. . . . For she is the brightness of eternal light,
the spotless mirror of God's majesty, and the image of his goodness* [Wis
7:7, 10bac, 11-12, 14, 22-26].

She is [as it is said] *more beautiful than the sun, and excels every arrangement of the stars. Compared to light she is found superior; for night
succeeds light, but wisdom conquers malice* [Wis 7:29-30]. *As it is said: She
reaches mightily from end to end, and she orders all things agreeably. . . .
For she teaches self-control and wisdom,[2] justice and courage; nothing in life
is more profitable for men and women than these* [Wis 8:1, 7].

For wisdom is a great treasure, and one who finds her will find
life, and one who possesses her will have the crown of immortality.
She it is that makes people stable in faith,[3] assured in speech, pleasant
in conversation, cheerful in giving, humane in mercy, agreeable in
responding, clever in distinguishing, meek in prosperity, fearless in
adversity, keen in thought, brilliant in deed,[4] candid in appearance,
brave in conflict.

*"Where then does wisdom come from? And where is the place of under-
standing? It is hidden from the eyes of all the living. . . . God understands
the way to it, and he knows its place. . . . For he said to humankind,
'Behold, the fear of the Lord is itself wisdom; and to depart from evil is
understanding'"* [Job 28:20-23, 28].

Let us love her, then, my friends, so that we may be loved by
her. . . . For the wisdom that is Christ says, *I, wisdom, live in counsel,
and I am present among learned thoughts. . . . Mine is counsel and im-
partiality; mine is prudence and mine fortitude. . . . I love those who love
me, and those who watch for me early will find me. With me are riches and
honor. . . . My fruit is better than gold and the precious stone. . . . I walk
in the ways of righteousness . . . to make rich those who love me, and to
fill their treasuries* [Prov 8:12, 14, 17-21].

For God loves those who love wisdom. [Wisdom prepares life for
her children, ministers justice to those who prize her, and bestows
prudence on those who love her.] In temptation she walks with such

---

[2] Smaragdus's text here reads *sapientiam* instead of the Vulgate's *prudentiam*.

[3] Here the *Diadema* has *stabiles in fide*; the *Via regia* has *stabiles in regno*, "stable
in kingship [or kingdom]."

[4] Here the *Diadema* has *perlucidos*; the *Via regia* has *placidos*, "placid."

as these, preparing a straight road for them; she bares her secrets and stores up for them knowledge and the understanding of prudence. And so those who hold her fast will inherit eternal life.[5]

<hr/>

[5] Smaragdus, Via reg 4; PL 102:941D–45A. The whole of this chapter of *The Crown* is found in Via reg 4, but not always in the same order; adaptations are made here for the monastic readership.

CHAPTER 8

On Prudence

Prudence is the ornament of all the virtues, the glory of our words, the distinction of our speech, as it is written: *To the prudent person teaching is a golden ornament, and like a bracelet on the right arm* [Sir 21:24]. Prudence guards the mouth, governs behavior, controls the heart, moderates the tongue, assesses all our words and weighs up our affairs. For so it is written: *The words of the prudent will be weighed in the balance* [Sir 21:28]. Hence Paul also says, *Let your speech always be gracious, seasoned with salt, so that you may know how you should answer each person* [Col 4:6].

Brothers and sisters, let us, too, love this outstanding virtue, so that it may provide direction of spirit and strengthen the mind's discretion. [For thus it is written: *The wise person is governed by much prudence* (Prov 14:29)].[1] Let us love prudence, that it may direct our steps in what we do and set in order our thinking activity. For it is written: *The prudent direct their steps* [Prov 15:21 Vulgate]. Let us love prudence, that it may build us a spiritual house, and raise it up and strengthen it once built. For it is written: *By wisdom a house will be built, and by prudence it will be strengthened* [Prov 24:3]. Let us love prudence, so that it may provide us with the adornment of upright behavior and virtues in plenty, put firmly in our mouth the law of truth, adorn in all sorts of ways wise and understanding speech, place in our speech an ornament of gold, and confer on our lips a gift of silver; may it set a constant guard over our behavior and award fitting glory.[2]

---

[1] This is the only quotation not found in Via reg 4; some of the later quotations come from earlier in Via reg 4.

[2] Smaragdus, Via reg 5; PL 102:945B–46A. The passage has adaptations, omissions, and additions appropriate to his monastic readership.

CHAPTER 9

On Simplicity

G reat indeed is the virtue of prudence, but it needs to be tempered by the virtue of simplicity. For thus says the Lord in the Gospel: *Be prudent as serpents and simple as doves* [Matt 10:16]. And the Lord says to the devil about the simple man Job: *Have you considered my servant Job? There is none like him on the earth, simple, upright, who fears God and shuns evil* [Job 1:8].[1]

So let us love this great virtue, friends; it proceeds from the treasury of the Most High, and though it belongs to all Christians, it is especially necessary for monks, who must adorn what they purpose in life with courtesy and simplicity.[2]

For it is written: *Think of the Lord in goodness and seek him in simplicity of heart, because he is found by those who do not put him to the test, and manifests himself to those who have faith in him* [Wis 1:1-2].

Let us then love simplicity of heart, so that it may direct our actions into the way of salvation. It is written: *The simplicity of the upright will direct them* [Prov 11:3]. Let us obey the words of Paul, the outstanding preacher, who admonishes us, saying, *I wish you to be wise in what is good, simple in what is evil* [Rom 16:19].[3]

For prudence in striving for what is good must continually sharpen the hearts of the elect, and simplicity temper the sharpness of prudence, so that prudence may not exceed the measure of uprightness, or simplicity grow sluggish through being deceived by ignorance.[4]

---

[1] Smaragdus, Via reg 6; PL 102:946B.

[2] No source traced for this passage; it may be an editorial addition of Smaragdus for this work.

[3] Possibly Smaragdus's adaptation with editorial addition of a couple of sentences from Via reg 6.

[4] Smaragdus, Via reg 6; PL 102:946CD.

For we read of Jacob: He was a simple man, living in his house [see Gen 25:27], because all who avoid being scattered in exterior cares and concerns are simple in their thinking and stand firm in the dwelling of their conscience . . . lest they covet many things outside and, having become strangers to their thoughts, withdraw from themselves.[5]

Let us, then, run by the paths of simplicity, so that through it we may deserve to reach our eternal homeland more quickly, and there merit to receive the garment of immortality and the rewards of simplicity.[6]

---

[5] Gregory, Mor 5.11; CCSL 143:232; PL 75:690A.

[6] Smaragdus, Via reg 6; PL 102:946D. The text is adapted and the word order slightly changed.

CHAPTER 10

On Patience

Concerning this virtue of patience the Lord says, *In your patience you will possess your souls* [Luke 21:19]. . . . And his disciple Paul says, *As God's chosen ones, holy and beloved, clothe yourselves with deep compassion, kindness, humility, modesty, and patience* [Col 3:12-13], *bearing with one another in love* [Eph 4:1]. Solomon also says, *A man's learning is known by his patience, and his boast is to overlook offenses* [Prov 19:11]. . . . In his preaching James the apostle says, *Patience brings the work to perfection, that you may be perfect and complete, lacking in nothing* [Jas 1:3-4]. And Paul again says, *Admonish the restless, encourage the fainthearted, help the weak, be patient towards all* [1 Thess 5:14].[1]

Therefore, dearly beloved, let us run all along this way of patience and let us love it, because there is nothing on it to make us stumble; it will in the future repay those who run all along it with complete and eternal joy. For great is the virtue of patience, my friends, which does not injure but rather loves those from whom one suffers injury; it forgives injuries to the one causing them, and does not return them; it does not hurt others when it could, but spares them. For the root and guard of all virtues is patience. Through patience we possess our

---

[1] Smaragdus, Via reg 7; PL 102:947AB, with the required adaptations and an inversion in the order of scripture quotations. The Proverbs 19:11 quotation replaces the *Via regia*'s Proverbs 25:15, which is more applicable to kings and rulers: *Patientia lenitur princeps, et lingua mollis frangit duritiem,* "With patience a ruler may be soothed, and a soft tongue breaks down resistance."

souls [see Luke 21:19]. The Lord showed that patience is the guard of our condition, because he taught that by it we possess ourselves.[2]

True patience is to bear evils from others with equanimity, and not to be moved[3] by any sorrow against one who inflicts evils.[4]

It is the virtue of patience that commends us to God, [guards us from all evils,] and preserves us. This virtue it is that tempers anger, curbs the tongue, and governs the mind; this it is that keeps the peace, exercises discipline [with moderation], crushes the onset of unlawful desire, represses violence, and extinguishes the flame of enmity. Patience restrains the power of the rich, assists the poor in their need. . . . It makes people humble in prosperity and brave in adversity and meek in response to injuries and insults. . . . It conquers temptations and bears with persecutions. . . . It is patience that fortifies the foundations of our faith, lifts our hope high, and directs the actions of our life. It patiently governs us so that we may be able to hold fast the way of Christ . . . and makes us inflexible in our resolve to persevere as children of God. . . .[5] Dearly beloved, we must joyfully esteem this virtue and embrace it with all our strength.[6]

For we shall speedily receive the fruit of patience and its reward if we persevere in its company to the end. For thus says James the apostle: *Behold, the judge is standing before the door!* [Jas 5:9], and will bestow on you the rewards of patience, and on your adversaries the penalty they deserve. *Before the door*, he says, because the Lord Jesus Christ is near to us, and is ready to forgive our faults when we pray, and to bestow the rewards of patience.[7]

---

[2] Smaragdus, Via reg 7; PL 102:947B. The last sentence is from Gregory, Past 3.9; PL 77:60D.

[3] Gregory's text has *morderi*, "to be bitten or vexed," whereas Smaragdus has *moveri*.

[4] Gregory, Hom ev 35.4; CCSL 141:324; PL 76:1261D–62A; see CS 123:305. The Migne and CCSL text of Gregory has *Patientia vero*, "But patience"; Smaragdus has *Patientia autem vera*.

[5] Cyprian, De pat 20; PL 4:659C–60A.

[6] Smaragdus, Via reg 7; PL 102:947BC. This section is quoted with the required adaptations, and omitting several of the repeated *ipsa est* that mark the more florid style of the passage in Smaragdus's earlier work.

[7] See Bede, In Jac 5:9; CCSL 121:219; PL 93:38A; see CS 82:59.

They used to say about Abba Isidore, who was the priest in Scetis,[8] that if anyone had a brother who was sick or fainthearted or given to acting wrongfully, and was wanting to drive him out, he would say, "Bring him to me." And he would take him and with his patience cure the spirit of that brother.[9]

Once robbers came to the monastery of a certain old man and said to him, "We have come to take away everything that is in your cell." And he said, "My sons, take whatever you like." So they took everything they found in the cell and departed. Now they forgot a little bag that was hidden in the cell. The old man followed, calling out after them, "My sons, take this as well. You overlooked it in the cell." Filled with wonder at his patience, they collected everything and restored it to his cell. And they all did penance, saying to one another, "This is indeed a man of God."[10]

---

[8] The Smaragdus text here has *in Scythia*; *Scyti*, the locative of *Scytus*, is its usual way of saying "in [at] Scetis."

[9] PL 73:970C (5); see also PG 65:219 [220]BC (1); *Sayings*, 82 [96], 1bis.

[10] PL 73:971CD (13); see *Wisdom*, 55, 206. Similar to the story told of Abba Euprepius, which does not mention the conversion of the thieves; see PG 65:171 [172]BC (2); *Sayings*, 52 [62], 2.

CHAPTER 11

On Humility

Although this virtue of humility should be characteristic of all Christians, it should especially find a dwelling and a resting place in the hearts of monks. Hence Isidore says that the highest virtue of a monk is humility; his supreme vice, pride. Anyone may judge himself a monk when he considers himself the least, even though he performs great acts of virtue. Those who leave the world and follow the virtues laid down in the precepts without humility of heart, fall more heavily from the heights because they are thrown down further through their being exalted by the virtues than they would have slipped through the vices. The conscience of God's servant must always be humble and sorrowful, so that through humility he may not give way to pride, and through a beneficial sorrow his heart may not grow slack and wanton.[1]

Of this supreme virtue the Lord says, *[A]ll who exalt themselves will be humbled, but all who humble themselves will be exalted* [Luke 18:14]. [And the apostle James says,] *Let the humble brother boast in his exaltation* [Jas 1:9]. Because every brother who humbly suffers adversities for the Lord will be lifted up to receive from him the rewards of the kingdom.[2]

[And so the blessed apostle Peter says,] *God resists the proud, but gives grace to the humble* [1 Pet 5:5; also Jas 4:6 and see Prov 3:34].

---

[1] Isidore, Sent 3.19.1–2, 3b; CCSL 111:249–50; PL 83:694AB.
[2] Bede, In Jac 1:9; CCSL 121:185; PL 93:12C; see CS 82:11.

He means all,[3] both the elders and the young folk, it seemingly being his aim subtly to encourage the mutual practice of the virtue of humility, the former in guiding, and the latter in obeying. . . . So he teaches all to introduce humility towards one another by example and also by word, because he knew well that the vice of pride is to be guarded against by all, seeing that it cast the angels down from heaven.

He goes on to expound what the grace is that he promises will be given to the humble, saying, *Humble yourselves therefore under the mighty hand of God, so that he may exalt you in the time of visitation* [1 Pet 5:6]. He bestows this grace on the humble, so that the more they are humbled on his account in time of combat, the more gloriously he may exalt them in time of recompense.[4]

And so the psalmist says, *The Lord is near to those of troubled heart, and he will save the humble of spirit* [Ps 33(34):18].

Now all humility is not so much in speech as in the mind; our conscience will know that we are humble, so let us never think that we know anything, or understand anything, or are anything. It is remarkable how the king and prophet David maintained humility when he said, *O Lord, my heart is not exalted, nor are my eyes raised on high* [Ps 131(132):1]. He also says, *A sacrifice to God is a broken spirit* [Ps 50(51):17]. And again, *See my humility and my toil, and forgive all my sins* [Ps 24(25):18].

So if the humbled heart is a sacrifice to God, that person offered sacrifice who said, *O Lord, my heart is not exalted,*[5] and so forth. If some hermit who spends his time in his cell were to say things like this, he would shine with praise for great patience; but because a king robed in purple and outstanding among prophets said it, let the Church, spread throughout the world, praise his example of humility. Humility rises to take a place of honor among distinguished virtues, because royal majesty has stooped to take it on.[6]

---

[3] Smaragdus has omitted the words in Bede citing Peter that supply the connection: "Manifest humility towards one another, all of you."

[4] Bede, In 1 Pt 5:5-6; CCSL 121:257–58; PL 93:65D–66AB; see CS 82:116–17. Smaragdus has brought the opening scripture quotation from later in this passage.

[5] Augustine, En in ps 130; PL 37:1706.

[6] Passage quoted in part by Smaragdus in his *Commentary*, 4.3; CS 212:267.

Abba Anthony said, "I saw all the snares of the enemy stretched out on the earth, and sighing deeply I said, 'Who, think you, will succeed in crossing over these?' And I heard a voice saying, Humility."[7]

Abba Serapion said, "I have done many bodily labors, more than my son Zachary, and I have not reached the level of his humility and reserve in speech."[8] Abba Moses said to Brother Zachary, "Tell me, what am I to do?" He took the cowl from his head, put it under his feet and trod on it, saying, "Unless a man is trampled under foot like this, he cannot be a monk."[9]

An old man, when asked why he was being troubled by demons, answered, "Because we have thrown away our weapons, which are enduring insults, humility, poverty and patience."[10] An old man, when asked what perfection was, answered, "A person's perfection is humility. The more people have advanced towards humility and been bowed down, the more they will be lifted up to their advantage[11] . . . because humility is a great and even a divine work. The way of humility is this: people should take up bodily labors, regard themselves as sinners and put themselves in subjection in all things . . . they should not pay attention to others' sins, but always consider their own, and pray to God without ceasing for forgiveness."[12]

---

[7] PL 73:953CD (3); see also PG 65:[77] 78AB (7); *Sayings*, 2 [2], 7.

[8] PL 73:957A (16); see also PG 65:[249] 250C (1); *Sayings*, 100 [117], 1. Smaragdus and the PL 73 text have Serapion, while the text in PG 65 has Carion.

[9] PL 73:957B (17a and c); see also 775CD (86) and 1032D–33A (2); PG 65:179 [180]AB (3); *Sayings*, 58 [68], 3.

[10] PL 73:964A (58); see also 798B (173) and 1048D–49A (1); *Wisdom*, 48, 169.

[11] PL 73:966D–967A (77); see also 797C (171b) and 1036B (5).

[12] PL 73:967BC (82); see *Wisdom*, 52, 192.

CHAPTER 12

On Peace

N one exalt themselves more with God than those who for God's sake humble themselves in their own estimation. The humble are exalted by God so as to be called children of God and heirs of Christ. Only let them pursue peace, because the children of peace must seek and pursue peace.

This is the thrust of the apostle's admonition when he says, *Pursue peace with everyone, and the holiness without which no one will see God* [Heb 12:14]. The Lord himself also says in the Gospel: *Blessed are the peacemakers, for they will be called children of God* [Matt 5:9]. Among his divine commands and saving teachings, when he was very near his passion the Savior entrusted this precept and commandment to us to keep, saying, *My peace I give to you; my peace I entrust to you* [John 14:27].[1] When ascending into heaven, the Lord left us this inheritance, and commanded us through his most faithful king and prophet David to pursue it. He said, *Turn away from evil, and do good; seek peace, and pursue it* [Ps 33(34):14]. If we are willing to pursue this with a sincere heart, we shall be heirs of Christ. But if we desire to be Christ's heirs, we must live in Christ's peace. If we are God's children we must be peaceful. For God's children must be peaceful and humble, meek in mind, simple in heart, pure in word, innocent in spirit, having the same mind and heart, cleaving faithfully and with one mind to one another.[2]

---

[1] Perhaps Smaragdus is relying on memory and misquoting. The Vulgate has *Pacem relinquo vobis, pacem meam do vobis*, "Peace I leave to you, my peace I give to you."

[2] Smaragdus, Via reg 17; PL 102:957CD.

CHAPTER 13

On Obedience

The blessed apostle Peter speaks in this way about obedience: *Therefore with the loins of your minds girded up, and sober* in all things,[1] *put complete hope in the grace that is offered to you, in the revelation of Jesus Christ, like obedient children.* [1 Pet 1:13-14]. He rightly wants those he referred to in the preface [of his letter] as *chosen [for sanctification by the Spirit,][2] for obedience to Jesus Christ and for sprinkling with his blood* [1 Pet 1:2] to be obedient children.[3]

Therefore obedience, when it faces adversity, must regard some of this as due to itself, while prosperity it must regard as in no way due to itself; this attitude is the more real in adversity the more perfect is the mind's detachment from the present glory which it receives by divine influence.[4]

We are commanded [by the Almighty Lord] to observe obedience until death, as Truth says, *I can do nothing by myself. As I hear, I judge* [John 5:30]. As he hears, he judges. Then he will also be obeying his Father when he comes as judge of this world. In case obedience to the end of the present life may seem laborious to us, our Redeemer points out that he observes it even when he comes as judge. What wonder is it, then, if sinful humans submit to obedience during the brief space of the present life, when the mediator between God and man, even when rewarding

---

[1] *In omnibus*, "In all things," is an addition of Smaragdus.

[2] Not in Bede (see next note) at this point, but inserted by Smaragdus.

[3] Bede, In 1 Pt 1:13-14; CCSL 121:230–31; PL 93:45D–46A; see CS 82:77–78.

[4] Taio, Sent 3.31; PL 80:888BC, quoting Gregory, Mor 35.14; CCSL 143B:1794; PL 76:767A.

the obedient, does not abandon obedience? We must know that evil is never done through obedience, but sometimes through obedience we must leave off some good we are doing. There was no evil tree in paradise that God forbade man to touch [see Gen 2:17]. Man was created good, but so that he might become better through the merit of obedience, God saw fit to keep him from a good thing. This was so that what he did would be so much more virtuous; by not engaging with the good thing, he should show himself more humble in subjection to his Maker.[5] . . . For it is written: *Obedience is better than sacrifice* [1 Sam 15:22]. And rightly is obedience put before sacrifices, because through sacrifices the flesh of another is slain, whereas by obedience one's own will is slain. Humans placate God the more quickly when they repress the pride of their own will before God's eyes and immolate themselves with the sword of his command.[6]

Hence when Abba Basil was asked how the brothers should obey one another, he replied, "As servants of the Lord, according as the Lord ordered: The one who wants to be great among you, let him become least of all and servant of all . . . just as the Son of Man did not come to be served but to serve" [see Matt 20:26-28 and Mark 10:43-45].[7]

A certain old man planted a dry stick in the desert, and wanting to test a brother's obedience, said to him, "Water that stick every day until it bears fruit." Now water was a long way away from them. When the brother had done this for three years that stick became green and bore fruit. The old man took some of its fruit, brought it to the church and told the brothers, "Take and eat the fruit of obedience."[8]

An old man used to say that God seeks nothing so much from those who are beginning their monastic life as the labor of obedience.[9]

---

[5] Taio, Sent 3.31; PL 80:888CD, quoting Gregory, Mor 35.14; CCSL 143B:1793–94; PL 76:766AB.

[6] Taio, Sent 3.31; PL 80:889A, quoting Gregory, Mor 35.14; CCSL 143B:1792; PL 76:765BC.

[7] RBas 115; PG 31:[1161] 1162A and RBas 64; CSEL 86:101.

[8] PL 73:948AB (3); see also PG 65:203 [204]C (1); *Sayings*, 73 [85–86], 1.

[9] PL 73:950D–51A (15).

A certain man of the world renounced the world, and came to the monastery, bringing with him his little son. The abba took the child and began to kiss him. He said to his father, "Do you love him?" He answered, "Of course." He said to him again, "Do you cherish him?" And he replied, "Of course." Afterwards the abba said to him, "If you love this child, take him and throw him into the burning oven." The father took him and threw him into the burning oven, and at once the oven became like dew. By this deed he won glory at that time as had the patriarch Abraham.[10]

An old man said, "A brother who has devoted his soul to obeying his spiritual father has a greater reward than one who has withdrawn alone to the desert. Those who remove themselves into the desert have withdrawn from the world by their own free will. But the kind who have devoted themselves to obey and cast off all their own desires depend on God and the command of their spiritual father, and so have greater glory than others. Therefore, my children, obedience done for God is good. Follow intently as best you can, then, my children, the path marked out by this virtue. Obedience is the salvation of all the faithful. Obedience is the mother of all the virtues. Obedience it is that finds the kingdom of heaven; it opens heaven and raises humans from the earth. Obedience cohabits with the angels. Obedience is the food of all the saints. It is by her they have been fed as with milk, and through her they have come to perfection."[11]

---

[10] PL 73:952B (18 abbreviated); for a similar saying see also Cassian, Inst. 4.27; PL 49:186B–88A; ACW:58:92–93.

[11] PL 73:952C–53A (19 abbreviated); see also PG 65: [389] 390CD–391 [392] A (2bis); *Sayings*, 177 [210–11], 2. In the Greek text the old man is Abba Rufus. The apophthegm is much abbreviated here.

CHAPTER 14

On Those Who Despise the World

The saints fly from what is dear to lovers of the world as if from things adverse to them, and rejoice in the world's adversities more than they delight in prosperity. There is general agreement that those to whom this world offers prosperity and every comfort are strangers to God. For God's servants, all the things of this world are felt to be harmful. The result is that while they experience adversity they are aroused to desire heaven more ardently. Great favor with God lights up one who is contemptible to this world. The reality is that one whom the world hates must be loved by God. . . . This is why holy persons yearn to despise the world and bring the movement of their mind back to things above, so that they can gather themselves together in the place from which they have slipped, and draw themselves up from the place where they have been dispersed. . . . Those who after renouncing the world pant after the heavenly country with holy desires are raised above their concern for earthly things as though by wings; with groans they regard the place they have slipped into, and with great joy apply their mind to the goal they will arrive at.[1]

Holy persons who entirely renounce the world die to this world to such a degree that they find their delight in living for God alone; and the more they withdraw from this world's manner of living,

---

[1] Isidore, Sent 3.16.1–3, 5, 7a; CCSL 111:244–45; PL 83:691CD–92AB.

the more they contemplate with the keen point of their mind the presence of God and the numerous assembly of the angels.

The life of the monk is a road without disordered desire or love for one to stumble over or stop at. For while each monk withdraws from association with the world, disordered desire does not bind him because he does not yield consent, nor does it torment him when he experiences it. It is good to be removed from the world in body, but much better to be so by choice. Both ways belong to the perfect man. The one who is separated from this world in body and heart is perfect. The wild ass, as Jeremiah says, despises the city [see Jer 2:24], and monks the general way of life of the citizens of the world. They desire the adversities of our life and look down on its prosperity, so that when they despise this life they may find the future life.[2]

---

[2] Isidore, Sent 3.17.1, 3–5; CCSL 111:246–47; PL 83:692D–93A–C.

CHAPTER 15

On Repentance

All sinners when they repent should heave a double sigh: that is, for not doing the good they should have done, and for doing the evil they should not have done. When we do not rise up to good works, we must bewail ourselves in these two ways, because we did not do what was right, and we did what was wrong. Through blessed Moses . . . the order is given for one turtledove to be offered for a sin offering, and another for a burnt offering [see Lev 5:7]. A whole burnt offering is called a holocaust. So we offer one turtledove for a sin offering when we utter sighs for faults; we make a holocaust of the other when we burn with the fire of sorrow, setting ourselves completely alight, because we neglected what was good.[1]

Blessed Job, making progress after the scourges, and striking himself in great self-reproach says, *Therefore I reprove myself, and do penance in dust and ashes* [Job 42:6]. . . . To do penance in dust and ashes is to recognize, after contemplating the Supreme Being, that one is nothing but dust and ashes. . . . In sackcloth the harshness and compunction for sins is shown, while in ashes is shown the dust of the dead. For this reason both are customarily used for penance, so that in the sackcloth of compunction we may know what we have done through our faults, and in the dust of ashes ponder what we have become through judgment.[2]

---

[1] Taio, Sent 3.42; PL 80:904CD, quoting Gregory, Mor 32.3; CCSL 143B:1628–29; PL 76:635C–36C.

[2] Taio, Sent 3.42; PL 80:904D–5A, quoting Gregory, Mor 35.5.6; CCSL 143B:1777–78; PL 76:753AB.

All faithful people well know that their thoughts are subjected to searching inquiry in the judgment, and so before the judgment they search into and closely examine themselves interiorly. They do this so that they may more calmly await the strict judge, who will come only to find the heart he draws near to examine already punished for its fault.[3] For when we ourselves punish the fault, he in no way judges it in the final examination. Paul witnesses to this when he says, *But if we were to judge ourselves, we would not be judged* [1 Cor 11:31].[4] Unless we wash it away with repentance, what we do outwardly is kept hidden in the secret of God's judgments, so that one day it may come out to the glare of judgment even from the seal of secrecy. But when we are wasted by the scourge of discipline for the evils we have done, and lament these through repentance, he takes note and cures our iniquity, because he does not leave things unpunished here, nor does he save them up for the judgment of punishment.[5]

Let the just judge themselves carefully in this life, so that they may not be judged by God with everlasting condemnation. People exact judgment of themselves when through worthy repentance they condemn their wrongful deeds. The bitterness of repentance causes the mind to examine more closely its deeds, and to remember with weeping the gifts of God that it has despised. There is nothing worse than to become aware of a fault and not bewail it. All sinners must have a twofold lament in repenting: through negligence they have failed to do good, and have done evil through sheer boldness. They have not done what they should have, and have done what they should not have.

Those persons do worthy penance who bewail their guilt by fitting satisfaction, condemning and weeping over what they have done, deploring it the more profoundly the more willful has been the sinning. Those persons do worthy penance who so deplore past

---

[3] Taio, Sent 3.42; PL 80:905AB, quoting Gregory, Mor 4.14; CCSL 143:181; PL 75:651BC.

[4] Taio, Sent 3.42; PL 80:905B, quoting Gregory, Mor 12.16; CCSL 143A:641; PL 75:996B.

[5] Taio, Sent 3.42; PL 80:905C, quoting Gregory, Mor 12.17; CCSL 143A:641; PL 75:996CD.

evils as not to commit them again in the future. For one who be-
wails a sin and then commits it again is like someone who washes
an unbaked brick: the more he washes it, the more mud he makes.

Though people be sinners and impious, if they are converted to
repentance they are believed able to obtain forgiveness.[6]

All must hasten to God by repenting while they can, in case
while they are able they refuse to, and when later they want to they
are quite unable. And so the prophet says, *Seek the Lord while he may
be found, call on him while he is near* [Isa 55:6]. If when people can sin
they repent, and so live their life as to correct it of all fault, there is
no doubt that when they die they pass over to eternal rest. But those
who live wickedly and do penance when in danger of death, just as
their condemnation is uncertain, so also is their forgiveness doubtful.
Although there is forgiveness of sins through repentance, a person
must not be without fear, because the satisfaction of repentance is
measured by divine, not human, judgment. Accordingly, because
God's mercy is hidden, we must weep without ceasing. Those who
repent ought not to have a feeling of security about sins, because
security breeds negligence, and negligence often draws the incau-
tious to their former vices. Although through repentance vices have
been driven out of them, if afterwards while overconfident of their
security any fault sneaks up on them unawares, immediately the
earlier delights of the vices quickly slip in; they strike those persons
and drag them more deeply into the former accustomed works,
so that *the last state of that person is worse than the first* [Matt 12:45].[7]

[6] Isidore, Sent 2.13.3–8; CCSL 111:120–21; PL 83:614D–15B.
[7] Isidore, Sent 2.13.13a, 14–15a, 18–19; CCSL 111:122–24; PL 83:616A–17A.

CHAPTER 16

On Confession

James says, *Confess your sins to one another, and pray for one another, so that you may be saved* [Jas 5:16]. But in this saying there needs to be this distinction, that we confess our daily less grievous sins to our equals, and believe that we are saved by their daily prayer.

Next, according to the law we bring to the priest the uncleanness of more serious leprosy, and following his judgment let us be careful to be purified in the manner and for the length of time he has commanded [see Lev 13].[1]

[And so David also says,] *Reveal your way to the Lord and trust in him* [Ps 36(37):5]. The thickness of sins is a kind of veil with which our way, that is, our life, is clothed and enveloped in darkness as with a garment. This is what we reveal when we very promptly confess our dark sins.[2]

[David again says,] *Confess to the Lord for he is good, for his mercy is forever* [Ps 106(107):1]. . . . He indicates this confession for applying the medicine in fullness.[3] Now there is no doubt that this also pertains to the public praise of the Lord, since divine compassion shows itself more glorious in pardoning one who confesses than

---

[1] Bede, In Jac 5:16; CCSL 121:222; PL 93:39D–40A; see CS 82:62.

[2] Cassiodorus, Ex ps 36(37):5; CCSL 97:326; PL 70:258D. Quoted in Commentary, 7.44–45; CS 212:295. The word *tenebrosa*, "dark," does not occur in the last phrase of Cassiodorus.

[3] Cassiodorus has *ad medicinam poenitudinis*, "for the medicine of repentance"; Smaragdus has *plenitudinis*.

44

it is to one who lives without offending.[4] . . . And lest the sheer number of their faults terrify any, he adds *for he is good.* Who would hesitate to have recourse to him, on hearing that he can come very swiftly to their aid? . . . He added, *for his mercy is forever.* In order that human negligence, having heard that the Lord is good, may not hang back from attentive and careful supplication, he mentions the cause of the remedy, so that by the Lord's gift they may hasten to make speedy confession.[5] Let us, then, brothers, confess to our Lord, for he is good and forgives sins.

That people acknowledge their iniquity, and by vocal confession lay bare what has been acknowledged, are testimonies of humility. It is a customary vice of the human race to slip and commit sin, and then not to admit the sin committed by confessing it, but rather to defend it by denying it, and thus to multiply the proven fault by defending it.[6]

The signs of a true confession are that when any say they are sinners, they do not contradict someone else who says the same about them. It is written: *The righteous in the beginning is his own accuser* [Prov 18:17]. . . . We must take the utmost care to admit of our own accord the evils we have done, and not deny them when others charge us with them. It is indeed the vice of pride for people to deign, as if of their own accord, to confess what they disdain to have others say about them.[7]

---

[4] In Smaragdus's *Expositio in Regulam S. Benedicti*, CCM 8:183 (*Commentary*): *quam viventi sine confessione praestare,* "than to one who lives without confessing." Cassiodorus and *Diadema* have *sine offensione.*

[5] Cassiodorus, Ex ps 105(106):1; CCSL 98:958; PL 80:754D–55AB. Quoted in Commentary, 7.46; CS 212:296.

[6] Taio, Sent 3.48; PL 80:905D–6A, quoting Gregory, Mor. 22.15; CCSL 143B:1113; PL 76:230D.

[7] Taio, Sent 3.48; PL 80:906B, quoting Gregory, Mor. 22.15; CCSL 143B:1115–16; PL 76:232D–33A.

CHAPTER 17

On Compunction

Compunction of heart is humility of mind with tears, arising from the remembrance of sin and fear of judgment. For those who are converted that sense of compunction is more perfect that repels all the longings of fleshly desires, and mustering all their mind's ability to apply itself fixes their attention on the contemplation of God. It is well known that there is a twofold compunction inspired by God that affects the soul of each of the elect, that is, when it considers the evils it has done, or when it sighs deeply with the desire for eternal life. There are four kinds of feeling by which the just person's mind is pierced with a salutary disgust: the memory of past sins, the calling to mind of future punishments, the consideration that one is a pilgrim for the duration of this life, the desire for the heavenly homeland—so as to be able to reach it as quickly as possible. When men and women are pierced with sorrow to the point of tears by the remembrance of sins, let them know that they are being quickened by the presence of God; when they blush inwardly at the thought of what they have lost they are already punishing themselves by judging themselves and repenting. For Peter wept when Christ looked at him [see Luke 22:61]. And the Psalm also says, He looked down [see Ps 32(33):13], and *the earth reeled and rocked* [Ps 17(18):7].[1]

David says about this virtue of compunction: *My tears have been my food by day and by night* [Ps 41(42):3]. The soul is nourished by its

---

[1] Isidore, Sent 2.12.1–5; CCSL 111:118–19; PL 83:613B–14A. Isidore may have conflated Psalm 96:4, *Vidit, et commota est terra* with Psalm 32:13's *respexit*, and words from Psalm 17:7, *commota est, et contremuit terra.*

mourning when in its weeping it is lifted up to heavenly joys and yet it bears inwardly the groaning of its sorrow; but it receives a strengthening food from the force of love that flows out through its tears.[2]

Every elect person's mind puts before its eyes on the one part the strictness of justice, on the other the fault's deserts. It considers the punishment it would deserve should the compassion of the one who spares fail, who is accustomed to deliver people from eternal punishments through the lamentations of the present time. Through the coming of the Holy Spirit, Almighty God afflicts the minds of carnal people [which formerly roamed about on this world's waves] with the grief of repentance, so that, with their pride crushed, those who were previously lifted up by the high wave of vanity and prosperity in the sea of this world may lie in a wholesome humility.[3]

There are four qualities by which the souls of the upright are vehemently afflicted in compunction: when they remember their evil actions while considering where they have been; or fearing the sentence of God's judgments, they search into themselves and think about where they will be; or paying close attention to the evils of the present life they think sorrowfully of where they are; or when they contemplate the good things of the heavenly homeland, and being not yet in possession of them they mournfully gaze at where they are not.[4]

[Hence the psalmist says,] *He has given us tears to drink in full measure* [Ps 79(80):5]. Those who deplore the sins they have committed must take care to wash away the evils they have done with full lamentation, in order not to be bound tightly by the debt incurred through what they have perpetrated, and fail to undo it by the weeping of their satisfaction. It is indeed written: *He has given us tears to drink in full measure* [Ps 79(80):5]. That is to say, everyone's mind is to drink the tears of its compunction as it remembers how parched and far from God it has become through its faults.[5]

---

[2] Gregory, Mor 5.8; CCSL 143:227; PL 75:686C.

[3] Taio, Sent 3.45; PL 80:900D–901A; a note in PL 80 says that this section is not found in Gregory.

[4] Taio, Sent 3.45; PL 80:901B, quoting Gregory, Mor 23.21; CCSL 143B:1175; PL 76:276A.

[5] Gregory, Past 3.29; PL 77:107C.

CHAPTER 18

On the Hope and Dread of the Elect

The upright person's mind generally deplores the wrong it remembers having done, and not only forsakes the wrong done but also punishes it with most bitter tears. Yet while it remembers what it has done it is sore afraid of judgment. All the elect have already been fully converted, but they do not yet lift themselves up in full security, because while they think about how strict the final examination is, they waver anxiously between hope and dread; and also because they do not know what the just judge will hold against them and what he will loose when he comes. For they remember how great is the wrong they have committed, but do not know whether they have worthily bewailed their actions. And they fear that the grossness of their fault exceeds the measure of their repentance. Generally truth already relaxes the blame, but the afflicted mind, exceedingly anxious for itself, still wavers concerning pardon.

So holy people receive mercy even here, but do not know that they have received it because they forsake their sin by correcting it and repenting, but are still very afraid of the strict judge regarding retribution for it. All the just freely sing the mercies of the Lord in eternity, where there is no longer any doubt about pardon for sin, where the remembrance of its fault no longer torments the secure mind, and where the heart does not waver under fear of sentence but exults in freedom because of forgiveness.[1]

---

[1] Taio, Sent 3.46; PL 80:902D–3AB, quoting Gregory, Mor 4.36; CCSL 143:215–16; PL 75:677CD–78A. For the last sentence see also Taio, Sent 5.35; PLS 4:1677.

[Those oppressed by fear and dread] are to be admonished [and encouraged] to regard as granted the mercy they are asking for, lest they perish by force of immoderate affliction. For the Lord would not in kindness set before the eyes of the delinquent sins for them to lament, had he wanted to smite them himself in strictness. It is certain that he has willed to hide from his judgment those whom he has made their own judges, anticipating them by showing mercy. . . . Thus Scripture says through Paul: *But if we were to judge ourselves, we would not be judged* [1 Cor 11:31].[2]

---

[2] Taio, Sent 3.46; PL 80:903CD, quoting Gregory, Past 3.29; PL 77:108AB.

CHAPTER 19

On Those Who after Shedding Tears Return to Sin

They are mockers, not penitents, who still do what they repent of; they seem not to implore God with subjection, but proudly to mock at him. Like a dog that returns to its vomit is a fool who reverts to his folly [see Prov 26:11 and 2 Pet 2:22]. Many shed tears unceasingly, yet do not cease to sin. We see some who receive tears for repentance, and do not produce its effects; through inconstancy of mind they at one time shed tears at the remembrance of sin, and at another again commit the very things they have lamented when the old habit comes to life again. Those who wish both to mourn the past and to attach themselves to worldly actions are not cleansed, because they still do what they could bewail by repenting. Isaiah says to sinners, *Wash; make yourselves clean* [Isa 1:16]. They wash themselves and are clean who bewail the past and do not commit again what would need to be lamented. They wash themselves and are not clean who bewail what they have done but do not forsake it, and after tears repeat what they have lamented.

Somewhere else the divine word rebukes the soul that repents and then sins again, saying, *How exceedingly vile you have become, retracing your ways* [Jer 2:36 Vulg]. Therefore all who deplore past faults must maintain this frame of mind, and bewail what they have committed in such wise as not again to commit what would need to be lamented.[1]

---

[1] Isidore, Sent 2.16.1–4a; CCSL 111:128–29; PL 83:619BC.

It is written in the book of Ecclesiasticus: *One who washes after touching a corpse, and touches it again, how does the washing bring benefit?* [Sir 34:30]. Those who do not guard innocence of life after shedding tears neglect to keep clean after their bath. For they wash but are quite unclean who unceasingly bewail what they have done, but who again commit what they need to lament. Those wash after touching a corpse who are cleansed of sin by their tears; but those who are eager for their fault after shedding tears touch the corpse after washing.[2] Hence Solomon says, Like a dog [is] one who repeats his folly [see Prov 26:11]. So when a dog vomits it obviously throws up the food that was making it feel ill; but when it returns to the vomit that made it feel relieved, it is again weighed down. Those who bewail their sins throw off in confessing it the wickedness by which they miserably sated themselves and that depressed their inmost mind; they take it up again when they repeat it after their confession. The sow washes by wallowing in the mud, and is made even dirtier [see 2 Pet 2:22]. Those who bewail a sin committed but do not forsake it become guilty of more serious fault; they despise the very pardon they could have obtained by weeping, and roll as if in muddy water, because while they withdraw cleanness of life from their weeping they make even their very tears unclean before the eyes of God.[3]

---

[2] Taio, Sent 4.37; PL 80:953C, quoting Gregory, Past 3.30; PL 77:110C. Taio places the quotation from Ben Sirach at the beginning, whereas it comes halfway through in Gregory.

[3] Gregory, Past 3.30; PL 77:110AB.

CHAPTER 20

On the Life and Way of Living of Monks

M onks are to be advised always to be circumspect, showing reverence for the monastic habit in behavior, speech, and thought; they are to forsake completely the things of the world, and present before the eyes of God by their conduct what they proclaim to human eyes by their habit. When passing prosperity smiles upon those chosen as monks, they ignore the world's favor as though not aware of it, and with firm step inwardly tread upon things that outwardly lift them up.

Chosen monks do not create a din with cries typical of wrongful behavior; they are not seized with turbulent and passionate desire for temporal things, but they escape being overly concerned with the inevitable cares of the present life. Though they often do good, monks still feel the paternal strokes so that they may come to the inheritance, brought closer now to perfection in that the discipline of the one who each day lovingly strikes purges them even of very small things.[1]

True monks[2] who fully renounce the world die to this world so completely that they find their delight in living for God alone; the more they withdraw from this world's mode of life, the more they

---

[1] Taio, Sent 2.46; PL 80:847C–48A; see Gregory, Mor 5.11; CCSL 143:231; PL 75:680AD.

[2] Isidore's *sancti viri*, "holy men" (Sent 3.17,1) is replaced by Smaragdus with *veri monachi*.

contemplate with the mind's inner eye the presence of God and the innumerable assembly of the angels.[3]

The more they despise themselves and abase themselves outwardly, the more they feed inwardly on the contemplation of revelations. For those whom the valley of humility keeps outwardly in lamentation, the ascent of contemplation raises up inwardly.[4]

For some precepts are given to the faithful living an ordinary life in the world, while others are given to those who renounce the world. The former are told to conduct all their affairs well, the latter to leave all their possessions. The former are bound by general precepts, which the latter transcend by their more perfect living. The perfect are only satisfied by denying all that is theirs and themselves as well. But what is it to deny oneself, if not to renounce one's own desires? What, if not for one who was proud to be humble, who was angry to study to be meek? For even if people renounce all they possess but do not renounce their bad habits, they are no disciples of Christ. Those who renounce their property deny what is theirs; those who renounce their bad habits deny themselves. Hence the Lord says, *If any want to come after me, let them deny themselves* [Matt 16:24].[5]

---

[3] Isidore, Sent 3.17.1; CCSL 111:246; PL 83:692C–93A.
[4] Gregory, Mor 30.19: CCSL 143B:1534; PL 76:559B. See end of chapter 29.
[5] Isidore, Sent 3.18.1–2; CCSL 111:247–48; PL 83:693CD–94A.

CHAPTER 21

On Those Who Love a Quiet Life

Because holy people seek nothing belonging to this world, their hearts are surely free from tumultuous emotions. With the hand of a holy way of life they cast out of the resting place of the heart all the disordered movements of the desires; they despise all passing things, and do not suffer the haughty boldness of thoughts born thereof. For they seek only the eternal fatherland, and because they love none of the things of this world, they enjoy great tranquility of mind. There is great rest of mind in driving out of the hidden place of the heart the disturbances of earthly desires, and single-mindedly panting after the eternal fatherland and loving intimate quiet. David sought withdrawal from the tumult of temporal affairs when he said, *One thing have I asked of the Lord, this will I seek after: that I may live in the house of the Lord* [Ps 26(27):4]. And when he said, *Behold, I went far away in flight; I abode in solitude* [Ps 54(55):7], he was persevering in his plan to withdraw.[1]

Abba Anthony said, "He who sits in solitude and is at peace is freed from three kinds of war, that is, of hearing, speech, and sight."[2]

Abba Arsenius prayed as follows: "Lord, direct me towards salvation." And a voice came to him saying, "Arsenius, flee from human beings, keep silence, be at peace, and you will be saved."[3]

---

[1] Taio, Sent 3.13; PL 80:864C–65B, quoting Gregory, Mor 4.30; CCSL 143:203–4; PL 75:668CD–69C.

[2] PL 73:858A (2); see also PG 65:[77] 78C (11); *Sayings*, 2 [3], 11.

[3] PL 73:858A (3a); see also 73:801A (190a); PG 65:87 [88]BC (1–2); *Sayings*, 8 [9], 1–2.

Abba Moses said, "A person who flees from human beings is like a mature grape, while the one who lives with human beings is like an unripe grape."[4]

Abba Nilus said, "One who loves quiet remains impervious to the enemy's arrows; one who mixes with the multitude will receive frequent wounds."[5]

---

[4] PL 73:859C (10); see also PG 65:283 [284]C–[285] 286A (7); *Sayings*, 118 [140], 7.

[5] PL 73:859C (11); see also PG 65:[305] 306C (9); *Sayings*, 129 [154], 9.

CHAPTER 22

On the Chosen Who Leave All

At the end of the world those who are now judged unjustly for God's sake will come with God as judges. Then their light will shine the more widely as the hand of the persecutors now restricts them more harshly. Then it will be obvious to the eyes of the reprobate that those who of their own will left all earthly things were supported by a heavenly power. . . . All who, roused by the goad of divine love, have here left possessions will no doubt obtain there the summit of judicial power, so that those who now of their own free will chastise themselves in view of judgment, will then come together with the judge.[1]

Our Redeemer decrees the sentence of judgment with the Church's holy preachers, as he says in the Gospel, *In the regeneration, when the Son of Man is seated on the throne of his majesty, you who have left all things and followed me will sit on twelve thrones, judging the twelve tribes of Israel* [Matt 19:28].[2]

All who are perfect now in the Church learned the uprightness of their perfection through the Gospel. United to our Redeemer,[3]

---

[1] Taio, Sent 2.21; PL 80:806C–7A, quoting Gregory, Mor 10.31; CCSL 143:575; PL 75:950CD–51A. Taio and the CCSL text have *spontanea paupertate*, "by voluntary poverty" where Smaragdus has *spontanea voluntate*, "of their own free will."

[2] Taio, Sent 2.21; PL 80:807AB, quoting Gregory, Mor 6.7; CCSL 143:290; PL 75:734BC. The Scripture text inserts *reliquistis omnia et*, "you have left all things and" before *secuti estis me*, "[you] have followed me."

[3] Gregory has *tunc ejus corpori uniti*, "then united to his body"; Taio: *Redemptori ergo nostro uniti* (see next note).

56

and joined to his majesty, those whose aim now was to do perfect works according to the Gospel precepts will appear with him as judges. Those who in this world obeyed the Lord's precepts will afterwards come with him as judges to judge the peoples, as it is said to the preachers who leave all: *You will sit on twelve thrones, judging the twelve tribes of Israel.*[4]

It is certainly right that those who at God's words completely forsake the present world should with God make the reckoning about the peoples in judgment. And they should afterwards come with God as judges who were his servants in voluntary poverty and in peace.[5]

[It is written:] *He called on the heavens above and on the earth, that he might judge his people* [Ps 49(50):4]. He indeed calls on the heavens above when those who left all that was theirs and held to a heavenly mode of life are called to sit with him in judgment, and when they come with him as judges. The earth is also called above when those who were obligated to earthly acts sought in them heavenly rather than earthly profits. He says to them at the end, *I was a stranger and you welcomed me, naked and you covered me* [Matt 25:35-36].[6]

The chosen who leave all are not judged, but reign; they go beyond the precepts of the law by the perfection of their virtue. Not at all content with doing only what the divine law lays on everyone, with all-consuming desire they long to show forth more than they were able to hear in the general precepts.[7]

[4] Taio, Sent 2.21; PL 80:807B, quoting Gregory, In Hiez 1.2, 18; CCSL 142:27–28; PL 76:803BC.

[5] Taio, Sent 2.21; PL 80:807BC, quoting Gregory, Mor 11.22; CCSL 143A:605; PL 75:969C. Near the end, Taio and Gregory have *prece*; this has become *pace* in Smaragdus. Gregory does not have *in voluntaria paupertate*.

[6] Taio, Sent 2.21; PL 80:807C, quoting Gregory, Mor 15.31; CCSL 143A:772; PL 75:1100C.

[7] Taio, Sent 2.21; PL 80:807CD, quoting Gregory, Mor 26.27; CCSL 143B:1305; PL 76:379D–80A.

CHAPTER 23

On the Mortification of Monks

The apostle Paul says, *Consider yourselves indeed dead to sin but alive to God* [Rom 6:11]. For sin does not reign in a dead person, or the desire for sin live there; fleshly concupiscence is immediately extinguished in that person, rage subsides, anger ceases, hatred is put to flight, and all vices at the same time fall quiet. And this is what it means to die to sin and to live to Christ. The apostle likewise says, *For you have died, and your life is hidden with Christ in God* [Col 3:3].[1]

Christ was crucified, died and was buried for our sake; let us crucify our wills and lustful desires in his likeness. . . . Christ has been crucified to sin, not partly but entirely, so that we may live to God. . . . That person lives to God who follows the footsteps of Christ by humility, holiness and compassion.[2]

A monk is mortified when he chastises his body by continual fasts, when he tempers his appetite within the limits of what is necessary, when he not only keeps himself from more delicate foods but also exercises temperance in the more ordinary types of food, when he allows nothing to his fleshly nature out of sheer desire, but does so out of the need to sustain life.[3]

When spiritual monks fully seek their own mortification, the closer they are brought to their end and the more ardent they show themselves in work. So they do not grow faint in working, rather they grow in spite of their labors, and the closer they reckon the

---

[1] No source traced for this passage.

[2] Primasius, In ep Pauli (ad Rom 6); PL 68:444A, 443D, 445C.

[3] Julianus Pomerius, Vita contem 2.22: PL 59:467C; adapted by Smaragdus; see ACW:4, 94.

rewards to be, the more pleasant it is for them to exert themselves in work to the point of perspiring.[4]

[All monks, when they leave the world,] do not cease to punish their wrongful deeds with weeping. They afflict themselves with a heavy sadness, because here they have been cast far away from the face of their Creator, and are not yet in the joys of the eternal country.[5] Sometimes monks do not arrive at contemplating[6] what they desire, so that their slowness meantime may serve to expand their capacity for what they desire as their minds unfold. By a remarkable arrangement it happens that the things involved, which could have diminished in importance, grow many times over through the delay. Most monks seek to mortify themselves in the present world in such a way that, if possible, they may contemplate the face of their Creator; but their desire's realization is deferred in order for it to progress, and it is nursed in the bosom of their slowness only in order to grow.[7]

Good monks withdraw completely from the restless and urgent desire of this world, abandoning the din of worldly activity, and through the pursuit of quiet their minds, intent on the virtues, sleep as it were a watchful sleep. No [monk] is brought to interior contemplation except by carefully withdrawing from exterior involvement. Hence the Truth itself says, *No one can serve two masters* [Matt 6:24]. And Paul too says, *No one serving God as a soldier gets involved in worldly affairs; the aim is to please the person enlisting* [2 Tim 2:4]. The Lord warns through the prophet saying, *Be still, and know that I am God!* [Ps 45(46):10], because interior knowledge is by no means conceived unless one ceases from exterior involvement.[8]

---

[4] Taio, Sent 2.45; PL 80:846D, quoting Gregory, Mor. 5.5; CCSL 143:223; PL 75:683B.

[5] Taio, Sent 2.45; PL 80:845C, quoting Gregory, Mor. 5.3; CCSL 143:220; PL 75:681A.

[6] Smaragdus has *ad contemplanda desideria*. Taio following Gregory (see next note) has *ad concepta desideria*, "[do not arrive] at the desires they have conceived."

[7] Taio, Sent 2.45; PL 80:846C, quoting Gregory, Mor 5.4; CCSL 143:222; PL 75:682D–83A.

[8] Taio, Sent 2.45; PL 80:847AB, quoting Gregory, Mor 5.31; CCSL 143:257; PL 75:709D–10A.

Hence Paul again says, *If we have died with him, we will also live with him* [2 Tim 2:11]. *But if we have died with Christ, we believe that we will live with him* [Rom 6:8]; *for as all die in Adam, so all will be made alive in Christ* [1 Cor 15:22]. For *if we endure tribulations* for him, as he did for us, *we will also reign with him* [2 Tim 2:12]; *it is through many tribulations that we must enter the kingdom of God* [Acts 14:21]. *For you have died, and your life is hidden with Christ in God* [Col 3:3].[9]

---

[9] This is very likely Smaragdus's contribution of relevant scripture texts.

CHAPTER 24

On the Contemplative Life

The active life entails good works done with integrity, while the contemplative life is the beholding of things above. The former is common to the many, but the latter belongs to the few. The active life makes good use of worldly things, while the contemplative life renounces the world and delights in living to God alone. Those who first make progress in the active life duly ascend to contemplation. For those who are found serviceable in the former are rightly raised up in the latter. . . . As those who have been buried are deprived of all earthly business, so those who apply themselves to contemplation turn away from active occupations. . . . Holy people go forth from the retirement of contemplation to activity in public, and again they return from the public domain to the retirement of intimate contemplation, so that they may praise God inwardly where they have received from him the strength to work outwardly for his glory. As it is the eagle's custom always to fix its eye on the sun's ray, and only to turn aside from it to get food, so also, holy people sometimes come back from contemplation to active life, considering the former to be beneficial in the highest degree, and yet the humble realities of the latter to be to some extent necessary because of our neediness.[1]

In the contemplative life the mind exerts itself greatly when it raises itself to heavenly things, when it extends the soul in spiritual

---

[1] Isidore, Sent 3.15.1–3a, 5a, 6–7; CCSL 111:241–42; PL 83:689C–91A; see Gregory, Mor 9.32; CCSL 143:489; PL 75:384D.

matters, when it endeavors to transcend all that seems bodily, and when it narrows itself so as to expand. Sometimes indeed it conquers, and overcomes the resistance of its darkness and blindness, and subtly and by stealth attains something of the uncircumscribed light. But at once it is beaten back towards itself, and from that light to which it passes over with longing it returns sighing to the darkness of its blindness.[2]

It is written in the book of Genesis: Abraham buried his wife in a double tomb [see Gen 23:19]. The active life is like a tomb, because it protects those who are dead from crooked works; but the contemplative life buries them more perfectly, because it separates completely from all the activities of the world.[3]

A certain brother went away to the cell of Abba Arsenius; he looked through the window and saw the old man as though totally on fire in contemplation. That brother was worthy to gaze on such things.[4]

They used to say about Abba Sisoes that unless he quickly lowered his hands when he stood at prayer, his mind was caught up into higher things. So if there happened to be some brother praying with him, he hastened to lower his hands in case his mind was seized and his attention held.[5]

A certain old man said that assiduous prayer quickly corrects the mind.[6]

A certain father said, "Just as it is impossible to see one's face in water that is stirred up, so also the soul can only pray contemplatively to God if it has been purged of alien thoughts."[7]

---

[2] Taio, Sent 3.21: PL 80:877CD, quoting Gregory, In Hiez 2.2, 12; CCSL 142:232–33; PL 76:955:AB.

[3] Taio, Sent 3.21: PL 80:877D, quoting Gregory, Mor 6.37; CCSL 143:325; PL 75:760C.

[4] PL 73:978A (1a); see also PG 65:95 [96]C (27); *Sayings*, 11 [13], 27a.

[5] PL 73:942D (11); see also PG 65:[428] 427 B; *Sayings*, 198 [236], 1, where Sisoes is Tithoes.

[6] PL 73:942D (12).

[7] PL 73:942D–43A (13).

CHAPTER 25

On Desire
for the Heavenly Kingdom

Loud is the cry of the saints, great their desire; the less one cries out, the less does one desire. The more fully we pour ourselves into our desire, the louder is the cry we express into the ears of the unbounded Spirit.[1] Often our desires, while not being quickly carried out, are receiving a favorable hearing, and what we ask to be speedily fulfilled fares better because of the delay itself. . . . Our desires are stretched by delay so as to make progress; they thus reach their full strength for what they are destined to receive. They are stirred up in the contest so as to be abundantly rewarded with greater prizes in the time of recompense. The toil of the fight is protracted, so that the crown of victory may grow.[2]

In as much as the just desire to cling to heavenly things through a ray of contemplation, they shrink from becoming established on the earth, where they know that they are strangers and pilgrims, as Paul says, *Our way of life is in heaven* [Phil 3:20].[3]

With the sword of the sacred word, holy people unceasingly render themselves dead to importunate desires for temporal things,

---

[1] Taio, Sent 3.37; PL 80:895A, quoting Gregory, Mor 2.7; CCSL 143:66; PL 75:560B.

[2] Taio, Sent 3.37; PL 80:895BC, quoting Gregory, Mor 26.34; CCSL 143B:1291; PL 76:368D–69A; see Hom ev 25.2; CCSL 141:207; PL 76:1190C; see CS123, 189–90.

[3] Taio, Sent 3.14; PL 80:866BC.

to useless cares and to the love of extreme and noisy disturbances;
they hide themselves within in the fold of their mind before the face
of God. And so the psalmist rightly says, *In the shelter of your presence
you hide them from human plots* [Ps 30(31):20] . . . so that their mind,
while it tends totally to the love of God, may not uselessly be torn
by any disturbance. The apostle Paul by contemplation had seen
disciples as dead and as if hidden in the tomb, and used to tell them:
for you have died, and your life is hidden with Christ in God [Col 3:3].
Those who seek to mortify themselves become extremely cheerful on finding the rest of contemplation. Let them hide themselves
within the fold of intimate love so as to be hidden from the world
like one annihilated, all disturbances arising from exterior things
being lulled to sleep.[4]

Sometimes the upright person's mind is admitted to a certain
unusual sweetness of inner flavor, and is at once somehow influenced
and renewed by a spirit of ardor; the more it tastes of certain things,
the more it is filled with longing for them. It desires to have within
itself what it inwardly judges to be sweeter than itself.[5]

Abba Theonas said, "Because our mind is impeded and called
back from the contemplation of God, we are led captive in fleshly
passions."[6]

Abba Arsenius said to a certain brother, "However great your
virtue, strive to ensure that your inner work is according to God
and conquers the passions of the outer man."[7]

Abba John used to say that he had once made a piece of interwo-
ven handle for two baskets, and used it all on one basket, but did not
realize it. For his mind was occupied in the contemplation of God.[8]

Abba Serapion said, "Just as the emperor's soldiers, when they
stand before him, do not dare look to the right or the left, so the

[4] Taio, Sent 3.14; PL 80:867BC, quoting Gregory, Mor 5.6; CCSL 143:224–25;
PL 75:684BC.
[5] Taio, Sent 3.14; PL 80:868A, quoting Gregory, Mor 23.21; CCSL 143B:1176–
77; PL 76:277B.
[6] PL 73:934B (12); see also PG 65:[197] 198C; *Sayings*, 69 [80], 1.
[7] PL 73:933B (1a); see also PG 65:[89] 90BC (9); *Sayings*, 9 [10], 9.
[8] PL 73:934C (14); see also PG 65:207 [208]AB (11); *Sayings*, 75 [87], 11.

monk, if he stands in the sight of God and is at every hour intent on fear of him, there is nothing with which the adversary is able to frighten him."[9]

Abba Hyperechius said, "Let your thought be always in the kingdom of heaven, and soon you will receive it as an inheritance."[10] He also said, "Let the monk's life be lived in imitation of the angels, burning up and consuming sins."[11]

Abba Matoes said, "The nearer a monk approaches to God, the more he sees himself a sinner. For Isaiah the prophet, on seeing God, said that he was wretched and unclean [see Isa 6:5]."[12]

A certain old man said, "Just as no one dares to hurt one who is alongside the emperor, so Satan will not be able to harm us in any way if our soul clings to God."[13]

[9] PL 73:937C (31); see *Wisdom*, 39, 136; see also PG 65:415 [416]C (3); see *Sayings*, 190 [227], 3.

[10] PL 73:938B (35); see also PG 65:[429] 430D–31 [432]A; *Sayings*, 200 [239], 7.

[11] PL 73:938B (36).

[12] PL 73:959D (28); see also 783D (123a); PG 65:[289] 290C (2); *Sayings*, 121 [143], 2.

[13] PL 73:939A (42a).

CHAPTER 26

On the Lax Way of Life of Monks

A lax monastic life leads many back into their former errors, and enfeebles them when it is time for being alive. . . . Those whose monastic life is lukewarm do not notice that idle words and empty thoughts are harmful. But if they awake from sluggishness of mind they at once become afraid of things they used to consider of no importance, thinking them dreadful and fearful. . . . Every one of this world's arts has its eager lovers who are very ready to exercise them. And this is so because the work involved has an immediate recompense. But the art of divine love has hangers-on who are mostly languid, lukewarm, and frozen hard in laziness and sloth. The reason for this is that the result of their toil is delayed for a future not a present recompense. And so when the recompense of a reward does not immediately result from their toil, their hope all but disappears and they grow listless. Hence great glory is prepared for those who by sure and steady growth bring to completion the beginnings of a good monastic life; they are made ready to receive a reward all the more glorious in proportion as they more firmly begin and complete the labors of a hard journey. Certain people in the first ardor of conversion gird themselves to acquire virtues. Progress is within reach, but as they apply themselves immoderately to earthly affairs, the dust of the basest desires clouds their vision.[1]

---

[1] Isidore, Sent 2.10.1a, 2, 4–5a; CCSL 111:112–14; PL 83:610CD–11A.

There are some who, after a wayward life, are eager to follow holy ways, but before good desires can grow strong in them, as we have said, some good fortune of the present world befalls them and involves them in exterior affairs. This draws their mind away from the ardor of their deepest longing, extinguishes it as though with cold, and kills all that seemed to be in them from their late fervor. If a weak and lukewarm monk has begun perhaps to do something good, before he grows strong in it through long practice he slips back into exterior things and wrongly abandons what he seemed rightly to have begun. The heart grows exceedingly cold in earthly acts if it has not yet been made firm through interior gifts.[2]

It is especially to be noted that this generally happens to monks who do not follow God in pure and simple attachment, because it is written in the book of blessed Job: *The gathering of the hypocrite is sterile* [Job 15:34]. They would not lose the good they have begun if they had not been hypocrites. Hypocrites gather good works, but their gathering is itself sterile, because they do not aim, through what they do, to receive the proceeds in eternal payment. To human eyes they appeared to be prolific and vigorous in their good works, but in the sight of the hidden judge they appear unfruitful and arid.[3]

The depraved minds of monks do not cease turning over within themselves the hustle and bustle of temporal affairs, even when they are free from work. They keep vividly portrayed in their thought the things they love, and although they may do nothing exteriorly, in their inmost selves they toil under the burden of restlessness even when at rest. If the administration of these affairs is entrusted to them, they abandon themselves entirely.[4]

---

[2] Taio, Sent 2.47; PL 80:848BC, quoting Gregory, Mor 12.53; CCSL 143A:665; PL 75:1014D–15A. Some of the same quotation occurs in Taio, Sent 4.37; PL 80:953B.

[3] Taio, Sent 2.47; PL 80:849BC, quoting Gregory, Mor 12.53; CCSL 143A:666; PL 75:1016A. Gregory's *haec semper eis eveniunt qui Deum . . . non sequuntur,* "these things always happen to those who do not follow God," becomes *plerumque monachis hoc evenire consuevit qui Deum . . . non sequuntur,* "this generally happens to monks who do not follow God."

[4] Taio, Sent 2.48; PL 80:849D–50A, quoting Gregory, Mor 5.11; CCSL 143:231; PL 75:689C. Taio has *pravae monachorum mentes* where Gregory has *pravae etenim mentes,* "for depraved minds."

When we are intent on worldly cares, we become inwardly less perceptive as we seem outwardly more zealous. With the care and concern of earthly desire the heart grows hard, and while it is becoming hard through its action in the world, it cannot be made soft for what pertains to the love of God.

Holy Church says about its weak members: *They placed me as keeper of the vineyards, but my own vineyard I have not kept* [Song 1:6]. Our vineyard is the actions that we cultivate by our daily labor. But placed as guards in the vineyards, we do not guard our own vineyard, because when we are involved in extraneous actions, we neglect the ministry of our own action.[5]

Abba Sisoes said, "Be contemptible, and cast your own desires behind your back. Be free and safe from worldly cares, and you will have rest."[6]

An old man said, "The life of a monk is this: work, obedience, meditation, not to judge, not to slander, not to murmur, not to exercise curiosity, not to find delight in hearing others' affairs. For it is written: *You who love the Lord, hate evil*" [Ps 96(97):10].[7]

[5] Taio, Sent 2.48; PL 80:850BC, quoting Gregory, Hom ev 17.14; CCSL 141:128; PL 76:1146B; see CS123, 144–45, where it is homily 19.

[6] PL 73:857A (17); see also PG 65:[405] 406AB (43); *Sayings*, 184 [220], 43.

[7] PL 73:857CD (22a); see *Wisdom*, 30, 93.

CHAPTER 27

On Abstinence

This is the perfect and reasonable fast: when our outer person fasts, the inner person prays. Prayer penetrates heaven more easily through fasting. For then being made spiritual, one is joined to the angels and is more freely united to God. Through fasting even the hidden dimensions of the heavenly mysteries are revealed, and the secrets of the divine sacrament are opened wide. In this way, Daniel, through the revealing angel, deserved to come to know deep mysteries [see Dan 10:3ff.]. For this virtue shows the manifestations of the angels and their pronouncements. Fasts are strong weapons against the temptations of the demons, who are quickly overcome through abstinence. Hence also our Lord and Savior forewarns us to overcome their incursions by fasts and prayers when he says, *This kind* of demon *is only cast out through prayer and fasting* [Mark 9:29]. The unclean spirits make their way in especially where they see more of food and drink.

As long as the saints dwell in the life of this world, they bear a body parched from their desire for heavenly dew. So we read in the psalm: *My soul has thirsted for you; in how many ways my flesh thirsts for you* [Ps 62(63):2]. The flesh thirsts for God when it abstains and grows dry through fasting. Abstinence both quickens and kills: it quickens the soul, but it slays the body.

Fasts are acceptable to God with good works. But those who abstain from food and yet act crookedly imitate the demons, who do not have food and yet are never lacking in wantonness. That person rightly abstains from food who fasts from acts of malice and worldly ambitions. . . . A fast that is refreshed in the evening with a great intake of food is not thought much of. That is not to be regarded as abstinence, when delicious fullness of belly follows. A fast that is compensated for with pleasure in the evening is scorned.[1]

When we tame our bodies through abstinence, what else are we showing the almighty Lord than fleshly sacrifices? As Paul says, *[I appeal to you] to present your bodies as a living sacrifice* [Rom 12:1].[2] The distinguished psalmist David, to show that there is no abstinence without concord, says, *Praise him with tambourine and chorus* [Ps 150:4]. In the tambourine a dry skin resounds, while in a chorus voices sing in concord. What else is designated by the tambourine than abstinence, and what by the chorus than the concord of charity? One who abstains in such a way as to abandon concord, praises indeed with the tambourine, but does not praise in chorus.[3]

A certain old man said, "I cut off from myself fleshly delights so that I may cut away even the occasions of wrath. For I know that it always fights against me on the side of pleasures, disturbs my mind and drives out my understanding."[4]

Abba John the Dwarf said, "If some king wishes to take possession of the city of his enemies, he first takes possession of their water and food, and thus his enemies being in danger from hunger and thirst submit to him. If a person lives in fasting and hunger, his enemies who vex his heart are first weakened."[5]

---

[1] Isidore, Sent 2.44.1–4, 8, 10–11a; CCSL 111:189–92; PL 83:651A–52B. The last few sentences are quoted or alluded to in Smaragdus's *Commentary*, 4:12 and 4:36; CS 212:175–77, 205–6.

[2] Taio, Sent 3.10; PL 80:862C, quoting Paterius, *Expositio* 5.9; PL 79:778BC.

[3] Taio, Sent 3.10; PL 80:862CD, quoting Gregory, In Hiez 1.8,8; CCSL 142:106; PL 76:858A; see Past 3.22; PL 77:89C.

[4] PL 73:866B (14, where Evagrius introduces the saying).

[5] PL 73:867A (19); see also 772:A (66), where the saying, with minor variations, is attributed to Abba Moses; PG 65:[205] 206A (3); *Sayings,* 73–74 [86]3.

CHAPTER 28

On Continence

ontinence is given by God [see Wis 8:21], but ask and you will receive [see Matt 7:7; Mark 11:24; Luke 11:9-10]. It is granted when one beats in God's direction with inner groaning. Virginity is a twofold benefit, because in this world it lets go of worldly solicitude, and in the world to come it receives the eternal prize of chastity. Isaiah testifies that virgins are happier in eternal life when he says, *The Lord says this to eunuchs, I will give them, in my house and within my walls, a place and a name better than sons and daughter; I will give them an everlasting name that shall not perish* [Isa 56:4-5]. There is no doubt that those who persevere in chastity and virginity become equal to God's angels. We must love the beauty of chastity; the delight of it, once tasted, is found sweeter than the delight of the flesh. For chastity is the fruit of sweetness, the inviolate beauty of the saints. Chastity is security of mind and health of body. For incorruption of body is of no benefit where there is not integrity of mind, and to be clean of body is of no avail to one who is defiled in mind.[1]

An old man said that peace of mind and reserve of speech and secret meditation bring forth chastity.[2]

The glory of a monk consists in abstinence from food and from much speaking.[3]

---

[1] Isidore, Sent 2.40.1, 3–5a, 8; CCSL 111:176–78; PL 83:643B–44B.

[2] PL 73:880A (25).

[3] PG 34:443A and PL 103:452B; from Pseudo-Macarius, Ep ad mon; see *Clavis* 313, 1843.

Abba Poemen said, "As a prince's official stands by him ever ready, so must the soul be ever ready against the spirit of fornication."[4]

Abba Anthony used to say, "It is well to know that there are three bodily movements: one is natural, the second comes from being full of food, while the third is from the attack of the demons. But against all of these it is good to observe what is written: *Keep your heart with all care*" [Prov 4:23].[5]

---

[4] PL 73:876A (8); see also 769C (59); PG 65:[325] 326B; *Sayings*, 142 [169], 14.

[5] PL 873D–874A (1c and 2b); see also PG 65:83 [84]AB (22); *Sayings*, 5 [6], 22, abbreviated.

CHAPTER 29

On Bearing Divine Correction

Sinners must not murmur at the scourges of God, because they are brought to amendment especially through being corrected. Now all people bear their suffering more easily if they dispel the evils for which a just retribution is inflicted on them. Those who suffer evils should learn not to murmur, even if they do not know why they suffer them; and they should think that they are suffering justly because they are being judged by one whose judgments are never unjust. Those who endure scourges and murmur against God find fault with the justice of the one who judges. Those who acknowledge that it is from the just judge that they suffer what they endure, even if they do not know for what precisely they are suffering, are already justified by the fact that they accuse themselves and praise God's justice. By a divine judgment and for their great profit the minds of the just are troubled by various temptations caused by the passions. If they thank God for this, and accept that they deserve it for their fault, what they put up with from passion will be imputed to them as virtue, because they both recognize divine justice and understand their own fault.[1]

The minds of the just not only weigh what they bear, but already fear what remains. They see the kind of things they suffer in this life, and fear lest they suffer weightier things hereafter. They mourn because they have fallen from the joy of paradise into the exile of this blindness; they fear lest, when exile is left behind, eternal death

[1] Isidore, Sent 3.4.1–2, 5; CCSL 111:202–3; PL 83:659BC–60AB.

may follow. Therefore they already bear the sentence in punishment, but still dread the threats of the eternal judge for their fault. [Rightly then] does the psalmist say, *Your anger has swept over me; your terrors have overwhelmed me* [Ps 87(88):16]. After the anger of the interior judge passes, terrors also disturb us, because we already suffer one thing from condemnation and we still dread something else from eternal vengeance.[2]

The glory of a monk is patience in his trials . . . and long-suffering with charity.[3]

The more holy persons despise themselves and abase themselves outwardly, the more they feed inwardly on the contemplation of revelations. For those whom the valley of humility keeps outwardly in lamentation, the ascent of contemplation raises up inwardly.[4]

[2] Gregory, Mor 7.6; CCSL 143:338; PL 75:769D–70A.
[3] Pseudo-Macarius, Ep ad mon; PL 103:452AB; see *Clavis* 313, 1843.
[4] Gregory, Mor 30.19; CCSL 143B:1534; PL 76:559B. See chapter 20.

CHAPTER 30

On the Scourges of God

There is order in God's compassion; here it first cleanses one of sin through scourges, and afterwards frees from eternal punishment. The elect of God are worn away by the sorrows of this life, so that becoming more perfect they may gain the rewards of the future life. God in no way spares the delinquent; he either smites sinners with a temporal scourge for their purging, or leaves them to be punished with an eternal judgment, or else they repent and punish in themselves their wrongdoing. And so it is that God does not spare the delinquent. Through temporal scourges the just advance to eternal joys. And so the just must rejoice in punishments, and the impious be afraid in prosperity. God does not withdraw mercy and justice from the just or the reprobate. Here he judges the good through affliction, and there he rewards them through compassion; here he rewards the evil through clemency in time, while there he punishes them through eternal justice. For in this life God spares the impious, and does not spare the elect; in that life he will spare the elect, but will not spare the wicked. Because they are loved by God, people are all the more taken to task with the scourge should they sin, for Amos the prophet says, *You only have I known of all the nations of the earth; therefore I will visit all your iniquities upon you* [Amos 3:2]. *For the Lord disciplines those he loves, and chastises every child whom he receives* [Heb 12:6].

It is very necessary for the just to be tempted in this life by the vices, and to be beaten with the scourge, in order not to become proud of their virtues while being pounded by the vices. While they are being worn away by sorrow whether of heart or body, they are being drawn away from love of the world. . . . God deals more harshly with his chosen in this life, so that while fiercer blows of the scourge are lashing them, they may not find delight in any diversion of the present life, but unceasingly desire the heavenly homeland where a sure rest is in store for them.[1]

The sick must be admonished to think themselves God's children, since the scourges of discipline chastise them. If he were not planning to give the inheritance to the children he has corrected, he would not bother to instruct them through annoyances. . . . The stones [of the Lord's sanctuary] have been struck repeatedly on the outside, so that in the actual construction of the temple they may be put in place without the sound of the hammer [see 1 Kgs 6:7]; that is, we are now struck repeatedly with scourges on the outside, so that afterwards inside we may be put in our place in God's temple without discipline and striking, inasmuch as the striking may now cut away whatever in us is excessive, and then only the harmony of charity may bind us in the building. . . . The sick are to be warned to preserve the virtue of patience, and thus never cease to consider how many evils our Redeemer bore from those he had created. . . . Why is it thought harsh for people to endure scourges from God for their evil deeds, if God endured such great evils from them in return for good things? Or who in their right mind would be ungrateful for being struck, if he who came here without sin did not depart from here without being scourged?[2]

[1] Isidore, Sent 3.1.2–6, 10–11a, 12; CCSL 111:194–96; PL 83:653BC–54BC.
[2] Taio, Sent 3.53: PL 80:909A,B,D–10A, quoting Gregory, Past 3.12; PL 77:67D.68AB.69C,D.

CHAPTER 31

On the Weakness of the Flesh

When God sees certain people refusing to be corrected of their own accord, he touches them with the stings of adversities, and when he foresees that certain ones can sin greatly against their salvation, he scourges them with weakness of body lest they sin. So it is more useful for them to be broken by bouts of feebleness than to remain in good health unto their condemnation. It is just as well for stronger and healthy persons to be sick and not sin, lest through the vigor of their health they be soiled by unlawful desires of lust and unchastity. It is a pernicious kind of health that leads one to disobedience, and it is a healthy sickness that through divine correction breaks the mind away from its hardness.[1]

Saint Syncletica said that the devil . . . by searching out certain weaknesses uses them against one whom he intends to tempt, so that making monks pusillanimous by their means he may disturb the charity they had towards God. But although the body is cut to pieces and set on fire with strong fevers, furthermore, even if the affliction is unbearable, if you who bear these things are indeed a sinner, call to mind the pains, the eternal fire, and the torments of judgment in the future age, and thus you will not grow faint because of what happens in the present; moreover, you will even rejoice that God has visited you, and will have that very famous saying on your tongue: *The Lord did indeed chastise me, but he did not hand me over to death* [Ps 117(118):18]. If you are iron, hope in the fire employed on

---

[1] Isidore, Sent 3.3.2, 5, 7; CCSL 111:201–2; PL 83:658B–59AB.

you . . . because if you are just and you suffer these things, you will advance from great things to greater. You are gold, but you will be more refined through fire. . . . If you are chastised with fevers or the rigors of cold, be mindful of what scripture says, *We went through fire and through water; and* he[2] *brought us to refreshment* [Ps 65(66):12].

If weakness is irksome to us, let us not grow sad, as though we cannot stand to pray or sing psalms aloud from bodily weakness or wound. All these things will be useful for us for destroying the desires of the body, because it is to counteract base pleasures that fasts and labors are appointed for us. So if sickness restrains these excesses, there is reason to observe these things. The body's deadly vices are cut away by sickness as by a large dose of strong medicine, and this is great virtue when weaknesses are patiently borne with and thanksgiving is offered to God. If we lose our eyes, let us not bear it reluctantly. We have lost a means of self-exaltation, and with interior eyes we gaze on the glory of the Lord. Have we become deaf? Let us not be concerned, because what we have lost is the ability to hear vain things. Our hands have been rendered weak by some suffering, but we have our interior hands ready against the enemy's temptations. Weakness grips our whole body, but health grows for our inner person.[3]

---

[2] The Vulgate and Hebrew texts and translations have the verb in the second person: *and you brought us to refreshment*. Smaragdus may have had a memory lapse while quoting this verse from Psalm 65(66).

[3] PL 73:895CD–96A–C (16 with omissions and 17); see also 792D–93A (157) and 1044D–45A (1); PG 65:423 [424]A–D (7 & 8); *Sayings*, 194 [231–32], 7 and 194–95 [232], 8. Of the four Latin collections only Pe follows the Greek in attributing this saying to Syncletica. See also chapter 70, note 5.

CHAPTER 32

On the Tribulations of the Just

The upright should recognize that they are being tested, not cast down, by adversity. Holy persons are more in dread of the world's favors than of adversities, because the world's favors cast down God's servants, while adversities instruct them. That is why the constancy of holy persons should bear adversities in such a way that it cannot be broken. The eyes of God are especially upon the just when heavenly providence allows them to be afflicted by the wicked. For when they are tested by present tribulation, eternal joys are being prepared for them. All this life's tribulations are compared with waters that pass by. The reason is that if some tribulation happens in this life, it does not last but quickly passes. Those who think diligently of the rewards of the future life bear with equanimity all the evils of the present life, because they temper the bitterness of this life with the sweetness of that life, and on account of the eternity of that life they despise the passing brevity of this. And because those who are burdened with bodily pain do not long for the evils of disordered desire and impurity and the rest of the vices, the temptation of the world is of more benefit to salvation than its prosperity. From prosperity one goes to the worse, and from the pain of temptation one advances to the better. Everyone must prepare the mind for temptation (see Sir 2:1). Temptation weighs less heavily when it is expected, but it presses harshly if it comes unexpectedly. It is for the wise to take thought beforehand against all adversities; and nothing should happen that their deliberations do not anticipate.[1]

---

[1] Isidore, Sent 3.58.1–5, 6b–9; CCSL 111:316–17; PL 83:730B–D.

The reason that the upright are allowed to be afflicted by the unjust is that when they hear of the future good things they long for, they may suffer even present evils that cause them to shudder, and torment may impel them to an easier departure when love summons them.[2]

The psalmist David says, *You are my refuge from the pressure that surrounds me, my exultation; redeem me from those who surround me* [Ps 31(32):7]. See how he mentions pressure as though in the night, and yet in the midst of the distress he calls his deliverer his exultation. Outside it was indeed night when pressure surrounded him, but within, songs resounded when he was consoled with joy.[3]

When all the chosen tell how they are surrounded by pressures, and yet call God their exultation, no doubt they as it were sing a song in the night so that they may happily come to the day of the next life.[4]

A certain old man said, "If the temptation comes to someone [for tribulations are multiplied on every side] to become pusillanimous and murmur,[5] do not become pusillanimous and take it amiss if some weakness of the body overtakes you, because God himself is taking thought for you concerning everything. You do not live without him, do you? You must then bear patiently, and ask him to give you what is expedient, that is, that you may do his will; sit with patience, eating what you have in charity."[6]

[2] Taio, Sent 3.16; PL 80:870A, quoting Gregory, Mor 26.13; CCSL 143B:1280–81; PL 76:360BC.

[3] Taio, Sent 3.16; PL 80:870A, quoting Gregory, Mor 26.16; CCSL 143B:1284; PL 76:362D–63A.

[4] Taio, Sent 3.16; PL 80:870B, quoting Gregory, In Hiez 1.9,32; CCSL 142:141; PL 76:884D. The last clause is not in Gregory at that place.

[5] PL 73:897A (22, the first sentence only).

[6] PL 73:904C (45). See *Wisdom*, 27, 81.

CHAPTER 33

On Temptations

The minds of the upright are pushed and pulled in this life by many temptations and calamities, and so they desire to be completely plucked out of this world to that place where they may be free of hardships and find unshaken security. . . . The devil tempts the elect no more than God's will allows. By tempting them he contributes to the progress of the saints. Although it is against his will, the devil nevertheless serves the advantage of the saints when he does not deceive them with his temptations but rather instructs them.

God's servants must be careful to understand the enemy's ambushes and at the same time beware of them, and be simple in innocence of life; but it behooves them to be prudent in their simplicity. One who does not combine prudence with simplicity is, according to the prophet, *[like] a dove, simple and without sense* [Hos 7:11]. A dove, because simple; without sense, because unacquainted with prudence. . . . In the eyes of the elect dread of him [the devil] does not count for much. Unbelievers fear him like a lion, but the strong in faith despise him like a worm, and his attack is repelled instantly. . . . The devil is a slippery serpent; if his head is not resisted at the very beginning of his suggestion he insinuates himself completely and unnoticed into the interior recesses of the heart.

In the beginning, the devil's temptations are tentative. But if precautions are not taken against them, and through practice they develop into habit, they finally become exceedingly strong and are never overcome, or only with great difficulty. Although all through life the devil wants people to act crookedly, he is more intent on

deceiving them at the end. Hence it is that in the beginning the
serpent was told in relation to the first man formed: *And you will
strike his heel* [Gen 3:15]. Those the devil has not tricked in the course
of their past life he plans to trip up and throw down at the end. So
even though people may be upright, it is never safe to feel secure
in this life, but be always humbly on guard, and fearful and anxious
not to fall at the end. . . .

The devil does not possess holy men by taking hold of them,
but he pursues them by tempting them. Because he does not reign
in them within, he fights against them without; and because he has
lost dominion interiorly, he wages war exteriorly. . . . When the
devil wants to deceive someone, he pays close attention to each one's
nature and applies himself to that area in which he has noticed that
a person is liable to sin. The devil tempts people on the side that he
observes them easily inclined to the vices because of temperament,
so that he may employ the temptation that best matches the person's
inclinations. Read about Balaam. In imitation of the devil he ordered pernicious snares to be laid against the people of the Lord on
the side where he thought they would slip and fall more easily [see
Num 23 and 24]. Those who are conducting water somewhere do
not take it by any other way than where they see it naturally flows.

It is one thing for the devil to enter someone's mind, and another
for him to dwell there. For he enters into the hearts of holy persons
when he insinuates evil suggestions; but he does not dwell in them
because he does not bring them over into his body. He dwells in
those who are in his body, because they are his temple. Although the
devil sneaks into the minds of the elect, he does not rest in them as
he does in the hearts of the reprobate, for he is soon roused by the
heat of faith to leave the elect. Some the devil has already devoured
with greedy mouth, but by the hidden compassion of divine judgment they are snatched from his mouth and restored to safety. The
divine power has often withdrawn from the ancient enemy's jaws
through repentance many whom he held submerged in the abyss
of unchastity. . . . The upright suffer many adversities in their soul
at the instigation of the demons, but they cannot be lost to eternal
life through such attempts, because a loving Lord does not count as
worthy of condemnation what people suffer and bear against their

will by permission of his majesty. For we commit sin when we turn aside through disordered desire or choice. But when we are violently given over, although there is no crime or disgraceful action, there remains a wretchedness as if for disgraceful action and crime. But one who praises God for this wretchedness is without doubt not guilty of committing a crime.[1]

---

[1] Isidore, Sent 3.5.1, 3–4a, 8, 13, 14b–16, 18, 24–25, 29–30, 37; CCSL 111:204–15. The whole of this chapter comes from Isidore's *Sententiae*; detailed references are given to the CCSL edition, but see PL 83:660B–67B *passim*.

CHAPTER 34

On the Manifold Ways of Sinning

There are four ways in which sin is committed in the heart, and four ways in which it is acted out in deed. It is committed in the heart by the suggestion of demons, by the delight of the flesh, by the consent of the mind, and by the self-defense of pride. It is committed in deed now secretly, now openly, now from habit, now from hopelessness. And so by these steps sin is committed in the heart and acted out in deed. Sin is committed in three ways: from ignorance, from weakness, and on purpose.[1]

It is more serious to commit a fault from weakness than from ignorance, and more serious to sin on purpose than from weakness. For a person sins on purpose who does evil with enthusiasm and with deliberation of mind. But one sins from weakness who is caught by surprise or while in a hurry. They sin more badly and on purpose who not only do not live good lives themselves but divert from the truth [if they can] even those who do. . . . There are light sins which are purged by beginners with daily satisfaction, but which are avoided by the perfect as great crimes. Now what must people do about great crimes, when the perfect mourn even any light sins as most serious?[2]

---

[1] Isidore, Sent 2.17.2, 3a; CCSL 111:130; see Gregory, Mor 4.27 *passim*; CCSL 143:193–97; PL 75:661–64. Again the whole of this chapter comes from Isidore's *Sententiae*; detailed references are given to the CCSL edition in this and the following footnotes, but see PL 83:619–25 *passim*.

[2] Isidore, Sent 2.17.4; 18.3; CCSL 111:131–33; PL 83:620B.621A.

After having experience of lesser sins one must not proceed to greater ones, in case those who did not know how to correct themselves[3] for small things are struck harder for great crimes. By a divine judgment those who disdain to curb their lesser misdeeds slip into more serious ones. Many fall from one crime into another; though they have knowledge of God they neglect to fear him, and him whom they know through intellectual knowledge they do not reverence through their action. And so by a divine judgment they are allowed to commit things deserving of punishment, and as punishment they add a worse sin to the sin they have committed. Often one sin is the cause of another sin; while it is being committed, another arises from it as though it were its offspring, as lust is usually born from the belly's gluttony. As punishment for one sin another is committed when God abandons someone; in return for one sin a person falls into worse sin, so that the sinner becomes even filthier. Therefore the first sin is the cause of the second, and the second is the penalty for the first. So earlier sins are the cause of crimes that follow, and those that follow are the penalty of the earlier ones. The penalty itself for earlier sins is called hardening, and it comes from divine justice. Hence the prophet says, *You have hardened our heart, so that we do not fear you* [Isa 63:17].[4]

It is one thing not to sin out of love for God's love, another not to sin out of fear of punishment. Those who do not sin out of love for charity toward God are in horror of all evil, embracing the good of justice; sin does not delight such as these, even should they be promised impunity for the sin. But those who repress vices in themselves only from the pain of punishment, although they may not complete the work of sin have the wish to sin alive in them, and they grieve because they know that what the law prohibits is not allowed them.

[3] Smaragdus's text has *qui . . . corrigi non noverunt*; the CCSL reading is *qui . . . corrigi noluerunt*, "who refused to be corrected."

[4] Isidore, Sent 2.19.1–5a; CCSL 111:133–34; PL 83:621B.622A. The full Isaiah text is actually a question, "Why, O Lord, have you made us wander from your ways, [why] have you hardened [etc.] . . . ?"

Those who do justice out of love receive the reward of their good work, but not so those who observe it unwillingly only out of fear of the penalties.[5] Before any sin is committed, one is more in horror of it. But when it becomes a habit it is considered light and is committed without any fear, no matter how serious it is. From these raw materials, as it were by certain stages, every sin is formed. For evil thought gives birth to pleasure, pleasure to consent, consent to action, action to habit, habit to necessity. And so, entangled in these bonds, people are held tight by the chain of the vices, so that they can in no way be plucked from it unless divine grace seizes the hand of those lying there. To commit sin is to fall into a pit. To form the habit of sinning is to narrow the mouth of the pit, so that one who has fallen in is unable to get out. But sometimes God frees even such people, when he changes their desperation to conversion leading to freedom. Sins are forgiven because he has compassion, and by his protection one does not move into a worse state by sinning. Accordingly, we who are confident that we can be saved in this way must be afraid in case, perhaps, when we expect to be healed of the vices we multiply them and fail to obtain salvation. So let us take care either not to fall, or to rise again from a fall by being quickly converted. Delaying in sin causes the enormity of a crime. And so the prophet says, *Woe to you who drag iniquity along with cords of vanity, and sin along like the chain of a cart* [Isa 5:18]. One who delays to be converted to God drags iniquity like a cord. To drag iniquity is to dally in it. Hence the psalmist says, *They have prolonged their iniquities: the righteous Lord has cut the necks of sinners* [Ps 128(129):3-4].[6]

[5] Isidore, Sent 2.21.1; CCSL 111:136–37; PL 83:623BC.
[6] Isidore, Sent 2.23.2–4, 9b, 12; CCSL 111:138–41; PL 83:624BC.625BC.

CHAPTER 35

That after Ruin One May Rise

Those who have experience of sins of the flesh should fear [to sin], at least after suffering shipwreck, and should dread the recognized perils of being lost. . . . [Those who have fallen must be told] to consider their past sins and avoid those that threaten, so that they should call to mind the faults they have committed and blush at the thought of being stained by future faults.

Those who have experience of sins of the flesh are to be warned to consider with watchful care how after sins God opens wide the bosom of his tender love to us as we return to him, saying to us through the prophet, *Your eyes shall see your Teacher and your ears shall hear the word of someone behind you, saying, "This is the way; walk in it"* [Isa 30:20-21].

[Almighty] God follows behind us, as it were, and warns us, because even after fault he persuades us to return to him. He calls back one who has turned away, he does not regard the sins committed, he opens wide the bosom of his tender love to the one who returns. So we hear the voice of one behind us warning us, if after sins we return [with humble and contrite heart]. Therefore we must blush at the tender love of the one who calls if we do not wish to fear his justice, because there is so much greater depravity in despising him when he still does not disdain to call even when despised.[1]

Through Micah the prophet the Lord says, *And you shall come to Babylon. There you shall be set free* [Mic 4:10]. By Babylon we under-

---

[1] Taio, Sent 4.3; PL 80:914A.BC.915AB, quoting Gregory, Past 3.28; PL 77:104B—5D *passim*.

stand confusion. For often those who have fallen in the confusion of
the vices and then, blushing for the evils they have perpetrated turn
back to repentance, raise themselves from their falls by their good
living. And what else have these done than come to Babylon and
there been set free? Sometimes people, ashamed of the evils they have
done, rise up against themselves and by doing good return to the state
of rectitude. And so one who by divine grace is shown to be saved
even from confusion is set free in Babylon. Therefore the prophet
speaks to the [people of the] transmigration when he upbraids those
who have fallen from a state of rectitude to the vices of error in the
transmigration.[2]

A brother asked an old man, "What happens if a monk falls into
sin and is afflicted on its account because from being a proficient he
has arrived at a worse state, and then labors until he rises again?" The
old man said in answer, "A monk who rushes into temptation is like
a house that has collapsed. If he is sober in his thinking he rebuilds
it, finding materials at hand useful for the building: foundations laid,
stones and sand and all else necessary for the work of building; and
in this way its fabric quickly advances. The monk, if he falls into
temptation and is converted to the Lord, is like this; he has a great
deal at his disposal: meditation on the divine law, psalmody, manual
work—these are the foundations of the spiritual edifice."[3]

[2] Taio, Sent 4.3; PL 80:915BC, quoting Gregory, In Hiez 1.10,22; CCSL
142:155; PL 76:894D–95A.
[3] PL 73:877CD–78A (18, slightly abbreviated); see *Wisdom*, 8–9, 36.

CHAPTER 36

On Thought

There are two ways of sinning, namely, in deed and in thought; one is called iniquity, which is performed in deed, the other injustice, which is committed in thought. The doing must first be cut off, and afterwards the thinking; first the wrong works, afterwards the crooked desires. Works proceed from thought, and thought in turn is born from works. Even if people are free from evil works, they will not be free of blame for the malice of wrongful thinking on its own.

And so the Lord says through Isaiah, *Take away the evil of your thoughts from my eyes* [Isa 1:16]. For it is not only by our acts that we sin; we also sin by our thoughts if we unlawfully take delight in those that come to us. For just as a female viper is destroyed if torn by the offspring in her womb, so too if our thoughts are nourished within they kill us, and when conceived interiorly they consume us with the poison of vipers and destroy our soul with a cruel wound. Divine enlightenment comes to people, and they are immediately attacked and troubled by shameful thoughts. But God's servants judge in the fear of God and reject the temptations, and by introducing good thoughts repel shameful ones. Great watchfulness is to be employed in guarding the heart, because both good and evil have their origin there. As it is written, *out of the heart come evil intentions* [Matt 15:19], and so if we first resist the wrongful thought, we do not incur a fall in what we do.[1]

[1] Isidore, Sent 2.25.1–4, 7–8; CCSL 111:142–44; PL 83:626BC.627AB.

Generally our good works let us know what purity of life we are fashioning in our thinking. Almost all good works proceed from our thought, but some flashes of thought also spring forth from our work. Just as our work issues from the mind, so again is the mind trained by our work.[2]

It is very necessary for the mind's eye to be called back immediately to works already done when thought strays beyond the usual.[3] [Sometimes sin is committed only in thought,] and because the fault is not acted out, repentance falls short of causing torment. The thought of affliction quickly sets the mind straight, whereas just the thought of iniquity defiles it.[4] Often what has been wiped out by tears in the sight of the judge returns to the mind through thought, and the fault previously conquered tries to insinuate itself again and bring delight; it is renewed by the age-old struggle and its long knocking, so that what was formerly in the body afterwards lodges in the mind as an importunate thought. When nothing is done exteriorly, but sin is committed within only in thought, the mind binds itself by a strict guilt, unless it cleanses this with anxious laments.[5] Generally a crowd of earthly thoughts closes the ear of the heart with its din; within the secret place of the mind, the more the voice of the presiding judge goes unheard, the less the sound of confusing cares is curbed.[6]

Sometimes in the very sacrifice of our prayer importunate thoughts press upon us, and these can snatch away or stain what in us we are immolating to God with tears.[7] All who long for unlaw-

---

[2] Taio, Sent 4.13; PL 80:926BC, quoting Gregory, Mor 10.15; CCSL 143:556; PL 75:935D–36A.

[3] Taio, Sent 4.13; PL 80:926C, quoting Gregory, Past 2.9; PL 77:22A.

[4] Taio, Sent 4.13; PL 80:926D, quoting Gregory, Past 3.29; PL 77:109C. The bracketed clause is in Taio but not in Gregory in this passage.

[5] Taio, Sent 4.13; PL 80:927A, quoting Gregory, Mor 9.55; CCSL 143:514; PL 75:904AB.

[6] Taio, Sent 4.13; PL 80:927AB, quoting Gregory, Mor 23.20; CCSL 143B:1172; PL 76:273B.

[7] Taio, Sent 4.13; PL 80:927D, quoting Gregory, Mor 16.42; CCSL 143A:829; PL 75:1146CD.

ful things or who wish to seem to be something in this world are hindered by the dense tumult of thoughts in their heart.[8]

The sea signifies the human mind, and the mind's thoughts are like the sea's waves; at times these swell with anger, or by God's grace grow calm, or through hatred flow quite away with bitterness.[9] The human mind suffers many temptations as though shaken by so many blasts. Generally the hubbub of thoughts presses down the human mind, anger disturbs it, and when anger recedes there comes upon it a joy that is out of place.[10]

A certain brother asked certain of the fathers whether a man is defiled when he thinks of sordid things. Some said, "Yes, he is defiled; we cannot be saved, we who are ignorant persons. But this contributes to our salvation, if we do not act out bodily the things we think of."[11]

A certain old man said, "We are not condemned simply because evil thoughts enter into us; but we are if we make bad use of our thoughts and give them our consent. In fact, our thoughts can cause us shipwreck, and our thoughts can win us the crown."[12]

[8] Taio, Sent 4.13; PL 80:928BC, quoting Gregory, Mor 4.30; CCSL 143:201; PL 75:667A.

[9] Taio, Sent 4.13; PL 80:928C, quoting Gregory, Mor 12.7; CCSL 143A:634; PL 75:991B.

[10] Taio, Sent 4.13; PL 80:928C, quoting Gregory, Mor 11.44; CCSL 143A:619; PL 75:980AB.

[11] PL 73:927A (78, the first part only, and much abbreviated).

[12] PL 73:928C (86).

CHAPTER 37

On Speech

W hen we do not avoid small morally questionable words, we
slide imperceptibly into great sins of the tongue. When we
freely and without fear commit certain acts that are not
serious, we slip into worse and dreadful crimes through the habit of
sinning.

Vain words must not be found in the mouth of Christians. Just
as good conversations correct bad morals, so *bad conversations corrupt
good morals* [1 Cor 15:33]. A guard is placed over the mouth [see Ps
140(141):3] when people acknowledge that they are not just, but
sinners [which is closer to the truth]. They put their hand over their
mouth [see Job 40:4] who cover the tongue's excesses with good
works. They put their hand over their mouth who cover the faults
of evil speech with the veil of good behavior.

There are four considerations to guide us in our need to foresee
what, when, to whom, or how one should speak. . . . One who
humbly announces what is right says something good and does it
well. . . . One who does not feign charity speaks well from the
heart. One who announces the truth speaks well with the mouth.
One who edifies others with good examples speaks well with
deeds. . . . The evil respond to good things with evil, and to favorable things with the opposite. The good respond to evil things with
good, and to adverse things with the opposite. We must respond with
the courage of patience when subjected to verbal insults, so that the
urge to reply with a word that wounds is defeated by the strength
of endurance and departs.[1]

---

[1] Isidore, Sent 2.29.1, 5–7, 14, 17a, 18, 22–23; CCSL 111:147–51; PL
83:629A–31B.

One of the fathers used to say that, sometimes when the seniors were sitting and talking about edifying things, there was among them one with insight who saw angels moving their hands and washing them. But when the talk had become worldly, the angels went away, and pigs full of foul odors wallowed in their midst and defiled them. But when they resumed speaking about edifying things, the angels came again and began washing them.[2]

The old men once came to Abba Anthony, and Abba Joseph was also with them. Wishing to test them, Anthony began talking about the Sacred Scriptures. He began asking the younger ones what this or that word meant. And all of them spoke according to their ability. But he said, "You have not yet found it." But after all had spoken, he said to Abba Joseph, "What do you say about this word?" And he replied, "I do not know." Abba Anthony said, "Truly, only Abba Joseph has found the way; his answer was that he did not know."[3]

A certain brother asked an old man, "If one of the brothers reports to me conversations from outside, do you want me, Abba, to tell him not to do so?" And the old man answered him, "No." And the brother said, "Why?" The old man replied, "Because we ourselves could not observe it." And the brother said, "What then must be done?" And the old man answered, "If we choose to observe reserve in speech, that very way of acting will be enough for our neighbor."[4]

---

[2] PL 73:993B (3); see *Wisdom*, 62, 228; see PL 73:762CD (36) for a much longer version.

[3] PL 73:953C (4); PG 65:79 [80]D (17); *Sayings*, 3–4 [4], 17.

[4] PL 73:964B (59); see also 1050D–51A (30, 2).

CHAPTER 38

On Reserve in Speech

The tongue is to be discretely curbed, but not bound without possibility of being loosed. For it is written: *The wise will be silent until the right moment* [Sir 20:7]. When they consider it opportune, they lay aside restrictive silence and make themselves useful by speaking appropriately.

About restrictive silence and speech, it is said through Solomon: *[There is] a time for keeping silence, and a time for speaking* [Eccl 3:7]. Discretion is needed in deciding when to change from one to the other, in case when the tongue should be restrained it pours out useless words, or when it can usefully speak it refrains out of laziness. When he considers how very useful is reserve in speech, the psalmist says, *Post, O Lord, a guard over my mouth, and a sentry at the door of my lips* [Ps 140(141):3]. He does not ask for a wall to be set on his mouth, but a door that, of course, can be opened and closed. We must, then, speak carefully, so that speech opens the mouth discreetly and at the fitting time, and reserve of speech closes it when that is fitting.[1]

All are to be warned that if they love their neighbors as themselves, they are not to keep silence with them about something on which they rightly censure them. The medicine of the word contributes to the salvation of both when wrongful behavior is restrained by the one who administers the medicine, and the one who takes it has the heat caused by the pain reduced as the wound is lanced.

---

[1] Taio, Sent 3.43; PL 80:899AB, quoting Gregory, Past 3.14; PL 77:72CD–73A; dispersed in Mor 7.37; CCSL 143:380; PL 75:801BC–2AB.

It is as if people who look upon their neighbors' evils and yet keep silence withdraw the use of medicine from wounds they can see; they thus become the cause of death, because they refused to attend to the virus when they could have done so.[2]

A certain brother asked a very young monk, "Is it better to speak or to be silent?" The boy said to him, "If the words are idle, let them be; if they are good words, do not spin them out unduly, but come quickly to the point of what you are saying, and then keep quiet."[3]

A certain old man said, "Pay attention to reserve of speech, and do not think about anything; attend to your thinking, whether resting in bed or rising with the fear of God. If you do this, you will not fear the assaults of the evil ones."[4]

Abba Poemen said, "Abba Moses asked Brother Zachary when he was dying: 'What do you see?' And he said to him, 'There is nothing better than keeping silence, Father.' He said to him, 'It is true, my son; keep silence.'"[5]

A certain person said to Abba Ammon, "If there is need to speak with a neighbor, do you think I should speak with him about the Scriptures or about the words and sayings of the seniors?" And the old man said to him, "If you cannot keep silence, it is better for you to speak about the words of the seniors than about Scripture. For there is no small risk here."[6]

An old man said, "If a man has words but not works, he will be likened to a tree that has leaves but no fruit. For just as a tree full of fruit is also full of green leaves, so speech follows a man who has good works."[7]

---

[2] Taio, Sent 3.43; PL 80:899D–900A, quoting Gregory, Past 3.14; PL 77:72C.

[3] *Wisdom*, 33, 105.

[4] PL 73:939C (47).

[5] PL 73:957BC (18a); PG 65:179 [180]C (5); *Sayings*, 58 [68], 5.

[6] PL 73:936B (20b); PG 65:127 [128]C (2b); *Sayings*, 27 [31–32], 2b.

[7] PL 73:928A (84); see also *Wisdom*, 35, 120. For a similar saying see PG 65:231 [232]C (4); *Sayings*, 89 [104], 4.

CHAPTER 39

On Much Speaking

I t is written: *In much speaking you will not avoid sin* [Prov 10:19].
And: *One who talks too much harms his own soul* [Sir 20:8]. And: *A
talkative man will not be directed upon the earth* [Ps 139(140):11]. And
if we are lifted up in much speaking, we are not absolved in the
presence of the Lord. So it is better to ask for this from the Lord and
say, *Post, O Lord, a guard over my mouth, and a sentry at the door of my
lips* [Ps 140(141):3]. And: *Do not turn my heart to evil words* [Ps
140(141):4].

Those who devote themselves to much speaking are to be warned
to look closely and see how from being upright they are going to
their ruin when they fall away through a multiplicity of words. The
human mind is like water; when surrounded by an enclosure it is
gathered to higher things, because it is seeking that from which it
descended; when released it loses itself, because it scatters itself uselessly through the lowest things. When it becomes dissipated from its
censoring silence by superfluous words, it is carried outside itself as
by so many streams. From there the mind is not able even to return
to itself interiorly, because being scattered through much speaking
it shuts itself out from the secret place of intimate consideration. It
exposes the whole of itself to the wounds of the enemy who lies
in ambush, because it does not surround itself on all sides with a
fortification to guard it. It is written in Proverbs: *Like an open city
without walls round about, is one who cannot control his spirit in speaking*

[Prov 25:28]. Because it does not have the silence of walls,[1] the city of the mind is open to the darts of the enemy, and when by words it throws itself outside itself, it shows itself open to the adversary.[2]

Generally the slothful mind that falls into the ditch is pushed there by degrees. When we neglect to beware of idle words we come to harmful ones; first we like talking about other people's affairs, then through detraction our tongue bites into their lives, and finally it breaks out into open insults. The unbridling of the tongue sows dissension, gives rise to quarrels, sets alight the torches of hatred and extinguishes peace of heart.

That anyone who is a slave to much speaking cannot hold to the uprightness of justice, the prophet testifies when he says, *The talkative man will not be directed upon the earth* [Ps 139(140):11]. And Solomon says again, *In much speaking you will not avoid sin* [Prov 10:19]. And the prophet Isaiah says, *The cultivation of righteousness is peace* [Isa 32:17]. He means that the mind's righteousness is forsaken when one does not refrain from immoderate speech. And so James says, *If any think they are religious, yet do not bridle their tongues but deceive their hearts, their religion is empty* [Jas 1:26].

Wayward people are hasty of speech and light of mind; they neglect silence and draw out the matter they are speaking about, and what is lightly conceived by the mind is straightway expressed by the light-minded tongue.

Truth itself admonishes us when it says, *On judgment day, people will have to give an account for every idle word they have spoken* [Matt 12:36]. An idle word is one that lacks the motive of rightly meeting a need or the intention of being lovingly useful. Therefore if an account is exacted for idle speech, let us estimate the penalty for much speaking, in which we sin through harmful words.[3]

---

[1] Smaragdus here has *murorum silentium*, while Taio (Sent 4.26) and Gregory (Past 3.14: Mor 7.37) read *murum silentii*, "a wall of silence," which yields a better sense.

[2] Taio, Sent 4.26; PL 80:942CD, quoting Gregory, Past 3.14; PL 77:73BC; Mor 7.37; CCSL 143:379; PL 75:800C–801A.

[3] Taio, Sent 4.26; PL 80:943A–C, quoting Gregory, Past 3.14; PL 77:73BC–74A; Mor 7.37; CCSL 143:378–79; PL 75:800A–C.

Abba Sisoes once said, "Really believe that for these last thirty years I have been beseeching God on account of sin, and I say this when I pray: 'Lord Jesus Christ, protect me from my tongue.' Even till now I fall and sin through it every day."[4]

Abba Macarius Senior used to say to the brothers in Scetis: "After Mass in church flee, brothers." One brother said to him, "Father, where are we to flee still more from this solitude?" And he answered by placing his finger on his mouth, saying, "This is what I say we must flee from." And so he entered his cell, and closing the door he sat alone.[5]

Abba Sisoes said, "Our pilgrimage consists in this, that a man controls his mouth."[6]

Abba Hyperechius said, "A monk who does not restrain his tongue in time of rage will never be able to check the rest of the passions."[7]

Abba Longinus said to Abba Lucius, "I have three thoughts: one, that I should go on pilgrimage." And the old man answered him, "If you do not hold your tongue, you will not be a pilgrim no matter where you go. But bridle your tongue here, and even here you will be a pilgrim."[8]

A brother asked Abba Sisoes, saying, "I desire to guard my heart." The old man said to him, "And how can we guard our heart, if our tongue has its door open?"[9]

A brother asked Abba Poemen, "How should a monk sit in his cell?" And he replied, "As regards what is in the open, that is, let him do his manual work, eat once [a day], keep quiet, and meditate. For he can make progress in a hidden way in his cell; that is, let each rebuke himself for his own excesses wherever he goes."[10]

---

[4] PL 73:870A (39); PG 65:[393] 394A (5); *Sayings*, 179 [213], 5.

[5] PL 73:868C (27); PG 65:[269] 270B (16); *Sayings*, 110 [131], 16.

[6] PL 73:870C (44); see also 1051C (4).

[7] PL 73:870D (49); PG 65:[429] 430C (3); *Sayings*, 200 [238], 3.

[8] PL 73:918AB (33a); PG 65:255 [256]C [partial quotation of 1]; *Sayings*, 103–4 [122], 1.

[9] PL 73:937A (27); see also 1051C (2); PG 65:427 [428]B (3); *Sayings*, 198 [236], 3. In the *Alphabetical Collection* the saying is attributed to Tithoes.

[10] PL 73:923B (64) [partial quotation]; see also PG 65:[361] 362C (168); *Sayings*, 160 [190], 168.

CHAPTER 40

On Holding Conference

Although reading is useful for instructing, greater understanding comes from holding conference. For to hold conference is better than to read. Conferring brings learning possibilities. When questions have been put forward they can be dealt with without delay, and often the hidden truth is established by raising objections. For what is obscure or doubtful is quickly seen by conferring.

Just as conferring usually instructs, so contention destroys. Contention generates quarrels when the feeling for truth is lost sight of, and by fighting with words it even blasphemes God.

Reading needs the help of the memory. If this is somewhat slow by nature, frequent meditation serves to sharpen it, and assiduous reading focuses it. By reason of its length, prolonged reading often obliterates the reader's memory. But if reading is short, once the book is put down the mind goes over the passage, and then one reads without toil. We reflect upon the things we have read, and they do not drop out of the memory.

Quiet reading is more agreeable to our senses than reading aloud. For the intellect gains more instruction when the reader's voice is quiet and the tongue moves in silence. Reading aloud tires the body, and the keenness of the voice is blunted.[1]

Abba Pelagius said, "It behooves the soul that is living according to the will of Christ either to learn faithfully what it does not know,

---

[1] Isidore, Sent 3.14.1–2, 4a, 7–9; CCSL 111:239–40; PL 83:688B.689AB.

or to teach openly what it does know. But if, although it can do both, it refuses to, it labors under the sickness of madness. A disdain for doctrine is the beginning of departure from God."[2]

Abba Poemen said, "A man who complains is no monk; one who detracts from a brother is no monk; one who is inclined to anger is no monk.[3] But one who is truly a monk is always humble and quiet and full of charity, has the fear of God before his eyes, and guards his heart."[4]

When asked what is meant when we read, "the road is narrow and confined," an old man replied, "'The road is narrow and confined' [see Matt 7:14] means that people are to do violence to their thoughts, and for God's sake cut off their own desires. This is also what is written: *Behold, we have left everything and followed you*" [Matt 19:27].[5]

An old man said, "A monk must daily, morning and evening, think within himself what he has done of the things God wills, and what he has not done. Acting in this way for his whole life and doing penance, he can be a monk."[6]

An old man said, "Whether you sleep or rise or do anything else, if God is before your eyes, the enemy will not be able to frighten you, and if such an attitude abides in a man, the power of God also abides in him."[7]

---

[2] PL 73:924A (67); Smaragdus has Abba Pelagius; PL 73 has Abba Palladius.

[3] PL 73:922A (54); see also PG 65:343 [344]BC (91); *Sayings*, 151 [179], 91.

[4] PL 74:391C (82).

[5] PL 73:927CD (81); see *Wisdom*, 35, 117; PG 65:123 [124]A (11); *Sayings*, 24 [28], 11. The Greek text says that the old man is Abba Ammonas.

[6] PL 73:938D (39); see *Wisdom*, 39, 132; PG 65:307 [308]C (5); *Sayings*, 130 [155], 5. Abba Nesteros in the Greek.

[7] PL 74:385C (24).

CHAPTER 41

On Love of Neighbor and Fraternal Correction

Two things must be observed with regard to love of neighbor: first, not to do evil, and second, to do good. First, that a person guard against inflicting hurt and so learn to do all that is good. Friendship is the association of minds, and it begins with two persons. There cannot be love between less than two persons.

Friends are truly loved if they are loved not for their own sake but for God. Those who love friends for their own sake embrace them in a foolish way. That person is much immersed in the earth who loves in a fleshly way one destined to die and more than is proper.[1]

One who is still a slave to the contagion of the vices must not correct another's vices. It is wrong for people to upbraid in others what is still worthy of censure in themselves. Those who truly wish to heal and correct their neighbors' weaknesses should aim to be useful to them and to admonish with a humble heart those they desire to correct; and they should do this from a sense of compassion because of a danger they have in common, so that they themselves may not be subject to temptation. Spiritual persons wait for the amendment of another's sin, whereas the impudent deride and insult sinners. As far as concerns them they think such people beyond healing; they do not bend their heart towards the mercy of fellow-feeling, but from their superior position detest and deride them.

[1] Isidore, Sent 3.28.1–2, 5a, 5b in part; CCSL 111:265–66; PL 83:702A–C.

Most people consider the correction they administer to be a duty
of charity, while most who are corrected out of charity take it as an
insult and an injury. And so it comes about that they are made worse
by the very thing that could have made them better had they obeyed.
The upright accept reproofs of their faults as being for their health
as often as they are given. . . . To the wicked truth is burdensome
and the discipline of justice is bitter; they only take delight in things
pleasing to their own weakness. . . . The hearts of the crooked are
slippery when it comes to consenting to evil, but are exceedingly
hard when it comes to consenting to the good. . . . Of such Solomon says, *Those who instruct scoffers do themselves injury* [Prov 9:7]. Of
the good he says, *Teach the righteous and they will hasten to accept* [Prov
9:9]. The evil turn in hatred against the ones who correct them.[2]

But if we keep silent from rebuking them because we dread the
hatred this might stir up against us, we are without doubt no longer
seeking God's gain but our own. It must by all means be known
that sometimes the crooked when they are rebuked become worse,
and pursue us with great hatred.[3] It is they whom we spare and not
ourselves if love for them makes us stop rebuking them. So we must
sometimes of necessity bear in silence with what they are, so that
they may learn by seeing in us what they are not.[4]

There is no need at all for the just to be afraid that when people
are corrected they may utter insults, but rather that being drawn to
hatred they may become worse.[5] Care is to be taken above all that
fondness for speaking does not unduly stretch the tongue and bring
us to make a sport of detraction, in case malice should arouse hatred
and incline us to hurling curses.[6]

---

[2] Isidore, Sent 3.32.1–3, 5–6a, 8a, 9, 10b, 10a; CCSL 111:269–71; PL
83:704A–5A.

[3] Smaragdus's insertion seems to be, ". . . and pursue us with great hatred."

[4] Taio, Sent 4.22; PL 80:939A, quoting Gregory, Mor 20.21; CCSL 143A:1038;
PL 76:165CD.

[5] Taio, Sent 4.22; PL 80:939AB, quoting Gregory, Mor 8.42; CCSL 143:434;
PL 75:842C.

[6] Taio, Sent 4.22; PL 80:939B, quoting Gregory, Mor 10.6; CCSL 143:540; PL
75:923C.

And so Solomon says, *Rebuke the wise, and they will love you; the foolish, and they will hate you all the more* [Prov 9:8]. *Those who love discipline love understanding, but those who hate the ones who rebuke them are stupid* [Prov 12:1].

But because the apostle says, *Admonish the restless, encourage the fainthearted, help the weak, be patient towards all* [1 Thess 5:14], we must put here helpful examples of correction given by the fathers.[7]

Once a brother gave offense in the community and was expelled. Now the one expelled from the community threw himself into a sedgy place and there began to weep. It happened that other brothers on their way to Abba Poemen heard him crying. They went down to him and found him unable to move on account of his distress. They begged him to go to the old solitary, but he would not agree, saying, I will die in this place. The brothers came to Abba Poemen, and told him about the man. He besought them to go and say to him, "Abba Poemen is calling you to himself." When they told him this he went directly to him. When the old man saw him all afflicted, he rose and kissed him. With great joy he asked him to take some food, and he did so.[8]

A brother questioned Abba Poemen and said, "I have committed a great sin, and I want to do penance for three years." But Abba Poemen said to him, "That is a lot." And the brother said to him, "Should I do one year?" And again the old man said to him, "It is a lot." Those who were present began to say, "Up to forty days?" The old man again said, "It is a lot." And he added, "I think that if a man repents with all his heart, God may accept even three days' penance."[9]

Abba Joseph questioned Abba Poemen, saying, "How must one fast?" And Abba Poemen said, "I want someone to eat every day, and keep back a little from himself so as not to reach satiety." And Abba Joseph said to him, "When you were a young man, did you not fast for two days at a time?" The old man said, "Believe me, brother, I

[7] An editorial insertion of Smaragdus.

[8] PL 73:910CD (7a); see also PG 65:319 [320]BC (6); *Sayings*, 139 [165–66], 6.

[9] PL 73:920B (40); see also PG 65:[325] 326AB (12); *Sayings*, 142 [169], 12. A similar saying is handed down under the name of Sisoes in PG 65:399 [400]AB (20); *Sayings*, 182 [217], 20.

fasted for three days, and even for a week at a time. But great seniors approved of all these things, and they found that it is good to eat every day, withdrawing a little from one's intake, and they showed us this royal way, because it is lighter and easy."[10]

[10] PL 73:920CD (44); see also 766CD (45); PG 65:[329] 330C (31); *Sayings*, 144 [171], 31.

CHAPTER 42

On the Zeal
of the Pastor's Office

All the spiritual zeal of the teacher parches his heart,[1] because it tortures him when he sees any weak person abandoning eternal things and finding delight in temporal things. There is no sacrifice as powerful with almighty God as zeal for souls, as the psalmist says, *Zeal for your house has consumed me* [Ps 68(69):9].

Just how pleasing to almighty God the parching of the heart that spiritual zeal causes is plainly shown when the law orders choice flour to be offered in sacrifice. It is written: *It shall be sprinkled with oil and roasted on a griddle; and the priest who by law succeeds his father shall offer it warm as a very sweet odor to the Lord, and the whole will be burnt on the altar* [Lev 6:21-22].

The choice flour is roasted on the griddle when the clean mind of the just is burnt through the ardor of holy zeal. The order is for the clean mind to be sprinkled with oil, and that happens when through the depths of charity and mercy it burns and shines in the sight of almighty God. . . . So the command is for it to be offered warm as a most sweet odor to the Lord, because if zeal does not have love, the choice flour that is offered from the griddle has lost its heat.

Particular note is to be taken of who is commanded to offer the choice flour, namely the priest who by right succeeds his father. That priest succeeds his father by right who shows himself to be a son of

---

[1] PL 76 has *animam*, "soul," where Smaragdus has *animum*, "mind" or "heart."

almighty God by his conduct, and who is not in disagreement with his deepest nobility by the unworthiness of his works. This nobility is ordered to be burnt whole on the altar so that it may become a holocaust.

The choice flour on the griddle is the clean mind of the just afflicted by spiritual zeal, which is parched through its solicitude for souls, and is reputed to be not only a sacrifice but also a holocaust to the Lord.

So let us take an iron griddle, and put it as an iron wall between us and the city [see Ezek 4:3], that is, let us take up strong zeal, so that we may find this afterwards a strong defense between us and the soul of our hearer. For we are going to find this iron wall then if we now hold it strongly, by teaching, guarding, persuading, rebuking, soothing, frightening, sometimes by acting gently, and sometimes also more severely.[2]

It is necessary for those moved by zeal for rectitude to attend to this above all, lest anger get beyond the mind's control; but in regard to punishment of sin considering the time and the measure, let them restrain and more carefully hold back the disturbance of the surging mind, repress animosity, and dispose with equity the heated movements, so that they may become more just avengers of others, as persons who have previously conquered themselves. Those moved by zeal for rectitude should correct the faults of wrongdoers in such a way that the ones correcting should first grow through patience, and make their judgment while looking beyond their fervor. They should act like this in case, roused by excessive zeal for rectitude, they wander far from rectitude.[3]

---

[2] Taio, Sent 2.46; PL 80:829D.830B–D, quoting Gregory, In Hiez 1.12,29, 30; CCSL 142:200–203; PL 76:932A–33AB.

[3] Taio, Sent 2.46; PL 80:831D–832A, quoting Gregory, Mor 5:45; CCSL 143:280–81; PL 75:727BC.

CHAPTER 43

On Discretion in Doctrine

One and the same teaching is not to be used for everybody, but let the exhortations of teachers vary according to characters. A sharp rebuke corrects certain people, but a gentle exhortation corrects others. Just as experienced doctors use different medications for the various illnesses of the body, so that for different wounds the medicine is different, so also the Church teacher will employ the remedy of teaching befitting each one, and will proclaim what each one needs according to age, sex, and occupation.

The first virtue is that of prudence, which ought to teach us how to assess a person. . . . We must act in one way towards those who are entrusted to our rule if they commit an offense, and in another way with those who are not entrusted to us. If the latter are upright we must show them reverence, but if they commit a fault they are to be corrected only out of charity, as occasion allows, but not with severity, as those entrusted to us are to be ruled.[1] Withdraw teaching and preaching, and you punish people who deserve it. For a deserving hearer, the ability to speak is granted to a teacher. It rests in the divine power for God to give a word of teaching to whom he wishes, or to withdraw it. And this is done either for the speaker's or the hearer's deserts, so that now the word is taken from the teacher because of the people's fault, and now it is granted for the deserts of both.

---

[1] Isidore, Sent 3.43.1–2, 4a, 6; CCSL 111:285–86; PL 83:711D–12A.C.

Those who receive the office of teaching should sometimes pass over in silence the deeds of a neighbor that they do not think they can correct at once. For if they are able to correct and pretend not to notice, they are really complicit in another's error. Generally holy teachers, being unable to amend the wicked because of the pertinacity of the evil, decide to keep silence in their regard; but not being able to bear the warmth of the spirit that drives them, they burst out in reproaches of the wicked.[2]

Those who are presiders[3] are condemned for the wickedness of subjects if they do not instruct them when they are ignorant nor rebuke them when they sin. The Lord says through the prophet: *I have given you to the house of Israel as a sentinel. If you do not speak so that the wicked guard themselves from their wicked ways, they shall die for their iniquity; but their blood I will require at your hand* [Ezek 3:17a, 18]. The presider must take care of those who are perishing, so that they may either be corrected from sins by his rebuke or, if they are incorrigible, be separated from the Church.[4]

One who is not corrected when reproved with a kindly word must be more sharply upbraided. For things that cannot be healed with mildness must with sorrow be cut off. One who, being secretly admonished, neglects to be corrected for sin is to be publicly rebuked, because the wound that cannot be healed in secret has to be amended openly. Public sins are not to be purged with a hidden correction. Those who openly do harm are to be openly rebuked, so that while they are being healed by an open scolding, those who have done wrong by imitating them may be corrected. While one is being corrected, many are amended. For it is better for one to be condemned for the salvation of many, than that many be imperiled for one person's dissoluteness. Therefore the word that corrects is to be uttered for wrongdoers as their health demands. But if there is need to sprinkle some health-giving medicine with a word of

[2] Isidore, Sent 3.44.1–2a, 5–6; CCSL 111:287–88; PL 83:713A–C.

[3] Where Isidore, has *sacerdos*, "priest or bishop," or its plural in this passage, Smaragdus has substituted *qui praeest*, "the presider or superior," or its plural, thus adapting the teaching to a monastic context.

[4] Isidore, Sent 3.46.1a, 4; CCSL 111:290–91; PL 83:714C–15A.

rebuke, one must retain mildness in the heart. Teachers sometimes wound their subjects with harsh rebukes without withdrawing from the love of those they are correcting.[5]

The role of a teacher calls for great subtlety of discretion, so that every church leader may know how to pardon discreetly the faults of delinquents, and lovingly cut them off. But those who forgive sins in such a way that they do not correct, or on the grounds of correcting so wound that they do not forgive, do not have the spirit of discretion.[6]

It is written in the book of Genesis: *If you offer rightly, and do not divide rightly, you have sinned* [Gen 4:7 LXX]. To divide offerings rightly is to think with discernment about all our good endeavors. When people pretend not to notice and so act, even if they offer rightly they sin. Often what we do with a good intention we neglect to discern carefully, and we do not know with what goal in mind to judge; and sometimes what is thought to be an exercise of virtue becomes a cause of blame and guilt.[7]

Therefore we rightly offer when we do a good work with a good intention; but we do not divide rightly if we have insufficient esteem for discretion in a good work.[8]

Abba Anthony said, "There are some who wear down their bodies in abstinence, and because they do not have discretion they become distant from God."[9]

Abba Daniel used to say that the soul dries up to the extent that the body flourishes; and to the extent that the body dries up, the soul flourishes.[10]

---

[5] Isidore, Sent 3.46.11–16; CCSL 111:293–94; PL 83:716AB.

[6] Taio, Sent 3.42; PL 80:898BC, quoting Gregory, In Hiez 2.9,20; CCSL 142:374; PL 76:1056A, with word order slightly changed in Taio. Smaragdus has mistakenly omitted the *non* modifying *habent* in the final clause.

[7] Taio, Sent 3.42; PL 80:898C, quoting Gregory, Mor 3.13; CCSL 143:129; PL 75:611A; see also In Hiez 1.11,12; CCSL 142:174; PL 76:910D–11A.

[8] Taio, Sent 3.42; PL 80:898CD, quoting Gregory, In Hiez 1.11, 12; CCSL 142:174–75; PL 76:910D–11A.

[9] PL 73:912B (1); PG 65:78 [77]B (8); *Sayings*, 2 [3], 8.

[10] PL 73:915B (17a); PG 65:155 [156]B (4); *Sayings*, 43–4 [52], 4.

Abba Poemen said, "Wickedness never drives out wickedness, but if someone does you evil, do him good, so that through your good work you may destroy his wickedness."[11]

A certain old man was asked by a certain brother, "How can I find God? In fasts or in labors, in vigils or in mercy?" And he replied, "In the things you have mentioned, and in discretion. For I tell you that many have afflicted their flesh, and because they did this without discretion, they went away empty handed."[12]

[11] PL 73:921D (53); see also 774C (79); 1032A (3); PG 65:[365] 366A (177); *Sayings*, 161 [191], 177.

[12] PL 73:928D–29A (91; Smaragdus omits the last sentence). See *Wisdom*, 29, 90. See PG 65:78 [77]B (23).

CHAPTER 44

On Divine Gifts

B y the secret regulation of an inner judgment Almighty God grants to one the word of wisdom, to another full faith, to another gifts of healing, to another the working of miracles, to another prophecy, to another the discernment of spirits, to another various kinds of tongues, to another the interpretation of tongues [see 1 Cor 12:9-10].

Our Creator and Mover arranges all things in such a way that those who could be lifted up because of the gift they have are humbled because of the virtue they do not have. And so it comes about that when he lifts someone up through a grace bestowed, he also subjects one person to another by bestowing a different gift.

The Almighty Lord[1] so arranges all things that every single thing belongs to everyone separately and, when a need of charity occurs, everything belongs to everyone individually. What individuals have not received they possesses in other people, so that they may humbly make available for another's possession what they themselves have received.[2]

Holy Church is the body of its heavenly head; in it one is the eye by seeing high things, another is the hand by performing right things, another the foot by running everywhere, another the ear by

[1] Smaragdus here has *omnipotens Dominus*, whereas Taio has introduced the quotation from Gregory with *omnipotens Deus*.

[2] Taio, Sent 3.19; PL 80: 872CD–73BC, quoting Gregory, Mor 28.10; CCSL 143B:1412–13; PL 76:460D–61A–C. In the second sentence of the previous paragraph Taio has replaced Gregory's *Sic cuncta moderatur*, "He arranges all things," with *atque ita fit*.

understanding the message of the precepts, another the nose by discerning the stench of evil things and the fragrance of good things. For in the manner of the bodily members they exercise for one another the offices they have received, thus making one body out of them all.[3]

By a wonderful plan our Author and Mover bestows on this one those things that he denies to another, and denies to another things that he bestows on the former. And so all who try to do more than has been given are endeavoring to go beyond the limits set for them. If every member of the faithful[4] [whose gift perhaps is only to treat of the hidden aspects of the precepts] attempts to shine with miracles as well; or if those whose gift is heavenly power only for performing miracles also strive to open up the hidden things of the divine law, they are stretching out their foot over a precipice and not attending to the limits of the measure set for them. [5]

They used to say of Abba Hor that he never lied, swore, or cursed anyone, and he did not speak to anyone if it was not necessary.[6]

At one time Abba Hilarion came from Palestine to Abba Anthony at the mountain, and Abba Anthony said to him, "You are welcome, light-bringer, who rise in the morning." And Abba Hilarion said to him, "Peace to you, column of light, who sustain the whole earth."[7]

A certain abba said that a certain solitary had lived in the desert forty years. When questioned by Abba John he replied, "From the time I began to be a solitary, the sun has never seen me eating." "Nor me being angry," replied Abba John.[8]

---

[3] Taio, Sent 3.19; PL 80:873C, quoting Gregory, Mor 28.10; CCSL 143B:1414; PL 76:462BC.

[4] Taio expands Gregory's *ut fortasse is cui tantummodo datum est*, "so that perhaps one (whose gift is only to treat of the hidden aspects of the precepts)" to *Unusquisque fidelium (cui tantummodo datum est)*.

[5] Taio, Sent 3.19; PL 80:874A, quoting Gregory, Mor 28.10; CCSL 143B:1414; PL 76:462C.

[6] PL 73:1008A (7); see also PG 65:[437] 438B (2); *Sayings*, 206 [246], 2.

[7] PL 73:973D (4); see also PG 65:[241] 242C; *Sayings*, 94,1bis; [111], 1.

[8] PL 73:867C (24b); see also PG 65:243D [244D]–246A [245A] (4b); *Sayings*, 97 [113–14], 4b. The solitary is identified as Abba Paësius in the *Apophthegmata*.

They used to say of Abba Arsenius that he would keep vigil all night, and when towards morning he wished to sleep, he used to say to sleep, "Come, bad slave." And he would steal a little sleep while seated, and would rise at once.[9]

---

[9] PL 73:865A (2); see also 807A (211); PG 65:91 [92]A (14); *Sayings*, 9 [11], 14.

CHAPTER 45

On the Grace of God

B y the grace of almighty God we can indeed attempt good works, but we cannot complete them if he who gives the order does not provide the help. . . . We must know that the evil we do belongs only to us, whereas the good we do belongs both to Almighty God and to us. For he who goes before us by inspiring us to will, follows after with his help so that we do not will in vain but are able to perform what we will to.

With grace anticipating and good will following, what is almighty God's gift becomes our merit. Paul explains this well in a short sentence when he says, *I worked more than all of them* [1 Cor 15:10]. For fear of appearing to attribute to his own power what he had done, he added, *Not I, but the grace of God that is with me* [1 Cor 15:10].[1]

Sometimes God does not withdraw his grace from us when we sin, so that the human mind may rise up to the hope of the divine forgiveness. . . . For all good things are given to us by him, with grace anticipating us. . . . A person's progress is God's gift; no one can do anything unaided, but can be amended by God. . . . The prophet testifies to this when he says, *I know, O Lord, that the way of humans is not in their control, nor is it for them to walk and direct their steps* [Jer 10:23]. Spiritual grace is not distributed to all, but it is given only to the chosen. . . . Different gifts of grace are given to

---

[1] Taio, Sent 2.30; PL 80:820BC, quoting Gregory, In Hiez 1.9.2; CCSL 142:123–24; PL 76:870B.CD.

different persons, and they are not given a possession as a result of which they have no need of anyone else. No doubt it can happen that those whom some surpass by the excellence of their virtues, may by God's sudden prevenient grace[2] come before them by a shortening of the process of acquiring holiness; and so while they are last by the time of their conversion, they are suddenly made first by reaching the summit of virtue.

When people receive some good, let them not desire more than they have merited, in case when they try to seize the positions of others they lose what they have already merited. Those who, not content with their own position, steal that of someone else disturb the whole order of the body.[3]

A brother asked a certain senior, "If I am in some place, and distress comes upon me, and I have no one to entrust myself to and reveal the suffering of my soul, what am I to do?" The old man said to him, "Believe in God, because he will send his grace and meet your need, if you ask him in truth." And he added, "I heard that such a thing happened in Scetis. There was a certain one there who was enduring temptations, and not having the trust in anyone to confess to, he packed his bag intending to leave. In the night the Lord's grace appeared to him in the form of a virgin, who told him, 'Do not go anywhere, but remain here with me; for none of the evils you have heard about will happen to you.' He believed her words and remained, and his heart was immediately restored to health."[4]

---

[2] Smaragdus's text here reads: *repentina praeveniente gratia.* Isidore has *repentina praeventi gratia,* "prevented by a sudden grace."

[3] Isidore, Sent 2.5.1a, 2b, 3a, 3c, 6a, 8–10; CCSL 111:99–102; PL 83:604A–C–605AB.

[4] PL 73:905AB (47); see *Wisdom,* 27, 83.

CHAPTER 46

On Good Subjects

Subjects are to be admonished not to censure rashly the life of their superiors if they happen to see them doing something deserving of censure. They may rightly contradict evils, and then finish up sinking lower through an impulse of pride. Subjects are to be admonished not to become less reverent toward their superiors when they consider their faults. If any of these faults are very serious, let them personally exercise discernment, so that bound by the fear of God they do not refuse to bear the yoke of reverence under them.[1]

Subjects of good disposition are to be admonished to rejoice in the good things of others, and so desire to have them as their own; they are to praise their neighbors' deeds, loving them so as to multiply them by imitating them. They should do this in case, while in the arena of this present life being ardent supporters at another's contest but slothful spectators, they remain without a prize after the contest. The reason for this would be that now they do not join in the contest. So they would then gaze with sad eyes at the palms waved by those in whose toil they are now too slothful to join. We sin greatly if we do not love the good that others do, but we get no reward if we do not imitate as much as we can the things we love.[2]

The good things that belong to others and that we love in them are ours, even if we cannot imitate them; and whatever they love in us becomes their property.[3]

---

[1] Taio, Sent 2.42; PL 80:841AB, quoting Gregory, Past 3.4; PL 77:55C.
[2] Taio, Sent 2.42; PL 80:842AB, quoting Gregory, Past 3.10; PL 77:62D–63A.
[3] Taio, Sent 2.43; PL 80:843A, quoting Gregory, Past 3.10; PL 77:63C.

Those who in the bosom of holy Church advance by means of great virtues must not look down on the life of their superiors when they see them applying themselves to exterior things; that they themselves securely penetrate interior things is due to the help of those who toil exteriorly against the storms of this world. For what grace and brightness would their fine linen retain if rain were to touch it? Or what splendor and brightness would their scarlet or hyacinth cloth show if dust were to soil them? Therefore let their outer wear be of the texture of sackcloth, strong against dust, and the color within be hyacinth, suitable for comeliness. Let those who apply themselves only to spiritual things adorn the Church. Let those burdened by the labor of bodily things protect the Church. Therefore in no way should one who within holy Church already shines spiritually murmur against his church leader who is dealing with exterior things. For if you in your sheltered life shine interiorly like scarlet cloth, why do you accuse the sackcloth that is protecting you?[4]

Abba Joseph asked Abba Poemen, saying, "Tell me how to become a monk?" And the old man said, "If you wish to find rest both in this world and in the world to come, in every situation say, 'What am I?' And do not judge anyone."[5]

A brother asked Abba Poemen, saying, "What am I to do, because I become faint of heart while I am sitting?" The old man said to him, "Judge no one, despise no one, do not condemn or slander anyone, and God will give you rest, and your sitting will be without disturbance."[6]

A certain holy man, when he had heard of someone sinning, wept bitterly and said, "He today, I tomorrow. But however anyone may sin before you, do not judge; but judge yourself a greater sinner than he."[7]

---

[4] Paterius, Expositio 2.41; PL 79:741C, quoting Gregory, Mor 25.16; CCSL 143B:1263–64; PL 76:347AB.

[5] PL 73:910B (5); see also PG 65:227 [228]C (2); *Sayings*, 87 [102], 2.

[6] PL 73:911A (8); see also 779CD (100); 1056A (2a).

[7] PL 73:1039C (3) see *Wisdom*, 52–3, 196.

Often seniors do something by way of exception, and juniors think it a mistake. Often the strong say many things that the weak pass judgment on because of ignorance. . . . And so some subjects extend their hand in blame, but through their temerity they at once fall from life itself. Thus the Levite stretched out his hand as if to help, but lost his life while trespassing [2 Sam 6:6-8], because when the weak blame things that the strong do, they are excluded from the lot of the living.[8]

---

[8] Paterius, Expositio 8.4; PL 79:799CD, quoting Gregory, Mor 5.11; CCSL 143:234; PL 75:690C–91A.

CHAPTER 47

That the Monk's Treasure
Is to Be Located in Heaven

The Lord admonishes us saying, *Store up for yourselves treasures in heaven, where neither moth nor rust drives out*[1] [Matt 6:20]. [And as to how everyone may come to the perfection of their monastic life,] he again says, *If you wish to be perfect, go, sell all you possess, and give the money to the poor, and you will have treasures in heaven; then come, follow me* [Matt 19:21; Mark 10:21; see Luke 12:33-34]. Let us, then, place our treasure in heaven, beloved, where we are not to fear any enemy or attacker. [Let us place the treasure of our works and virtues in heaven,] where we are not to fear the hidden thief [or the violent plunderer]. For our homeland is paradise. Since we are going to receive them afterwards in our homeland, we must lay up now the manifold treasures of the virtues, [where after the end of this world we may deserve to receive fruit a hundredfold. For the saints, says the prophet, will possess a double portion in their land (see Isa 61:7), that is, they will have happiness of mind and also of body in the land of the living: When the Lord Jesus Christ *will transform the body of our lowliness, now conformed to the body of his glory* (Phil 3:21)]. For there a great number of people dear to us is waiting for us; a large crowd of parents, brothers, and sisters longs to see us, secure already of their own immortality, but still anxious for our salvation. There the choir of patriarchs and the order of prophets, apostles [and virgins,] and the ranks of all the saints long to behold

---

[1] Smaragdus here has *exterminat*, where the Vulgate has *demolitur*, "demolishes."

us. Oh, how great is the joy, to arrive at the fellowship of all the saints, to come to the happy embrace of them all! Oh, how supreme and perpetual is the happiness, there to behold the glorious choirs of apostles, and to see the sacred order of prophets abounding in joy, and to be right there among the white ranks of virgins, martyrs and confessors![2]

Abba Hyperechius said, "The monk's treasure is voluntary poverty. Therefore, brother, store up treasure for yourself in heaven, because the ages are for endless rest."[3]

Abba Evagrius used to say, "When you sit in your cell, gather your mind to yourself and remember the day of death, and then you will see what it means to mortify your body. Think of the destruction, accept the sorrow, avoid the vanities of this world. Be modest and solicitous, so that you may be able always to remain in the same resolve of quiet, and you will not grow feeble. . . . Remember also the good things that are laid up for the just. Have confidence before God the Father and his Christ, in the presence of the angels and the powers and all the people of the kingdom of heaven, and think of its gifts, its rest and its joy. Rejoice over the good things laid up for the just, and exult for joy, and hasten to enjoy these things."[4]

---

[2] Smaragdus, Via reg 13, with the customary adaptations to a monastic audience; PL 102:953D–54B; see Cyprian, *De mortalitate*, at the end; PL 4:624AB.

[3] PL 73:891A (14); see also PG 65:[429] 430D (6); *Sayings*, 200 [238], 6.

[4] PL 73:860D–61AB (3); PG 65:173 [174]D (1bis); *Sayings*, 54 [63–64], 1. Smaragdus or his source in using this apophthegm has abbreviated it, omitting the meditation on hell and the judgment of the wicked that it contains.

CHAPTER 48

On Counsel

S olomon admonishes us about this virtue of counsel, saying, *My child, listen to advice and accept instruction, that you may be wise for the future* [Prov 19:20]. *My child, do nothing without counsel and you will not repent after acting* [Sir 32:24]. [*For the astute person does everything with counsel* (Prov 13:16).] *Those who take advice for all they do are endowed with much wisdom* [Prov 13:10]. *Where counsel is lacking, plans go wrong, but where advisers are many, they succeed* [Prov 15:22]. *The heart is delighted with ointment and various odors, and the soul is sweetened by the good counsels of a friend* [Prov 27:9 Vulgate]. *War is begun with planning, and where there are many counselors there is safety* [Prov 24:6]. [*The knowledge of the wise will abound like a flood, and their counsel remains like a spring of life* (Sir 21:13).]

Good counsel is something quite important, and very necessary for monks. [Therefore all who have wished to climb to the heavenly homeland have loved the virtue of counsel on earth.][1] . . .Through this virtue of counsel the martyrs delivered up their mortal bodies to death in order to receive eternal life from the Lord. Through this virtue of counsel the virgins and confessors persevered to the end in the service of the Lord.[2]

---

[1] This last sentence is proper to the *Diadema*, and at this point Smaragdus omits a long list of examples from the Old Testament of counsel given and received by kings and leaders.

[2] Smaragdus, Via reg 20; PL 102:959A–60A. The Scripture quotations vary slightly in order and wording.

The heart's weighty counsel banishes all wandering and inconstancy. There are souls that fleetingly desire now this, now that. And so, since he does not regard these light fluctuations of mind as unimportant, Almighty God turns his gaze from wandering hearts; but when by grace he does have regard, he fixes wandering minds in the stability of counsel. When Almighty God mercifully deigns to regard the light-minded movements of humans, he forthwith forms them in mature constancy, and with the regard of heavenly grace suddenly brings their hearts to the seriousness of counsel.[3]

In every work you think of doing, think first of God, and examine carefully if what you are thinking is according to God. And if it is right in God's presence, do it; but if it is not right, cut it off from your soul.[4]

So, beloved, let us do all that we do with counsel, because it is written: *Before every work let a truthful word go before you* [Sir 37:20]; *and in everything beseech the Most High that he may direct your way in truth* [Sir 37:19]. *If the great Lord wills it, he will fill* you *with the spirit of understanding; he will send you words of wisdom like the rain* [Sir 39:8-9], and he will open your mouth in prayer and direct your counsel in the good, and your memory will not be blotted out for ever [see Sir 39:6-7, 9].[5]

At the beginning of his monastic life, Abba Evagrius came to a certain old man seeking counsel, and said to him, "Tell me, Abba, a word by which I may be saved." And he said to him, "If you want to be saved, when you go to anyone do not speak first before he inquires of you." Pierced by this word, Evagrius said, "Believe me, I have read many books, and I have never found such learning." And he went out greatly benefitted.[6]

---

[3] Taio, Sent 3.49; PL 80:906CD, quoting Gregory, Mor 19.5; CCSL 143:961; PL 76:100BC. The last clause seems to be Taio's addition.

[4] Pseudo-Basil, *Admonitio* 12; PL103:694A.

[5] Smaragdus, Via reg 20; PL 102:960AB. The Scripture quotations vary slightly in order and wording.

[6] PL 73:915CD (19); see also PG 65:171 [172]D (7); *Sayings*, 53 [62], 7. In the Alphabetical Sayings this apophthegm is under the name of Abba Euprepios.

Abba Poemen said, "He who teaches and does not do what he teaches is like a canal; it can slake the thirst of all who come to it and wash their stains, yet it cannot cleanse itself, but all filth and uncleanness is in it."[7]

A brother asked Abba Poemen, saying, "What is the meaning of what is written: 'One who is angry with his brother without cause?'" [see Matt 5:22]. And he replied, "For every matter with which your brother should wish to burden you, do not be angry with him, until he thrusts out your right eye; otherwise you are angry with him without cause. But if someone wants to separate you from God, be angry for this."[8]

[7] PL 73:921C (50); see also 799C (183); PG 65:327 [328]D (25); *Sayings*, 143 [170], 25.

[8] PL 73:921B (47); see also PG 65:351 [352]D–[353] 354A (118); *Sayings*, 155 [184], 118.

CHAPTER 49

On the Sanctification of Heart and Body

Among other things, Paul speaks as follows to the Thessalonians about sanctification: *This is the will of God, your sanctification: that you abstain from fornication* [1 Thess 4:3]. *This is the will of God,* he says; that is, this is pleasing to God, that you be sanctified in heart and also in body. If this had not been pleasing to him, he would not have ordered us, saying, *Be holy, for I the Lord your God am holy* [Lev 19:2; see Lev 20:7]. But truly and without any doubt, the holiness and splendor by which those who are holy and splendid become holy with God consists in the sanctification of our same Creator, as it is written: *Holiness and splendor are in his sanctification* [Ps 95(96):6]. Hence also the Lord says, *Keep my statutes, and observe them; I am the Lord who sanctify you* [Lev 20:8].

Although this virtue of sanctification must be in all Christians, it is especially fitting and becoming to the priestly order. For this reason the Lord also says to Moses, *You shall clothe Aaron and his sons, and sanctify them, so that they may exercise the priesthood for me* [Exod 30:30]. *Let not a priest defile himself for the dead* [Lev 21:1], for he is holy to his God, and he offers the show bread [see Lev 21:7-8]. *Therefore they shall be holy, for I the Lord, who sanctify you, am holy* [Lev 21:8].

For indeed, unless a priest offers sacrifice to God with heart and body sanctified, it will not be agreeable to him, who knows the priest's heart to be polluted with the contagion of fornication. Hence in this place too the apostle exhorts not only the Thessalonians [1 Thess 4:3] but all who believe in Christ to abstain from fornication; because as through humility of mind chastity of the flesh is safeguarded, so through pride of heart one enters into the uncleanness of impurity.[1]

That is why the demons associate familiarly with the sexually impure and the proud more than with the rest of sinners, because through impurity of the flesh the devil binds them up with his own chains, so that separated from God and associated with the demons, they cannot possess the kingdom of heaven with the saints.[2]

John the Apostle also says this about this virtue of sanctification: *And all who have this hope in him sanctify themselves, just as he is holy* [1 John 3:3]. Many say they have hope of heavenly life in Christ, but they make this confession empty by their negligent living. Those who are careful to apply themselves to good works show a clear sign of heavenly hope, being certain that they will only reach likeness to God in the future if they imitate God's holiness in the present by sanctifying themselves, that is, by renouncing *impiety and worldly desires*, and by living *lives that are sober, upright, and godly* [Titus 2:12]. . . .Those who have hope in God sanctify themselves as much as they can by looking towards him[3] and in everything entreating his grace, who says, *Without me you can do nothing* [John 15:5], and by saying to him, *Be my helper, do not forsake me* [Ps 26(27):9].[4] . . . Therefore he makes us holy, *just as he is holy* [1 John 3:3]. But he is holy in virtue of eternity, we are holy in virtue of faith.[5]

In olden times bishops, priests, and deacons were ordained as men having only one wife [see 1 Tim 3:2]; but now, since purity has increased in distinction because of its connection with holiness, the rule of the sacred canons prohibits them from all carnal intercourse. In the Old Testament priests withheld themselves from intercourse with their wives only when they were ministering at the altar. But

---

[1] No source traced for this passage.

[2] See Isidore, Sent 2.39.4; CCSL 111:171; PL 83:640D.

[3] Bede's text (In 1 Jo 3:3) has *quantum potest ipse nitendo*, "as much as he [they] can by striving"; Smaragdus has *quantum potest ipsum intuendo*.

[4] Bede, In 1 Jo 3:3; CCSL 121:302–3; PL 93:99D–100A; see CS 82:186–87.

[5] Bede, In 1 Jo 3:7; CCSL 121:304; PL 93:101B; see CS 82:190.

now, because we must daily consecrate the Lord's body at the altar, or receive it, we must daily abstain from sexual intercourse. Thus Paul admonishes Timothy, saying, *Be an example for believers in speech and conduct, in love, in faith, in chastity* [1 Tim 4:12]. For those who have to give an example in speech to others must not neglect their manner of speaking, but must diligently attend to what, to whom, when, and how they must speak, so that their speech is not foolish, but, according to the Lord's precept, let it be seasoned with the salt [see Col 4:6] of wisdom. Those persons offer a good example to others in behavior who live chastely, piously, and justly in this world [see Titus 2:12]. Those persons give a good example to others in charity who love God with their whole heart, their whole mind, and their whole strength, and their neighbor as themselves [see Deut 6:5; Matt 22:37; Mark 12:30; Luke 10:27]. Those persons give a good example in faith who by believing rightly live well, and by living well keep a right faith.[6] Those persons give a good example to others in chastity who love the beauty of chastity, and preserve it not only in body but safeguard it also in mind from wrongful thoughts, because incorruption of body is of no benefit where there is not integrity of mind.[7]

---

[6] This sentence incorporates a saying recorded for the first time in Auctor incertus, *Sermones suppositii* 108; PL 39:1959 near the end, and repeated in Isidore, Sent 2.2.1; PL 83:601B; see also Defensor, Scint 32, quoting Isidore; PL 88:662D; Bonifatius Moguntinus, Sermo 7; PL 89:857AB.

[7] No source traced for this passage, apart from the sentence referred to in the previous note, and the last two clauses of the final sentence, for which see Isidore, Sent 2.40.8; CCSL 111:178; PL 83:644B.

CHAPTER 50

On the Call
of the Divine Kindness

The call of the divine kindness, which is made in different ways in different ages and at different times, is not due to human merit but is always made freely by God alone in his kindness. As the apostle says, *The gifts and the call of God are irrevocable* [Rom 11:29]. He also says to Timothy, *He freed us and called us with a holy calling, not according to our works but according to his own purpose and grace* [2 Tim 1:9].

People are called in different ways, as was said. Some who are healthy only in body are called, being divinely inspired; others afflicted with weakness of the flesh are called, as are others again who are oppressed by diverse defects or various trials. They are called at different ages: some in infancy, some in adolescence, others in youth, others in old age, and some even in extreme old age. They are called at different hours of the day: some early in the morning, others at the third or the sixth or the ninth hour, and others at the eleventh hour. None of these is called to uncleanness, but all are called by a holy God to holiness of heart and of body. The holy God always wishes to have holy ministers, as he says in the Gospel: *For their sake I sanctify myself, so that they also may be sanctified in truth* [John 17:19].[1]

A certain old man said, "Two brothers were neighbors, one a foreigner, the other a native-born. The foreigner was somewhat

---

[1] No source traced for this passage.

negligent, while the native-born was very zealous. Now it happened that the foreigner fell asleep in peace. The old man who was their neighbor, being gifted with foresight, saw a multitude of angels leading his soul away. When he had come to enter heaven, the question was put about that soul. And there came a voice from above saying, 'It is clear that he was somewhat negligent, but open to him on account of his living in a foreign country.' And afterwards that native-born person fell asleep, and all his kindred came to him; but that old man did not see any angels come to lead his soul away. Surprised, the old man said, 'How is it that the foreigner, although he was somewhat negligent, had such glory, and this man, although he was zealous, did not merit anything of the kind?' And a voice came, saying to him, 'When this zealous man came to die, he opened his eyes and saw his relatives weeping, and his soul was consoled. But that foreigner, although he was somewhat negligent, did not see any of his own, and he groaned and wept, and God consoled him.'"[2]

They used to say of Abba Sisoes that on the day of his falling asleep, when the fathers were sitting around him, his face shone like the sun, and he said to them, "Behold, the choir of prophets and apostles has come." Again he said, "Behold, the angels have come to take me." And again his face became like the sun, and they were all afraid. He said to them again, "See, behold the Lord is coming, saying, 'Bring to me the chosen vessel of the desert.'" And at once he rendered up his spirit. And that whole place was filled with brightness and a sweet odor.[3]

[2] PL 73:994CD–95A (12); see *Wisdom*, 63–64, 236.
[3] PL 73:1007CD (6); see also 793CD–94A (162); PG 65:395 [396]BC (14); *Sayings*, 180 [214–15], 14. Smaragdus's version is abbreviated here, while the full version is given in chapter 88 of this work.

CHAPTER 51

On the Love and Grace of God

C oncerning this heading the apostle says, *But God, who is rich in mercy, on account of the great love with which he loved us even when we were dead through our sins, made us alive together with Christ—by his grace we have been saved—and raised us up with him and made us sit with him in the heavenly places in Christ, so that he might show the abundant riches of his grace in kindness towards us in Christ Jesus. For by grace we have been saved through faith* [Eph 2:4-8].

Now God is said to be rich in mercy because he is omnipotent and the earth is full of his mercy. God is said to be rich in mercy, because he mercifully draws all sinners to repentance, and mercifully grants them perseverance in it. And he is said to be rich on account of his exceeding great love with which he loved the human race. For almighty God loved us so much that he delivered up his Son to death for us, as it is written: *God did not spare his own Son, but gave him up for us all* [Rom 8:32]. For it is exceeding great love to deliver up his only-begotten Son for sinful slaves, and to love those same rebel slaves as children. And so, beloved, we must consider how much the Lord loves us his holy ones, who deigned to love sinners so much, who, *even when we were dead through our sins, made us alive together with Christ* [Eph 2:5]. On account of his mercy he granted us to have one and the same perpetual life with him. The soul is said to be dead when it is befouled with death-dealing vices, as also the apostle says, *You were dead through the trespasses and sins in which at one time you openly lived* [Eph 2:1-2]. Sin is said to be the death of the soul, as the prophet says, *The soul that sins will die* [Ezek 18:20].

The soul of any human being sins in two ways, that is, by not doing what it was ordered to do, and by doing what has been forbidden it.

By grace we have been saved [Eph 2:5], he says, that is, not by the former works of our life, but by faith alone and the grace of baptism we have received the remission of our sins. For the Lord himself, our Lord, who is rich in mercy, beloved, on account of his exceeding love with which he loved us has raised us up with him and made us sit with him in Christ Jesus. Consider, brothers and sisters, what thanks we must render to our Creator, since it was in our nature that Christ our Creator and Redeemer himself rose from the dead, ascended into heaven, and sits at the right hand of the Father. It is in that nature that we too rose with him, we ascended and we sit at the right hand of the Father. Hence holy people, though living in the flesh, have their real life in heaven, and do not hesitate to say that the saints already sit and reign with Christ at the right hand of the Father.[1]

How great the benefit and how manifold the grace by which he made us sit with the Lord and made us reign with Christ! This is proved by the fact that we, who were once held fast by the law of the underworld, now reign in Christ and sit with him. Grace is truly abundant; it not only forgave our sins, but after we were raised up with Christ it also placed us at the right hand of God.[2]

An angel said to a certain bishop, "*God so loved* this *world that he gave his only Son* for it [John 3:16]. Therefore will not he who, when people were his enemies, chose to die for them, much more absolve them from punishment now that they have become members of his household and are doing penance for what they did? And will he not give them the good things that he has prepared? . . . Therefore know this, that no human trespasses surpass God's clemency. Let people only through patience[3] wash away by their good acts the evil that they did before. Since God is merciful, he knows the weaknesses of your race, the strength of your passions, and the power and cun-

---

[1] No source traced for this passage.

[2] See Jerome, In Eph 2:7; PL 26:469B.

[3] Smaragdus here has *patientiam*, while the three source texts listed below have *poenitentiam*, "repentance."

ning of the devil; he, so to say, forgives people while they are falling by sin, and in all patience towards them awaits their correction. He has compassion on those who turn and beseech his goodness as on people who are weak; he at once relieves their anguish, and gives them the good things that have been prepared for the just."[4]

---

[4] PL 73:999AB (16, extract from a long *apophthegm*); see also 794D–95B–C (166) and 1046CD (1).

CHAPTER 52

That the Saints
Are Called Children of Light

The apostle John says, *We announce to you that God is light, and in him there is no darkness at all* [1 John 1:5]. Rightly then does the apostle call those who are children of God children of light, when he says, *You are all children of the light and children of the day; you do not belong to the night or to darkness* [1 Thess 5:5]. Just as those who have in them love and peace are called children of love and children of peace, so too those who have in them the light of faith and knowledge are called children of light. Hence also Paul says, *You were at one time darkness, but now you are light in the Lord. Live as children of light* [Eph 5:8]. Or they are called children of light—that is, children of God, as the Lord says, *I am the light of the world. Those who follow me do not walk in darkness but will have the light of life* [John 8:12]. And they are children of the day, he says, that is, of the Lord Jesus Christ, who said to his disciples, *Are there not twelve hours in the day? Those who walk during the day do not stumble* [John 11:9]. He wished to indicate himself by the day and the apostles by the hours. For he himself is spiritually the true day, because it is said of him: A sanctified day has shone upon us.[1] Now the twelve hours, as was said earlier, are his twelve apostles, because to show that he is the day he chose twelve apostles.

[1] *Dies sanctificatus illuxit nobis*, Gregory, *Liber Antiphonarius*, In Die Natalis Domini; PL 78:646C. Verse used in the Alleluia of the Third Mass of Christmas.

Those who do the truth come to the light [John 3:21]; they are light and children of light and of the day [see 1 Thess 5:5]. Just as none exist of themselves, so too none are enlightened by themselves, but the one who enlightens is the one of whom it is written: *There was the true light that enlightens everyone who comes into this world* [John 1:9]. Whoever has risen from the darkness of ignorance and from sin and been enlightened by him who said, *I am the light of the world. Those who follow me do not walk in darkness but will have the light of life* [John 8:12], is rightly called a child of light and of the day.[2]

For we are God's children not by nature but by imitation, as the Savior says, *so that you may be children of your Father who is in heaven* [Matt 5:45].[3]

---

[2] No source traced for this passage.
[3] Auctor incertus, In Eph 5:1; PL 30:835C.

CHAPTER 53

On Hope

Concerning this chapter on hope the apostle Paul says, *Now faith is the substance of things to be hoped for, the conviction of things that are not apparent* [Heb 11:1]. *For who hopes for what is seen? But what we do not see we wait for with patience* [Rom 8:24-25].

Hope is the expectation of future good things,[1] which expresses a feeling of humility and the compliance of assiduous service. It is called hope [*spes*] because it is the foot by which one advances, as though saying *est pes*, "it is the foot." On the other hand despair is so called because one who despairs lacks the means of advancing, for while people love sin they cannot expect future glory.[2] That person waits trustingly who faithfully keeps God's commandments. The apostle rightly says that hope is blessed when we shall merit to be God's children and heirs: *Heirs indeed of God, and joint heirs with Christ* [Rom 8:17]. *When he appears, we will be like him, for we will see him as he is* [1 John 3:2]. Then sin will not rule over us and eternal life will be bestowed; then we shall obtain the brightness of the sun and the company of the angels.[3]

Hence the same apostle says elsewhere: *Because of the hope that is laid up for us in heaven* [Col 1:5]. For hope of future good things is not visible to our fleshly eyes now, but it is still laid up for us in heaven. The same apostle says about this hope: *What eye has not seen, nor ear*

---

[1] See Isidore, Diff 2.36.139A; PL 83:92A.

[2] See Isidore, Etym. 8.2.5; Lindsay, vol. 1 (at reference, as pages are not numbered); PL 82:296A.

[3] Smaragdus, Collect, Oct Nativ Dom; PL 102:56BC.

heard, nor has it entered the human heart, the things God has prepared for those who love him [1 Cor 2:9].

The hope of all the elect is eternal life, which is still laid up for us in heaven in Christ: *When Christ your life has appeared, then we too will appear with him in glory* [Col 3:4]. And elsewhere the same apostle says, *Now may our Lord Jesus Christ himself and God the Father, who loved us and gave us eternal comfort and good hope in grace* [2 Thess 2:16].[4] Hope is called good because it is written: Those who hope in the Lord shall not lack any good [see Ps 33(34):10]. It is also called hope of mercy: *Because those who hope in the Lord, mercy will surround* [Ps 31(32):10].

Peter calls it living hope [see 1 Pet 1:3], because it promises us eternal life. The noun "hope" is given an adjective in keeping with the quality of the gift. Now it can be understood here much more clearly and more excellently as a good hope by grace—that is, the one who with the Father and the Holy Spirit is alone good, the Lord Jesus Christ, of whom the psalmist sings, *The Lord is my hope since my youth* [Ps 70(71):5].[5]

It is greatly to be feared that, through the hope of pardon which God promises we may persevere in sin, or that because he justly punishes sins we may despair of pardon. Avoiding both dangers, let us turn away from evil and also hope for pardon from the Lord's kindness.[6]

---

[4] The quotation from 2 Thessalonians is incomplete; the passage concentrates on the hope mentioned near the end.

[5] No source traced for this passage.

[6] Isidore, Sent 2.4.2a; CCSL 111:98–99; PL 83:603C.

CHAPTER 54

That We Are to Pray without Ceasing

I t seems to me possible to pray without ceasing in two ways: with the intention of the heart, or by the practice of mercy. Those inspired by the desire of heavenly contemplation and totally dedicated in the love of their Creator pray with the intention of the heart. For this continual practice of love for God is prayer without ceasing.

Prayer without ceasing is also practiced when the treasure of alms is stored up in heaven, since the Lord says, *Store up for yourselves treasures in heaven* [Matt 6:20]. For those who store up treasure in heaven, their treasure, laid up in the Lord's sight, is always (whether they walk, sit, eat, drink, talk, keep quiet or sleep) praying to the Lord without ceasing. Hence also the Lord himself says, *Hide an alms in the bosom of a poor person, and it will pray to the Lord for you* [Sir 29:15].[1]

Those who, after prayer, strive to keep themselves in prayer in the way they were during prayer, pray without ceasing (according to some). This is what we read about Hannah when she prayed; she remained in the very attitude of compunction with which she prayed until she obtained from the Lord what she asked for [see 1 Sam 1].[2]

They used to say of Abba Arsenius that on Saturday evening, as Sunday's light was approaching, he would turn his back to the sun

---

[1] Smaragdus's text has *ad Dominum*, which is not in the standard Vulgate text.
[2] No source traced for this passage.

and extend his hands to heaven in prayer, until on Sunday morning the rising sun lit up his face, and then he would sit down again.[3]

Certain monks, called Euchites, that is, "people who pray," once came to Abba Lucius, and the old man asked them, "What is your manual work?" And they said, "We do not touch manual work, but as the apostle says, *Pray without ceasing*" [1 Thess 5:17]. And the old man said to them, "And do you not eat?" They said, "Yes, we eat." And he said to them, "So when you are eating, who prays for you?" And he asked them again, "Do you not sleep?" And they said, "We do sleep." The old man said, "And when you are sleeping, who prays for you?" And they could not find an answer to these questions. And the old man said, "Forgive me, brothers, for behold, you do not do as you said. But I can show you that I pray without ceasing while working with my hands. For I sit down and with God's help soak a few small palm leaves, and I make from them a woven handle, and I say, *Have mercy on me, God, according to your great mercy; according to the abundance of your mercy blot out my iniquity*" [Ps 50(51):1]. And he said to them, "Is it prayer or not?" And they said to him, "Yes." And he said, "When I remain working and praying the whole day, I make more or less sixteen coppers,[4] and I put two of them at the door, while the rest I use for food. The person who receives those two pennies prays for me at the time when I am eating or sleeping, and so through the grace of God there is fulfilled in me what is written: *Pray without ceasing*" [1 Thess 5:17].[5]

---

[3] PL 73:941A (1); see also 807A (211a); PG 65:[97] 98C (30); *Sayings*, 12 [14], 30.

[4] The Latin word translated here is *nummus*.

[5] PL 73:942A+C (9); see also 807BC (212); PG 65:[253] 254BC; *Sayings*, 102 [120–21], 1.

CHAPTER 55

That We Are to Be Simple, as Children of God

Those people give no grounds for complaint who, as far as human frailty allows, strive to lead a life without fault. Faults committed against God or neighbor give rise to complaints. So those people live without giving grounds for complaint who do not lead lives soiled with vices, nor commit faults for which complaints may be justly brought against them.[1]

And you are to be simple, says the apostle, as children of God [see Phil 2:15]. For God is simple in nature. So those who are already children of God through adoption, and desire to be so through imitation, must needs *be simple as doves* [Matt 10:16]. For it is written: *The simplicity of the upright will guide them* [Prov 11:3].[2]

Nothing is happier than a simple heart, because those who show themselves innocent with regard to others have no need to fear suffering anything from others. Their simplicity is for them a kind of strong citadel; they have no thought of suffering what they do not remember having done.[3]

Be spotless, *without reproach* [Phil 2:15]. Paul teaches and desires God's children to be very well supplied with virtues and upright, for one who sins is stained. The impious action of sin is itself a stain

---

[1] This paragraph occurs again at the end of chapter 66.

[2] No source traced for this passage.

[3] Taio, Sent 3.28; PL 80:886C, quoting Gregory, Mor 12.39; CCSL 143A:655; PL 75:1007A.

that soils and contaminates the one who commits it. But with God's help the children of God are spotless and can live without reproach if they do nothing deserving of reproach, although they may suffer reproach from people of ill will. *Happy are those who are spotless in the way, who walk in the law of the Lord* [Ps 118(119):1].[4]

Saint Syncletica said, "Let us become prudent as serpents and simple as doves [see Matt 10:16], so that we may be astute in understanding the devil's snares. For it was said that the prudent become like serpents so that we may be alert to the attacks of the devil and his wiles. One charge is overcome by something similar. And the simplicity of the dove also points to purity of action."[5]

[4] No source traced for this passage.
[5] PL 73:993AB (2); see also PG 65:427 [428]A (18); *Sayings*, 196 [234], 18.

CHAPTER 56

That We Should Do Everything without Murmuring

Those who murmur against the Lord's precepts and those of his teacher are doubtless unsure as regards receiving the rewards of their labor. All those of the children of Israel who murmured against the Lord and Moses in the desert perished in the same desert from the poisonous bites of serpents, and did not receive the inheritance in the promised land among their brothers [see Num 14 and 21].

Any of us who desire to possess the inheritance among God's chosen as among brothers in the land of the living, must live in the present age without murmuring. The more people murmur about what they have to do in the present, the less hope they have of receiving the eternal recompense of their labor. Those who do not doubt about the hope of receiving the reward, despite finding themselves among difficult tasks, do not in any way murmur against their instructor, the Lord. For a son who is instructed by his father in order to receive an eternal inheritance must not murmur, but rather rejoice in his father's instruction.[1]

When a perverse mind is corrected through a verbal rebuke, or someone tries to persuade it through the sweetness of preaching, it becomes worse as a result of the correction, and where it ought to be restrained from iniquity it is further inflamed by the vice of

---

[1] No source traced for this passage.

murmuring.[2] Those who are struck because of sin and do not resist with murmuring are already beginning to be just by the fact that they do not find fault with the striker's justice.[3]

And so Paul says, *And do not murmur as some of them murmured . . . and were destroyed by serpents* [1 Cor 10:10, 9; see Num 21].

The book of Numbers tells how the people, wearied in the desert by their long march and hard toil, murmured . . . and so the Lord sent fiery serpents against them. . . . So the plagues of the fiery serpents are the poison of the vices that bring spiritual death on the soul they touch. And rightly were the people laid low by the serpents' bites for murmuring against the Lord. This was so that they might recognize from the manner of the exterior scourge how much harm they were suffering interiorly by their murmuring.[4]

Abba Joseph said that three ways of acting are honorable in the Lord's sight: first, when a person is sick, and temptations are laid on him, and he receives them with thanksgiving; second, when someone does all his works with a pure intention before the Lord, and seeks nothing human in them; third, when someone sits in subjection and obeys spiritual precepts without murmuring, and renounces self-will completely.[5]

---

[2] Taio, Sent 4.33; PL 80:949C, quoting Gregory, In Hiez 1.9,32; CCSL 142:140; PL 76:884C.

[3] Taio, Sent 4.33; PL 80:949C, quoting Gregory, Mor 23.18; CCSL 143B:1168; PL 76:270D–71A.

[4] Smaragdus, Collect, Heb 10 post Pent; PL 102:416AB, and Dom oct Pent, 102:342BC, quoting Bede, In Jo 3:14-15; PL 92:671BC.

[5] PL 73:856A (9); see also PG 65:241 [242]BC; *Sayings*, 94 [110], 1. PL does not have PG's ending.

CHAPTER 57

On Circumcising the Vices

On this subject Paul says, *We are the circumcision, who serve God in spirit and make our boast in Christ Jesus* [Phil 3:3]. It is as though he should say to those circumcised in the flesh: You are circumcised in the skin of your foreskin; we are circumcised in our heart and body. You cut away from you a good creature of God; we circumcise from us spiritually vices and sins. And so we who worship God in the Spirit are the circumcision, not you who bring the stain of circumcision on your body. When he says, *We are the circumcision, who serve God in spirit,* it is as if he said, We are the righteousness of spiritual circumcision, because being made spiritual by righteousness, we serve our Author spiritually. For he did not say, We are circumcised, or, We have circumcision, but he says, *We are the circumcision*—that is, we are the cleanness and righteousness of a spiritual circumcision, by having spiritual righteousness and cleanness. For in the law and the prophets we are ordered to be circumcised in two ways: namely, in the flesh and in the heart. In the flesh, when he says, *You shall circumcise the flesh of your foreskin* [Gen 17:11]; in the heart, when he says, *Circumcise the foreskins of your hearts* [Deut 10:16; see Jer 4:4]. Now we are circumcised in the flesh if we cut off from ourselves the vices of the flesh: adultery, fornication, uncleanness, gluttony, drunkenness, and all other things like these, which work through the concupiscence of the flesh. We are circumcised in the heart if we cut off from ourselves spiritual vices: pride, boasting, anger, quarrelling, hatred, envy and the like. So the casting off of all these vices and the acquisition of the virtues make a person righteous. And this righteousness of circumcision by which people are made upright, Paul calls circumcision.

[We] who worship God in spirit [Phil 3:3], he says. *God is spirit* [John 4:24]. And as those who adore God must adore in spirit and truth,

so too one who serves God ought to serve him in spirit and truth. [*We*] *boast of Christ Jesus* [Phil 3:3]. As though to say, We who serve God in spirit do not glory in a fleshly way in the circumcision of the flesh, but we glory in Christ Jesus in a spiritual way; from him we have received the virtue of faith, through which we glory in him.[1] For the Lord was circumcised on the eighth day, and on the thirty-third day after being circumcised he was carried to the temple [see Luke 2:22], so that a victim might be offered for him and he might be called the Holy One of the Lord. The mystical meaning of this is that none are worthy to be presented in the Lord's sight unless they are circumcised from vices; none will be able to reach perfection and climb to the joys of the heavenly city unless they are freed from the bonds of mortality.[2]

James the apostle exhorts us to perform this circumcision of the carnal and spiritual vices when he says, *Cast off all uncleanness and the abundance of wickedness, and receive with meekness the implanted word* [Jas 1:21]. First he orders the body and mind to be circumcised[3] from vices so that we can be worthy to receive the word of salvation. He names all uncleanness as belonging to body and soul; but wickedness he designates as belonging only to the crookedness of the inner person.[4]

Peter the apostle admonishes us when he says, *Beloved, I beseech you as aliens and exiles to abstain from the desires of the flesh* [1 Pet 2:11]. He openly teaches us to abstain from carnal desires that war against the soul; and while the flesh is being feebly subjected to flattering lusts, the army of the vices is being strongly armed against the soul.[5]

Abba Ammonas said that he spent fourteen years in Scetis praying God night and day to give him the strength to overcome the flesh.[6]

---

[1] No source traced for this passage.

[2] See Bede, In Lc 2:22; CCSL 120:61; PL 92:341A; Smaragdus, In Oct Nativ Dom; PL 102:59BC.

[3] Bede here has *iubet expurgare*, "he orders [us] to purge . . . ." Smaragdus has *iubet circumcidi*. Smaragdus has "we" in this text where Bede has "they."

[4] Bede, In Jac 1:21; CCSL 121:191; PL 93:17A; see CS 82:19.

[5] See Bede, In 1 Pt 2:11; CCSL 121:238–39; PL 93:51D–52A; see CS 82:88–89; see Commentary, 4.59; CS 212:231.

[6] PL 73:893B (3); PG 65:119 [120]B (3); *Sayings*, 22 [26], 3.

CHAPTER 58

On the Fruit of Righteousness

[The apostle James says,] *And the fruit of righteousness is sown in peace for those who make peace* [Jas 3:18]. All that we do in this life is the seed of future recompense. And the recompense itself is the fruit of present works, on the witness of the apostle who says, *For what one sows, this one will also reap. One who sows in the flesh will reap corruption from the flesh. But one who sows in the spirit will reap eternal life from the spirit* [Gal 6:8]. And so it is rightly said that *the fruit of righteousness is sown in peace for those who make peace.* The fruit of righteousness is eternal life, which is recompense for works of righteousness, because those who seek peace pursue it. As though with the best seed, they sprinkle the earth of their heart with the very peace on which they are intent, so that through the daily growth of their good works they can reach the fruit of heavenly life. Of this it is written elsewhere: *Those who are sowing in tears will reap in joy* [Ps 125(126):5].[1]

And so Paul also says, *Being filled with the fruit [of righteousness] through Jesus Christ for the glory and praise of God* [Phil 1:11]. In the letter to the Galatians he called this fruit of righteousness the fruit of the Spirit when he says, *Now the fruit of the Spirit is love, joy, peace, patience, kindness, goodness, gentleness, meekness, faith, modesty, self-control, chastity* [Gal 5:22-23]. He wants us to be filled with this manifold fruit on the day of Christ Jesus, to the glory and praise of God, because for all the good things we have received from him we

---

[1] Bede, In Jac 3:18; CCSL 121:210–11; PL 93:31CD; see CS 82:46–47.

must with the psalmist give to him, and not to ourselves, glory and praise, saying, *Not to us, Lord, not to us, but to your name give the glory* [Ps 113B(115):1].[2]

Once two brothers came to a certain old man, whose custom it was not to eat every day. When he saw the brothers he received them gladly and said, "Fasting has its reward." And again, "He who eats because of charity fulfills two commands, because he forsakes his own will and fulfills the command while refreshing the brothers."[3]

A certain father said, "Unless you first hate vices you will not be able to love. Therefore unless you hate sin you will not do righteousness. It is written: *Turn away from evil, and do good* [Ps 33(34):14]. But in all these things the mind's intention is everywhere sought. While living in paradise, Adam transgressed God's command, but while seated on the dung heap, Job kept it. From this it is clear that God seeks from humans a good intention, and that they always fear him."[4]

---

[2] No source traced for this passage.

[3] PL 73:945C (10).

[4] PL 73:940D–41A (54).

CHAPTER 59

That We Are to Return to the Innocence of Childhood

The Lord says in the Gospel: *Truly I tell you, unless you change and become like little children, you will not enter the kingdom of heaven* [Matt 18:3]. The Lord gave this command not only to the apostles but also to all who believe in him and desire to enter the kingdom of heaven. We are not ordered to have the age of children, but to lead an innocent way of life; we are to possess through the purity of innocence what they possess through their age, so as to be children in wickedness, not in wisdom.[1]

Thus the Lord also says again, *Therefore whoever becomes humble like this little child is the greatest in the kingdom of heaven* [Matt 18:4]. As though to say, Just as this child, whose example I offer you, does not remain angry, does not remember injury, does not take pleasure when he sees a beautiful woman, does not think one thing and say another, so you too, unless you have such innocence and purity of mind, will not be able to enter the kingdom of heaven.[2] How we may come to the innocence of childhood, the apostle Peter sets out when he says, *Putting off, therefore, all malice and all guile, pretence, envy, and all slander, like newborn infant, long for the pure milk that has no guile, so that by it you may grow into salvation* [1 Pet 2:1-2]. As though to

---

[1] Jerome, In Mt 18:3; PL 26:133A.

[2] Smaragdus, Collect, In Natale S. Archangeli Michaelis, In Mt 18; PL 102:478BC, quoting and conflating Bede In Mt 18:3; In Mc 10:15; CCSL 120:559; In Lc 18:17; CCSL 120:326; PL 92:83B.230D–31A.553D.

say, Because you are already reborn through the water of baptism, and through the grace of the Holy Spirit you have become God's children through baptism, be now through zeal for a good manner of life like children, who are naturally incapable of doing harm in virtue of their age; that is, without malice or deceit or pretence or slanders; and let all bitterness, rage, anger and indignation, shouting and blasphemy be removed from you together with all wickedness. And in this way returning to childlike innocence, desire to receive in you the word of the Sacred Scriptures like mother's milk, so that growing in it you may set out to eat that bread *which comes down from heaven and gives life to the world* [John 6:33].[3]

Now Paul says of himself and his followers, *We became as little children among you, like a nurse who nourishes her own children* [1 Th 2:7]. For he knew that gospel saying uttered by the Lord: *Whoever becomes humble like this little child is the greatest in the kingdom of heaven* [Matt 18:4]. And so he humbled himself in the midst of his disciples to give them an example of humility and to acquire for himself the reward for being humbled.

But let us see how he could say in a way deserving of praise, *we became children*, since he says in another place: may we not become children [see 1 Cor 14:20]. How did they become children voluntarily though not wanting to be children? What kind of children Paul desires us to be he himself explains when he says, *Be little children in evil* [1 Cor 14:20]. And what kind of children he does not desire us to be he shows when he adds, Would that we may not become little children, wavering, and blown about by every wind of doctrine [see Eph 4:14].

Therefore we become children in two ways: by having and by not having, that is, by having humility, purity, and innocence; by not having malice, guile, and envy. Now the apostles became children by not having malice, guile, and envy; they became great by having humility, purity, and innocence, and by having also an abundance of teaching, with which Paul like a nurse nourished his children, to whom he also said, *Like little children in Christ, I gave you milk to drink, not solid food* [1 Cor 3:2-3].[4]

---

[3] See Bede, In 1 Pt 2:1-2; CCSL 121:232–33; PL 93:47BC; see CS 82:80.

[4] No source traced for this passage.

CHAPTER 60

About the Fact That the Just Are Called Living Stones

Peter in his Letter says, *And like living stones you yourselves are being built into a spiritual house* [1 Pet 2:5]. He says that they are being built on him, because without the Lord Jesus Christ—that is, the living stone—no spiritual building can stand. *For no one can lay any other foundation besides him* [1 Cor 3:11]. By sharing in him the faithful, who had been dead stones through infidelity— that is, they were hard and unfeeling—become living stones. It could rightly be said to them, *I will remove from you the heart of stone and give you a heart of flesh* [Ezek 36:26], [a heart docile for receiving the Gospel teaching,] so that they may be fitted as living stones to form a spiritual building; that is, with superfluous acts and thoughts cut off through the discretion of a learned teacher, they are squared as by the blow of an axe.[1]

[A square stone that is turned on any side stands just as well.[2] Now the upright person who is not lifted up in prosperity or broken by adversity, or cast down by censures, or drawn to evil by persuasion, is a square stone.][3]

For just as stones are placed in order in a wall, some stones being carried by others, so the faithful are carried in the Church by those upright ones who precede them. These through their teaching and

[1] Bede, In 1 Pt 2:5; CCSL 121:234; PL 93:48BC; see CS 82:82.
[2] Gregory, In Hiez 2.9,5; CCSL 142:359; PL 76:1044C.
[3] See Gregory, In Hiez 2.9,5; CCSL 142:359; PL 76:1044CD.

bearing carry those that follow, [and in this way some upright persons are carried by others] right up to the last upright person. And since the latter is carried by those who go before, that person will not have someone coming after who must be carried. Now the one who carried the whole edifice, and whom no one else carries, is the Lord Christ. And so he is called by the prophet a precious stone, a sure foundation [see Isa 28:16]. Again the apostle calls the elect living stones so as to insinuate the need for exertion in their good action. . . . For wherever dead—that is material—stones are laid by the builder . . . they remain without feeling, or they even slip and fall down. So blessed Peter does not want us to imitate the lack of feeling of such stones, but he wants us to be built as living stones on the foundation that is Christ, so that with God's grace helping us, we may *live lives that are sober, upright, and godly* [Titus 2:12]. Therefore those who without growing weary are careful to apply themselves to good works are, by Christ's gift and with his help, built by him as living stones in his house.[4]

In the living and holy temple only living and holy stones can be laid. And so we must make every effort to be those stones of which it is written: *Living stones are rolled upon the earth* [Zech 9:16 LXX], and when we are living stones hewn on every side, let us be built into the temple; and let us be with the apostles and prophets a holy, spiritual *dwelling place for God* [Eph 2:22], *not made with hands* [Heb 9:11].[5]

[4] Bede, In 1 Pt 2:5; CCSL 121:234–35; PL 93:48B–D–49A; see CS 82:82–83.
[5] Jerome, In Eph 2:19-22; PL 26:475AB. Whole phrases here are word for word, others are paraphrases.

CHAPTER 61

On Enduring Temptations

B lessed are those, says James the apostle, who endure temptation. Such as these have stood the test and will receive the crown of life that God has promised to those who love him [Jas 1:12]. Similar to this is the saying in the Apocalypse: Be faithful until death, and I will give you the crown of life [Rev 2:10] that God has promised to those who love him [Jas 1:12]. He openly warns that we ought to rejoice more in temptations, since it is clear that God often imposes a greater weight of temptations on those he loves, so that through the training provided by such temptations they may be proved perfect in faith. And when they have been proved truly faithful, that is, perfect and whole and lacking in nothing [Jas 1:4], they will receive the promised crown of eternal life.[1]

There are two types of temptation, one that deceives, another that proves. About the type that deceives it is written: No one, when tempted, should say, "I am being tempted by God"; for God himself does not tempt anyone [Jas 1:13]. About the type that proves: God tested Abraham [Gen 22:1]. Of this temptation the prophet asks the Lord and says, Prove me, O Lord, and test me [Ps 25(26):2].[2]

And elsewhere it is written: The kiln tests the potter's vessels; and tribulation tests the upright [Sir 27:6].

Temptation comes about in three ways: by suggestion, delight, and consent;[3] by the enemy's suggestion, by delight, and also by

---

[1] Bede, In Jac 1:12; CCSL 121:187; PL 93:13CD; see CS 82:13.

[2] Bede, In Jac 1:13; CCSL 121:187; PL 93:14AB; see CS 82:14.

[3] Gregory, Hom ev 16.1; CCSL 141:110; PL 76:1135C; see CS 123:102, where it is homily 14.

consent of our frailty. But if the enemy suggests something and we refuse to take delight in sin or consent to it, temptation itself results in victory for us, so that by it we merit the crown of life. . . . Job was tempted in many ways, but because he did not prefer possessions or health of body to divine love, he could indeed be tempted by the enemy's suggestion, but could in no way consent to sin or find any delight in it.[4]

Abba Anthony said to Abba Poemen, "This is man's great work: each one is to lay the blame on himself before the Lord, and expect temptation to the very end of his life."[5]

A certain old man said, "When we are tempted, we humble ourselves the more. God, knowing our weakness, protects us; but if we boast, he removes his protection and we perish."[6]

They told the story of a certain old man. Sitting in his cell and putting up with temptations he would see the demons quite clearly and despise them. Now when the devil saw that he was beaten by the old man, he came and showed himself to him and said, "I am Christ." When the old man saw him he closed his eyes. The devil said to him, "I am Christ. Why have you closed your eyes?" The old man answered him and said, "I do not want to see Christ here, but in that other life." When he heard this, the devil stopped appearing.[7]

---

[4] Bede, In Jac 1:15; CCSL 121:188–89; PL 93:14C.15A; see CS 82:15.
[5] PL 953B (2); see also PG 65:[77] 78A (4); *Sayings*, 2 [2], 4.
[6] PL 73:965C (67).
[7] PL 73:965D (70); *Wisdom*, 50, 180.

CHAPTER 62

On Knowing
Our Lord Jesus Christ

Peter the apostle says, *May grace and peace be yours in fullness in the knowledge of our Lord Jesus Christ, of how everything needed for life and godliness has been given us from his divine power, through the knowledge of him who called us by his own glory and goodness* [2 Pet 1:2-3]. . . . As though to say, May grace abound for you in him, that you may know our Lord Jesus Christ perfectly. And may you also know through him how all that belongs to his divine power has been given to us through his grace—all that suffices for obtaining life and preserving godliness. . . . The more perfectly one knows the Lord, the more deeply does one experience the greatness of his promises.[1]

[Hence Paul also says, *To know him and the power of his resurrection* (Phil 3:10).] For knowledge of the mystery of his incarnation, passion, and resurrection is the perfection of life and the treasure of wisdom.[2]

Through knowledge of our Lord and Savior Jesus Christ we come to know all the mysteries of his divinity by which we are saved.[3]

For by the witness of Scripture we have learned that we come to the knowledge of Christ in three ways: first, by believing that he

---

[1] Bede, In 2 Pt 1:2-4; CCSL 121:261–62; PL 93:68D.69A+C; see CS 82:124–25.

[2] Ambrosiaster, In Phil 3:8-11; PL 17:416A.

[3] Bede, In 2 Pt 1:3; CCSL 121:262; PL 93:69B; see CS 82:125.

is the Son of God the Father Almighty, and with the Father and the Holy Spirit is one God in Trinity; second, by loving him with our whole heart, our whole soul, our whole strength [see Mark 12:30], because as John says, *Everyone who loves is born of God and knows God. Those who do not love do not know God* [1 John 4:7-8]; third, by keeping his commandments. The same John is witness when he says, *Any who say they know him, and do not obey his commandments, are liars* [1 John 2:4]. In this we are sure that we know him and the power of his resurrection, if we observe his commandments. For we know the power of Christ's resurrection when we believe that *God raised the Lord, and has also raised us* with him *by his power* [1 Cor 6:14],[4] and snatched us from the condemnation of death, and those he thus snatched he placed at the Father's right hand in an eternal inheritance as his children.[5]

For on the eighth day of his rising from the dead the Lord showed us an example of the future resurrection and the mystery of the new life.[6]

---

[4] Smaragdus's text reads: *Deus suscitavit eum, et nos cum illo* suscitavit *per virtutem suam.*

[5] No source traced for this passage.

[6] Bede, In 1 Pt 3:21; CCSL 121:250; PL 93:60B; see CS 82:105.

CHAPTER 63

On the Glorification of Our Lord Jesus Christ in the Saints

Concerning the Lord Jesus Christ the apostle Paul says, *When he comes to be glorified in his saints* [2 Thess 1:10]; he who by nature is always glorious in his glory and always remains glorified, when he comes in judgment to judge the living and the dead and the world by fire, will glorify his saints, being himself glorious with them and appearing in his glory and glorifying them with the brightness of his power. As the same Lord says to the Father, *And the glory you have given me I have given them* [John 17:22]. And elsewhere he says, *Then the righteous will shine like the sun in the kingdom of my Father* [Matt 13:43]. Glorified with the glorious and perpetual glory, the elect will appear in judgment with Christ. So he will come, he will come in judgment to appear glorified in his saints, he who appeared to the wicked in his passion as contemptible.

In his first coming he appeared lowly and puny before Pilate and the chief priests of the Jews; in his second coming he will appear as the glorious, great and most high God, and admirable in all who have believed. For our Lord Jesus Christ, who is always admirable in his divinity, became admirable for us also in his humanity: admirable in his conception, admirable in his birth, admirable in his resurrection and ascension. He will still appear wonderful in all who believed [as was necessary] when the revelation of the last judgment occurs, so that made wonderful by the Wonderful One, they may be glorified and live with him forever.

For he is the wonderful God, of whom Isaiah also says, *And his name will be called Wonderful Counselor, Mighty God*, etc. [Isa 9:6].

And David says, *God is wonderful among his holy ones* [Ps 67(68):35]. The Christian peoples have seen the glory of his resurrection and believed it, and in the judgment only the chosen will see the glory of his majesty.[1]

---

[1] No source traced for this passage.

CHAPTER 64

We Should Walk Worthy of God, and Be Filled with Knowledge of His Will

After receiving the stream of sacred baptism and the grace of the Holy Spirit through the imposition of the bishop's hand, the chief thing for human beings is to be filled with knowledge of God's will [see Col 1:9], so that they may do all that God wants, and live in everything according to his will. In proportion as people have knowledge of God's will, they will also have fear of his majesty; they will hold firm the heart's love towards him, and be able to walk worthy of God, pleasing him and bearing fruit in every good work.

So they walk worthy of God who daily by good works increase the faith they received in baptism through God's grace, mortify their members that are on the earth so as to live spiritually to God, and please him to whom they have commended themselves by living in a just and godly manner. *Pleasing to him in every way* [Col 1:10]. So no one can please God and reach true happiness except by mortifying the vices and taking up the virtues, through right faith and holy conduct. No one obtains the grace of sanctification in this world or will possess eternal life in the world to come without these two things, if there be time for working: *[a]s you bear fruit in every good work* [Col 1:10].

Those really bear fruit in every good work who, after receiving the seed of the word in their hearts, like good and very good earth produce fruit in patience, some thirtyfold, some sixtyfold, and some a hundredfold [see Matt 13:8; Mark 4:20; Luke 8:15]. It is to be noted that in this place he tacitly reproves the slothful minds of those who do not grow better or advance in virtues by doing good, but think it enough that they do not do evil and have left the world in body only; they do not realize that a person becomes new each day, growing and pleasing God through the exercises of wisdom, through meditating the Sacred Scriptures and through the power of good works.[1]

Abba Poemen said, "Just as bees are expelled by smoke in order for the sweetness they produce to be removed, so also bodily rest expels the fear of the Lord from the soul and takes away from it every good work."[2] He also said, "All bodily rest is an abomination."[3]

---

[1] No source traced for this passage.

[2] PL 73:868D–69A (32); see also PG 65:335 [336] AB (7); *Sayings*, 146–47 [174], 57.

[3] PG 65:331 [332]A (38); *Sayings*, 145 [172], 38.

CHAPTER 65

That We Do Not Have to Please Everyone

Thus Paul says, *If I were still wanting to please people, I would not be a servant of Christ* [Gal 1:10]. That is, if I had agreed with Jews living after a fleshly manner in observing the law, and with Christians living in a depraved way in their depravity, I would not be a servant of Christ. This statement is not at all contrary to the one where he says, *Be without offense to Jews and to Gentiles and to the church of God, just as I, too, try to please everyone in everything* [1 Cor 10:32-33]. For he himself explains why he would please all, adding, *not seeking what is useful to me, but to the many, so that they may be saved* [1 Cor 10:33]. It was not unfitting that he who was seeking the advantage and salvation of all would say that he pleased all.

Taking this apostolic example, good monks must not be content to seek what suits their own advantage, but rather what is fitting for their neighbors, each one not considering his own interests but those of others [see Phil 2:4]. Those who consider only their own interests, that is, what is needful only for themselves, and are not concerned about their neighbors' salvation or their temporal advantage, without doubt depart from the way of charity, on which the salvation of souls is entirely dependent. But those who are solicitous for their own and their neighbors' advantage and salvation are fully intent on doing whatever they can that is of advantage to their neighbors as though they were the superiors; through this humble obedience they gain more abundant joys of the heavenly life.

Therefore Paul pleases people and does not please them; in all his behavior, speech and acts he pleases all those who live well, justly and rightly; but he opposes all who live in depravity and evil, and pleases them neither in speech nor in behavior. For in this very broad and magnificent Church of Christ that is spread through the four corners of the world there are two kinds of persons, those with a good will and those with an evil will. Paul pleases those with a good will in everything, but he displeases in everything those with an evil will. For just as in a threshing floor grain is mixed with straw, so for the Church still living on earth those of good and evil will are mixed.

Concerning this mixture of the good and the evil we read in the letter Paul sent to Timothy: *In a large house not only are there vessels of gold and silver, but also of wood and clay; some are held in honor, some in disregard* [2 Tim 2:20]. Now by a great lord's large house can be understood the Church of Christ, spread through the whole world, in which are vessels of gold, that is, the hearts of people filled with spiritual understanding, and shining like gold of Ophir with the various virtues. There are also vessels of silver, bright with the gleam of eloquence and outstandingly lucid in the office of preaching. There are vessels of wood—that is, proud, foolish, and insensitive hearts. And there are vessels of clay, fragile and earthy, taken from the earth and given to earthly acts. But those of gold and silver are held in honor in this great Church of Christ. *Those who have ministered well* [1 Tim 3:13], says the apostle, are to *be held worthy of a double honor* [1 Tim 5:17]. But those of wood and clay are rightly held in disregard, because having a foolish and proud mind they have not kept their Lord's just precepts.[1]

Saint Syncletica said, "We ought to govern our souls through discretion, and while remaining in the congregation seek not what is ours, nor serve our own will, but according to faith obey the spiritual father."[2]

A certain old man said, "I have never desired work that would be advantageous to me and cause loss to my brother, since my hope is that winning my brother is a work of great fruitfulness to me."[3]

---

[1] No source traced for this passage.

[2] PL 73:950A (10a); PG 65:427 [428]A (17); *Sayings*, 196 [234], 17.

[3] PL 73:977D (24); see *Wisdom*, 61, 222.

CHAPTER 66

That We Are
to Forgive One Another's Faults

The Lord says in the Gospel, *If you offer your gift at the altar and remember that your brother or sister has something against you, leave your gift there before the altar; and go, first be reconciled with your brother or sister, and then come and offer your gift* [Matt 5:23-24]. Although this precept is to be kept literally, we must always fulfill it spiritually.

Spiritually our inner person is our temple, our faith is the altar, and the gift is prophecy, teaching, prayer, hymn, and psalm. If the person who has something against us is present, we will be able to soothe that person without pretense and with a sincere mind, and by asking pardon bring the person back to a favorable attitude; that is, provided we do this in the presence of God, not with a sluggish movement of the body but with a very swift movement of love.[1]

On this matter the apostle Paul also says, *Support one another in charity, and if anyone has a complaint against another, forgive each other, just as the Lord has forgiven you* [Col 3:13]. The apostle exhorts us to bear with one another, that is, that for Christ we behave, act, and speak patiently, and bear all our burdens mutually out of fraternal charity. Those who love others as themselves patiently bear and endure everything for them.

For *charity*, according to the apostle, *bears all things, endures all things* [1 Cor 13:4.7]. *Forgive each other*, says the apostle, *if anyone has a*

---

[1] Smaragdus, Collect, Heb 7 post Pent; PL 102:405CD.

complaint against another [Col 3:13]. Someone has a complaint against another when the latter injures the former, even without meaning to. *As the Lord has forgiven you,* do you also forgive. As though to say, As the Lord has forgiven you all your sins through the stream of sacred baptism, so also must you forgive others from your heart not just some but all their sins; because it is most just in relation to God that we forgive all others all the sins that they have committed against us, according to the measure of the kindness with which he forgave us, so that we can say freely to God, *Forgive us our debts, as we also forgive our debtors* [Matt 6:12].[2]

And may we thereby be ready to pardon all the faults committed against us, if we desire to be pardoned.[3]

People should not hold onto something against their own interests by refusing to forgive, and then have it held against them (by God) through this very refusal to pardon. For the Lord says of the wicked slave who refused to forgive his fellow slave his fault: *And in anger his lord handed him over to the torturers until he should pay the entire debt* [Matt 18:34]. He warns us to beware of his example when he says, *So my heavenly Father will also do to you, if you do not, each one of you, forgive your brother or sister from your heart* [Matt 18:35].

Do not say with your tongue, I pardon, and have something different in your heart. For God sees into your conscience.

So do you want God to forgive you all your debts? Forgive your debtor everything. This is the rule you lay down; by this pact and agreement you are bound with God when you say, *And forgive us our debts, as we also forgive our debtors* [Matt 6:12]. Hence in another place the Lord says, *Forgive, and you will be forgiven; give, and gifts will be given you* [Luke 6:37-38].[4]

---

[2] No source traced for this passage, except for "because it is most just ... with which he forgave us"; see Smaragdus, Collect, Dom post Ascens; PL 102:314B, quoting Bede, In 1 Pt 4:8; CCSL 121:254; PL 93:62D–63A; see CS 82:110.

[3] Smaragdus, Collect, Heb 23 post Pent; PL 102:499C, quoting Augustine, Serm de Script 83.4; PL 38:516.

[4] Smaragdus, Collect, Heb 23 post Pent; PL 102:499A–500A. Smaragdus appears to have edited this section from a long quotation in the *Collectiones* taken

An old man was asked, "What is humility?" And he replied, "If you forgive your brother who sins, before he does penance in your presence,[5] and if you do good to those who do you evil."[6]

Abba Anthony said, "Death and life come from the neighbor. For if we win our brother, we will win God; but if we scandalize our brother, we sin against Christ."[7]

Abba Hyperechius used to say, "Snatch your neighbor from sins as far as in you lies, without harsh reproach, because God does not repel those who turn to him. Do not have a word of malice and wickedness in you heart against your neighbor, so that you can say, *And forgive us our debts, as we also forgive our debtors*" [Matt 6:12].[8]

About this point it is written elsewhere: *So that you may be blameless and simple, as children of God* [Phil 2:15]. Those people give no grounds for complaint who, as far as human frailty allows, strive to lead a life without fault. Faults committed against God or neighbor give rise to complaints. So those people live without giving grounds for complaint who do not lead lives soiled with vices, nor commit faults for which complaints may be justly brought against them.[9]

---

from Saint Augustine, using approximately 18 lines from more than 150; see Augustine, Serm de Script 83.4; PL 38:516.

[5] PL 73:964B (60); see also 1037A (12); *Wisdom*, 48, 171.

[6] PL 73:964C (63a).

[7] PL 73:973C (2); see also PG 65:[77] 78B (9); *Sayings*, 2 [3], 9.

[8] PL 73:975BC (13).

[9] The section after the Scripture quotation is repeated from the beginning of chapter 55.

CHAPTER 67

That We Are Children of God, His Heirs and His Inheritance, and He Ours

Paul says on this subject, *And because you are children of God, he has sent the Spirit of his Son into your hearts, crying, "Abba! Father!"* [Gal 4:6]. We would never dare to say, *Our Father in heaven,* if we were not conscious of the Spirit dwelling in us.[1]

So that we might know for certain that we have been adopted by God as his children, he gave us his Spirit to show that the sign of the Father is in the children, and so we dare to say, *Abba,* which means Father, something not granted to the Jews long ago to say.[2]

We are, then, no longer slaves but children; and if children, heirs also through God [see Gal 4:7]. That is to say, if we are children, then the inheritance of the Father is due to us. We have become his children through receiving the Spirit of God's Son, and so brought from slavery into freedom we are heirs of God the Father and coheirs of Jesus Christ his Son.

For the same apostle says in another place: *giving thanks to* God *the Father, who has made us worthy to share in the inheritance of the saints in the light* [Col 1:12]. The sharing in the lot of the saints is the gathering of all the elect united and joined in one society, as he also says elsewhere, *And may the Lord make you increase* [1 Thess 3:12], under-

---

[1] Jerome, In Gal 4:6; PL 26:374A.
[2] Ambrosiaster, In Gal 4:6; PL 17:360A.

stand, in the number of his elect, that you may be *holy and spotless* [Eph 1:4], gathered in the bosom of the saints. The sharing in the lot of the saints takes place in the light; and one is enlightened by the light when one comes to be in Christ and is enlightened by Christ, because by "lot" is usually meant "inheritance," as it is written: *He divided the land for them by lot with a measuring line* [Ps 77(78):55]. Let us say that all the people of the elect are the lot and measuring line of the Lord's inheritance, since Scripture says, *The lot of the Lord is his people; Jacob is the measuring line of his inheritance* [Deut 32:9]. Likewise the Lord himself is the portion and inheritance of the lot of the saints, as he said to Aaron: *I am your portion and your inheritance in the midst of the children of Israel* [Num 18:20]. Now that we are associated with the apostles and all the saints, *giving thanks to* God *the Father* [Col 1:12], let us pray that he may make us worthy of a portion of the lot of the saints in light [see Col 1:12]; that is, that we may merit to be the Lord's portion, lot, and inheritance and blissfully possess our Lord and Savior himself as an eternal lot and inheritance, and being enlightened in him and through him, may we abide forever blissfully in the light.[3]

---

[3] No source traced for this passage.

CHAPTER 68

How a Person May Gain Christ

If a monk mortifies his members that are on the earth [see Col 3:5], and takes up his cross and follows Christ [see Matt 16:24], and if being dead to the world he fastens the trophy of his mortification to the wood of the Lord's passion so that he can say with Paul, *For through the law I am dead to the law, so that I may live to God. I have been crucified with Christ* [Gal 2:19],[1] he will be able to gain Christ. For Christ is called Truth, and Charity, and Wisdom, and Justice, and Sanctification. One who acquires for himself all these things by living well without doubt gains Christ, and one who gains his brother, who is Christ's member, by preaching and by showing good example, gains Christ.[2]

For Blessed Augustine says, "If you see something amiss, do your best to correct it, and do not grow slack in amending it. Do whatever you can for the person you are carrying. Do not leave off gaining Christ, because you have been gained by Christ."[3] According to the understanding of this saying, those who understand that Christ became man, suffered, died and rose from the dead and ascended into heaven for their sake, despise everything that belongs to the world, and by a straight course follow Christ so that they may grasp him by whom they have been grasped; such as these blissfully gain Christ.[4]

---

[1] See Jerome, In Gal 2:19; PL 26:345C. Between Jerome and Smaragdus the text has been adapted to monks, with the insertion of *monachus* near the beginning.

[2] See PG 65:[77] 78B; *Sayings*, 2 [3], 9. Similar, but not the same.

[3] Smaragdus, Collect, Feria 2a post vicesimam; PL 102:156CD. Quoted also in part in the Via reg 18. Introduced here as a quotation from Augustine.

[4] See Ambrosiaster, In Phil 3:11; PL 17:416A.

Hence the same apostle says elsewhere, *Far be it from me to boast except in the cross of our Lord Jesus Christ, by which the world has been crucified to me, and I to the world* [Gal 6:14]. The monk must not boast of his own righteousness, or in any doctrine, but in faith in the cross of Christ, through whom he hopes that all his sins are forgiven him. So they must be dead to one another, the world to the monk and the monk to the world. And the monk must not covet anything belonging to the world, and the world must not have anything to covet in the monk. So only that person can boast of the cross of Christ who takes it up and follows the Savior [see Matt 16:24], who crucifies the flesh with its vices and concupiscences [see Gal 5:25], who is dead to the world [see Gal 6:14], and does not contemplate things that are seen but things that are not seen and are eternal [see 2 Cor 4:18].[5]

---

[5] No source traced for this passage.

CHAPTER 69

That the Lord's Mighty Acts Are Ever to Be Proclaimed by Monks

On this matter the apostle Peter says, *So that you may proclaim the mighty acts of him who called you out of darkness into his wonderful light* [1 Pet 2:9]. For just as those who were freed through Moses from Egyptian slavery sang to the Lord a triumphal song after the crossing of the Red Sea and the drowning of Pharaoh's army [see Exod 15], so we too ought to return worthy thanks for heavenly benefits after receiving remission of sins in baptism, and always proclaim his mighty acts.[1]

If almighty God were to keep his mighty acts quiet, no one would recognize or love him. So he proclaims his mighty acts not in order to derive advantage from his praises, but so that those who have known him in his praise may come to a perpetual inheritance.[2]

God, then, declares his praises so that we who hear them may be able to know him, and knowing him may come to love him, and loving him may follow him, and following him may attain to him, and attaining to him may enjoy the vision of him. Thus the prophet says, *He will show his people the power of his works, to give them*

---

[1] Bede, In 1 Pt 2:9; CCSL 121:237–38; PL 93:51B; see CS 82:87–88. The last clause is not in Bede at this point.

[2] Taio Sent 2.2; PL 80:777BC, quoting Gregory, In Hiez 1.9,19; CCSL 142:133; PL 76:878C.

the heritage of the nations [Ps 110(111):6]. As though to say openly, He subtly introduces the power of his working so that those who hear of it may be enriched with spiritual gifts.[3]

To advance in spiritual gifts is to walk worthily in God, and from day to day to advance in holy virtues until one can arrive at the vision of the Almighty, so that it can be said of him with the rest of the saints: *They will go from strength to strength; and the God of gods will be seen in Zion* [Ps 83(84):7]. He whom we will see in Zion, that is, in heavenly contemplation, is he who has called us into his kingdom and glory. He called us first through faith, but afterwards he will call[4] us through vision, when we will see him face to face, and hear that voice, so worthy of desire, of the one who says, *Come, blessed of my Father, inherit the kingdom prepared for you from the foundation of the world* [Matt 25:34]. In this kingdom, the glory is eternal and the life without end.[5]

Blessed Job says about this proclamation of his mighty acts, under the figure of our Redeemer: *O earth, do not cover my blood* [Job 16:19]. For the earth did not cover the blood of Christ, because Holy Church has already preached the mystery of his redemption in all parts of the world. . . . The very blood of redemption that is received is the cry of our Redeemer. . . . In order then that the sacrament of the Lord's passion may not be unproductive in us, we must imitate what we receive, and preach to everyone else what we venerate. Thus blessed Job again says, *Let my outcry find no hiding place in you* [Job 16:19]. His cry finds a hiding place in us if the tongue keeps silent about what the mind believes. But so that his cry may not be hidden in us, it remains for each and everyone according to their measure to make known to their neighbors the mystery of their being made to live.[6]

---

[3] Taio, Sent 2.2; PL 80:777C, quoting Gregory, Mor 18.7; CCSL 143A:894; PL 76:45AB.

[4] The Migne text has *vocavit*, "he has called."

[5] No source traced for this passage.

[6] Taio, Sent 2.14; PL 80:795AB, quoting Gregory, Mor 13.23; CCSL 143A:683; PL 75:1029AB.

CHAPTER 70

That It Is Given to the Saints to Suffer for Christ

Paul the apostle says among other things, *It has been granted you not only to believe in Christ, but also to suffer for him as well* [Phil 1:29]. Note that both the faith by which we believe in Christ and the sufferings that we suffer for him are given to us by God the Father for Christ's sake. For it is not given to others but to Christ's lovers to suffer for him. That is why we must not be sad in our sufferings for Christ, but we must rather rejoice and be glad; as the apostles *left the council, they rejoiced that they were considered worthy to suffer insult for the name of Jesus* [Acts 5:41].[1]

Not only is there nothing hurtful to good people who return good to those who do them evil, but they are also given reason for greater happiness . . . according to the gospel saying: *Blessed are those who suffer persecution for righteousness' sake, for theirs is the kingdom of heaven* [Matt 5:10].[2]

And so Paul also says elsewhere, *For this reason I suffer these things. But I am not ashamed* [2 Tim 1:12]. *For this reason*, he says—that is, on account of the preaching of the Gospel and the faith of our Lord Jesus Christ. To suffer for Christ ought not to be a source of confusion for the faithful but a great reason for boasting. For Christ, says the apostle, *became for us righteousness* [1 Cor 1:30]. For *blessed*, says

---

[1] No source traced for this passage.

[2] Bede, In 1 Pt 3:14; CCSL 121:245; PL 93:56D–57A; see CS 82:99. Smaragdus completes the Scripture quotation.

the Lord, *are those who suffer persecution for righteousness' sake, for theirs is the kingdom of heaven* [Matt 5:10]. Therefore let those who persecute the elect for righteousness' sake be put to confusion, because an eternal torture awaits them. Let not the elect be put to confusion; to them eternal joy is given for brief tribulations, and also the kingdom of heaven.

Hence Peter says, *If you do suffer for righteousness' sake, you are blessed* [1 Pet 3:14]. Not only does nothing hurt you, he says, who inflict good on those who do you evil, but also when the enemy assails you because of the good that he loathes, he gives you a reason for greater happiness when he exercises the strength of your patience. Again he says, *For it is better to suffer for doing good, if such should be God's will, than for doing evil* [1 Pet 3:17]. This saying is a rebuke to the foolishness of those monks who, when rebuked by the brothers for their faults, or even excommunicated, do not bear it patiently.[3] If without having committed a fault they suffer verbal insults or any adversities from their superiors, they straightway burst out in anger; and those who previously seemed quite harmless render themselves culpable and harmful through impatience and the boldness of murmuring. If I were given a choice, I would prefer . . . to be judged or suffer adversities without fault, than with fault to be subject to strokes or excommunication. . . . One who is just and suffers without fault imitates Christ; but one who is corrected with scourges imitates the thief who came to know Christ on the cross and after enduring the cross entered paradise with Christ. But one who does not cease from faults even amidst scourges imitates the thief on the left, who mounted the cross because of sins and after suffering the cross was cast into the infernal regions.[4]

Saint Syncletica said, "Although your body is struck down with sicknesses and inflamed with severe fevers, do not fail under the

---

[3] Where Bede has *poenis coercentur*, "they are forced by penalties," Smaragdus has *excommunicantur*. The *Diadema* text has *patienter non tolerant* where Bede's text and Smaragdus's Commentary have *patienter omnino tolerant*, "bear it with complete patience." Smaragdus substitutes Bede's reference to neighbors with superiors.

[4] Bede, In 1 Pt 3:14.17; CCSL 121:245–46; PL 93:56D–57A.C.D–58A; see CS 82:98–101.

pressures, but rather be glad, because the Lord has visited you, and you will say, *The Lord did indeed chastise me, but he did not hand me over to death* [Ps 117(118):18]. If you are iron, hope that fire will be applied to you. You are gold, but you will be more fully tried by fire [see 1 Pet 1:6–7]. But if you are upright and suffer these things, you will advance from great things to greater."[5]

A certain brother asked an old man, saying, "Tell me the one thing I should observe so that I may live by it." And the old man said to him, "If you can suffer and endure insult, this is a great thing, and above all the virtues. One who patiently bears contempt and injury and loss can be saved."[6]

---

[5] PL 73:895CD–96AB (16); see also 792D–93A (157) and 1044D–45A (1); PG 65:423 [424]A–C (7); *Sayings*, 194 [231–32], 7. An extract from Syncletica. See also chapter 31, note 2.

[6] PL 73:967C (83 and 84).

CHAPTER 71

That Christ Gave Himself up for Love of Us

Paul the apostle says, *Grace to you and peace from God our Father and the Lord Jesus Christ, who gave himself for our sins* [Gal 1:3-4]. And elsewhere he says, *He loved us, and gave himself up for us* [Eph 5:2]. For Christ loved our life so much that he laid down his own life for it. The Lord Jesus Christ gave himself to death to deliver us from the danger of death, and thus delivered to adopt us for his Father as children. For he died so that we would not be afraid to die. He has risen so that we may be able to rise through him: *he snatched us out of the present evil age* [Gal 1:4] so that he might bestow on us glory as well as life.

For the Son of God delivered us from the unjust robber in order to return us to our rightful Lord. Christ delivered us from the present evil age when he changed our life, all nourished as it was with vices, into a better life. To such an extent did he change our way of life into something better and raise it up to something more sublime, that with Paul we can say, *Our way of life is in heaven* [Phil 3:20]. Therefore rightly does Paul say that his and their citizenship is in heaven, seeing that, abandoning earthly things, with their whole desire they think of heavenly things, and with a pure and devout mind they desire not what is earthly and perishable, but what is heavenly and eternal.

For it was the will of God the Father that the Lord Jesus Christ should be handed over for our sins. And it was the will of Christ that he should do the Father's will, as the same Lord says through the prophet, *so that I might do your will, O my God* [Ps 39(40):8].[1]

---

[1] No source traced for this passage.

For we are what he has made us, created in Christ Jesus for the good works God has prepared beforehand for us to walk in them [Eph 2:10]. This means, the fact that we live, that we hope, that we understand and can believe belongs to him, for he is our creator, and we are his handiwork.[2] We are said to be created for this in Christ Jesus, and created not because we did not exist before, but because we are reborn in Christ, and created for the good works that God has prepared to be our way of life. *Rooted and established in love* [Eph 3:17]. Charity is Christ, and we must be rooted and grounded in charity—that is, in Christ, so that we may firmly persevere in his love. *For no one can lay any other foundation besides him, which is Christ Jesus* [1 Cor 3:11]. *But doing the truth in charity, we must grow up in every way into him who is the head* [Eph 4:15]. Truth is Christ, and charity is Christ, and righteousness, and sanctification, and peace is Christ [see 1 Cor 1:30]. So the one who does all these things which Christ is, and moreover keeps his commandments, does the truth and grows daily in charity, that is, in Christ.[3]

---

[2] Jerome, In Eph 2:10; PL 26:470BC.
[3] No source traced for this passage.

CHAPTER 72

That the Apostle Says:
Do Not Extinguish the Spirit

I t is as if he says, Do not by your bad life extinguish the grace of the Holy Spirit [see 1 Thess 5:19] which after you were baptized you received through the laying on of hands and the anointing of chrism, but keep it whole and inviolate in your heart and body. And so the same apostle says to the Ephesians, *And do not grieve the Holy Spirit of God, with which you were sealed for the day of redemption* [Eph 4:30]. For we received the seal of the Holy Spirit on the day we were baptized and confirmed, and we must faithfully keep it. So one who believes in God is signed with this seal of the Holy Spirit, in order to keep it and show it on the day of redemption pure and sound, in no way diminished.[1]

Hence John the Apostle also says, *Let the anointing that you received from him abide in you* [1 John 2:27]. As though to say, With the Lord's help, endeavor to keep whole in your heart and body the Holy Spirit's grace which you obtained in baptism, and *do not extinguish the Spirit* [1 Thess 5:19]. . . . The anointing John speaks of, and the spirit of which Paul says, *Do not extinguish the Spirit*, can be understood to be *the love of God*, which *has been poured into our hearts through the Holy Spirit that has been given to us* [Rom 5:5]. This love that fills the heart inflames it very quickly to observe God's commandments.[2] It is extinguished by those living bad lives, through hatred and envy and discord.

---

[1] Jerome, In Eph 4:30; PL 26:514C.
[2] Bede, In 1 Jo 2:27; CCSL 121:298; PL 93:96CD; see CS 82:180–81.

The spirit of preachers, who preach the word of salvation to their hearers, is extinguished by the malice of hearers who contradict, resist, and rebel, so that preachers prefer to keep silent rather than preach; and thus it comes about that the word is taken away from preachers through the rebellion of the hearers. And so the Lord says to Ezekiel, *And I will make your tongue cling to the roof of your mouth, and you will be mute, unable to reprove them, for they are an irritating house* [Ezek 3:26].[3]

A certain old man came to another old man and one of them said, "I am dead to this world." The other said to him, "Do not trust in yourself until you depart from this body, because if you are dead, Satan is not."[4]

Abba Poemen said, "A person must always breathe humility and the fear of God unceasingly, like the breath that he inhales and exhales through his nostrils."[5] Again he said, "To cast oneself down in the sight of God, and not to lift oneself up, and to fling one's own will behind one's back, these are the tools with which the soul does its work."[6]

---

[3] See Gregory, Mor 30.27; CCSL 143B:1547; PL 76:569D–70A; Hom ev 17.3; CCSL 141:118; PL 76:1139D–40A; see CS 123:135–36, where it is homily 19.

[4] PL 73:938D (38); see also 782A (116) and 1035A (5); *Wisdom,* 39, 134.

[5] PL 73:960D (32); see also PG 65:[333] 334D (49); *Sayings,* 146 [173], 49.

[6] PL 73:960D–61A (34); see also PG 65:331 [332]D (36); *Sayings,* 145 [172], 36.

CHAPTER 73

On the Harmful Curiosity of Monks

The apostle Paul says, *We urge you, brothers and sisters, to live quietly, to go about your own business, and to work with your hands* [1 Thess 4:10-11]. As though to say, Keep yourselves completely from the vice of restlessness and curiosity, so that having become quiet you may attend to your own affairs. Therefore those people attend to their own affairs who put aside the vice of curiosity and are unceasingly solicitous for their own salvation. For that monk attends to another's affairs who from the vice of curiosity forgets to examine his own vicious life and is over-anxious to investigate someone else's life.

That is why he also says to the same persons in a second letter: *For we hear that some of you are living restlessly, not doing any work, curious in regard to others' business* [2 Thess 3:11]. In this short sentence Paul censures many of the vices of monks, namely, restlessness and idleness and curiosity, and much speaking, in which according to Solomon there is no escaping sin [see Prov 10:19]; so restlessness, which by another name is called curiosity, is a great vice, which does not allow the body to be quiet or the soul without sin. For while it agitates and impels one to go around the dwellings of others or to inquire with curiosity into what others are doing, it doubtless offends in many things. For idleness unceasingly accompanies the vice of curiosity.

Idleness is the enemy of the soul [RB 48.1; RBas 192; see Sir 33:29]. So it is better for monks to be obedient to their superiors with an obedience that redounds to their own advantage, and to eat their bread in silence, as strangers to every vice of restlessness and curiosity and verbosity, working with their hands, and to understand concerning themselves the saying of the psalmist: *You shall eat the work of your hands; you shall be happy, and it shall be well with you* [Ps 127(128):2].[1]

A certain old man used to say, "We do not make progress because we do not know our limits and we do not have patience in the work we have begun; we want to possess virtues without any toil."[2]

Abba Poemen used to say that Abba Isidore once addressed the group of brothers, saying, "Brothers, did we not come to this place to work? And now I see that there is no work here. So I am going to leave the brothers and go where there is work, and where I do not find rest."[3]

The brothers used to ask a certain old man to rest from hard toil, but he answered them, "Believe me, my sons, when Abraham sees the great and admirable gifts of God, he will regret that he did not engage more in the contest of hard work."[4]

---

[1] No source traced for this passage.

[2] PL 73:897C (23); see *Wisdom*, 47, 164.

[3] PL 73:895BC (14); PG 65:331 [332]D (44); *Sayings*, 145 [173], 44. The conclusion in Smaragdus is the opposite of that in PG, PL and the Ward translation, which reads: "and there I shall find peace."

[4] PL 73:900BC (29). See *Wisdom*, 22, 65. Smaragdus or his source here treats *decertare* as a deponent verb.

CHAPTER 74

On the Rule Laid Down by the Apostles

On this matter Paul the Apostle says, *All those who follow this rule—may peace be upon them, and mercy* [Gal 6:16]. The teaching of God is a certain rule in language that judges between what is just and what is unjust; those who follow it will have in themselves peace that surpasses all understanding, and after peace they will obtain mercy.[1] Christian generation means a new creature, because Christ the new man came into the world and gave it new precepts, and upon those who observe them there is peace and mercy.

Again the apostle says, *As regards what we have attained, so that we are of the same opinion—let us remain in the same rule* [Phil 3:16], that is, let us remain in the service of the faith to which we have come at Christ's call. In the living of the faith let us think of nothing outside the discipline of the rule, but think of what is common and unassuming, remaining in the gospel truth and in the same rule of faith.[2]

The word "rule" in this place means the Catholic faith. It is called a "rule" because it guides correctly and rules rightly. Hence those institutes of the Fathers that teach the Catholic Church to live rightly are called canons. What in Greek is called a "canon" is called a "rule" in Latin.[3]

[1] Jerome, In Gal 6:16; PL 26:437AB. Smaragdus has rounded off his quotation from Jerome with *consequentur*, "they will obtain."

[2] No source traced for this passage.

[3] See Isidore, Etym 6.16.1; Lindsay, vol. 1 (at reference, as pages are not numbered); PL 87:1117B.

And so Paul says elsewhere, *Now we command you, beloved, in the name of our Lord Jesus Christ, to keep away from every believer who lives* restlessly and *in a disorderly way* [2 Thess 3:6]. This warning is not to be made light of by the hearers, because it is supported by royal authority when made in the name of our Lord Jesus Christ. And although it is full of apostolic charity, it contains royal authority, which leads the crowd of all the faithful in a wholesome way to the right rule of souls. For he says, *keep away from every believer who lives* restlessly, *and not according to the tradition that they received from us* [2 Thess 3:6]. Hence the Church of the saints received from the apostle a clear authorization to withdraw from perverse people. But the apostles handed down to the faithful the rule of walking well, that is, of living well and uprightly and piously, and the Church of all the faithful must hold it firmly, since she wants to direct her own life according to that of the apostles. So the norm for applying that rule became for all Christians the life of the apostles themselves. For this reason he adds, *For you yourselves know how you ought to imitate us* [2 Thess 3:7]. As though to say, We have already often told you in words and shown you by examples; therefore you know how you ought to imitate us. But do willingly what we exhort you to do, if you wish to hold the rule of faith we have handed down.[4]

A certain old man said, "It is written: *The righteous will flourish like the palm tree* [Ps 91(92):12]. This saying signifies a good act, high and upright and sweet. For there is in the palm one heart [*incardium*] and it is white, with all its working in itself. Similarly in the just person there is found to be one simple heart, gazing only at God. It is white, having the enlightenment of faith, and all the working of the just is in the heart. For its sharp defenses are a fortress against the devil."[5]

---

[4] No source traced for this passage.

[5] PL 73:993D–94A (6).

CHAPTER 75

That Monks Are to Be Vigilant

Paul the Apostle warns us saying, *Let us not sleep like the rest, but let us keep awake* [1 Thess 5:6]. That is, let us not sleep like the rest, unbelievers, unjust, unfair, those weighed down by the sleep of ignorance and of the body, who are burdened by the weight of their sins and cannot foresee what will happen to them in the future. They sleep so heavily and shamefully that they do not open their eyes to guard their heart; they have no thought for future glory but are always thinking of the present life. They do not think about things invisible and eternal, but always about the corruptible and temporal things they can see. Let us not sleep like them, but keep awake.

That is why Mark the Evangelist also gives us this wholesome warning when he says, *Therefore, keep watch, for you do not know when the master will come. Otherwise he may find you asleep when he comes suddenly* [Mark 13:35a, 36].[1]

Blessed are those slaves whom the master finds watching when he comes [Luke 12:37]. For they keep watch who have their eyes open for the sight of the true light. They keep watch who observe in their work what they believe. They keep watch who drive away the darkness of sluggishness[2] and negligence.[3]

---

[1] No source traced for this passage.

[2] Gregory's text has *torporis*, "of sluggishness," which is more likely than Smaragdus's *corporis*, "of the body."

[3] Gregory, Hom ev 13.3; CCSL 141:91; PL 76:1124CD; see CS 123:153, where it is homily 20.

Hence the apostle says the same elsewhere, *[so that] whether we keep watch or sleep, we may live together with Christ* [1 Thess 5:11]. That is, whether we keep watch so as to guard our salvation, or whether we sleep from the harmful cares of this world, let us live together with him, that is, let us always be in and with Christ, who for our sake *died and rose again* [Rom 14:9; see 1 Thess 5:10].

Concerning this wholesome wakefulness and sleep, Solomon says in the Song of Songs, *I sleep, but my heart keeps watch* [Song 5:2]. As though to say, The more I rest from earthly cares as though sleeping, the more freely does my heart keep watch to contemplate its creator. For that soul will always and forever live with God that clings to him here through love and never retreats from following behind him. Hence the Lord says, *The one who* loves me *must follow me, and where I am, there will my servant be also* [John 12:26]. That is, he will live with me forever, and will reign ever glorious and immortal.[4]

Abba Evagrius said, "If you lose heart, pray, as it is written. But pray with fear and trembling and toil, soberly and watchfully. Thus ought one to pray, most of all because of those malign ones who are intent on wickedness, our invisible enemies, who strive to hinder us especially in this." He said again, "When a harmful thought comes into your heart, do not seek something in its stead through prayer, but sharpen the sword of tears against the thought that is attacking you."[5]

---

[4] No source traced for this passage.
[5] PL 73:941CD (4 & 5).

CHAPTER 76

On the Battle of the Virtues

Holy persons are more truly wiped clean of the filth of the vices when they pit individual virtues against individual vices. . . . For one must fight against the attacks of the vices with the contrary virtues: cleanness of heart must be employed against impurity; love must be made ready against hatred; patience must be put forward against anger; one must employ confidence against fear, joy against sadness; against accidie, fortitude; against avarice, generosity; humility must be set against pride; and thus the individual virtues restrain the vices that spring up against them. . . . Abstinence tames sexual desire, because to the extent that the body is broken by fasting, the mind is called back from unlawful desire. And endurance struggles against anger. . . . And the hope of eternal joy overcomes the bitterness of sadness. And those whose disturbed minds cause them upset from exterior things are soothed by the sweetness of interior tranquility. Charity is made ready against envy, and against the heat of anger the tranquility of meekness is employed. . . .[1]

When we go against the dominion[2] of the vices, when we struggle against the iniquity that separates us from God, when we strenuously resist habit and, treading down perverse desires, vindicate our right to our innate freedom against these things; when we resist the massed troops of the vices with energetic determination, when

[1] Isidore, Sent 1.37.1a, 2 (less the last clause), 3–4a, 5–6; CCSL 111:165–66; PL 83:638B–D. Most of this passage also appears in Taio, Sent 4.25; PL 80:942A–C.

[2] Smaragdus here has *dominio vitiorum*, while Taio (Sent 4.25) has *domino vitiorum*, "the lord of the vices," and Gregory has simply *domino*.

we strike at faults by repenting and wash the stains of filth with tears, we are struggling bravely against the vices.[3]

Abba Agathon said, "I have never deliberately gone to sleep while retaining sadness in my heart against anyone, and I have not let another go to sleep while having anything against me."[4]

Abba Macarius said, "Act with assurance, my son, for I have not taken my fill of bread or water or sleep these twenty years. I would take a measured weight of bread and a measure of water, and for sleep I simply leaned against a wall and snatched a few moments."[5]

Abba Isidore said, "If we do not have thoughts, we are like wild animals. But if the enemy demands what is his, we must also fulfill what is ours. Let us be instant in prayer, and the enemy is put to flight. Apply yourself to meditation on God and you conquer. Perseverance in the good is our victory. Fight and you will be crowned."[6]

Abba John said, "The door to God is humility, and the fathers, driven by many insults, entered rejoicing into the city of God, because humility and fear of God surpass all the virtues.[7] Therefore the monk must have humility before all else. This is the Savior's first command among the eight beatitudes when he says, *Blessed are the poor in spirit, for theirs is the kingdom of heaven*" [Matt 5:3].[8]

---

[3] Taio, Sent 4.25; PL 80:941D–42A, quoting Gregory, Mor 4.36; CCSL 143:215; PL 75:677C.

[4] PL 73:974A (6); see also 777D (95); PG 65:[109] 110B (4); *Sayings*, 17–18 [20], 4.

[5] PL 73:1018CD (18); *Praktikos*, 94.

[6] PL 73:1018D–19A (21). Abba Isidore is named as the speaker in the preceding apophthegm.

[7] PL 73:958A (22); PG 65:211 [212]D (22); *Sayings*, 77 [90], 22. In *VP* the Abba John is John the Dwarf.

[8] PL 73:958A (23); PG 65:[233] 234D (2bis); *Sayings*, 90,1bis [106]1. This saying is attributed to John of the Thebaid.

CHAPTER 77

On Hatred
and Fraternal Correction

Paul the Apostle says, *If any do not obey what we say in this letter, take note of them; do not mix with them, so that they may be ashamed. Do not regard them as enemies, but take them to task as believers* [2 Thess 3:14-15]. As though to say, If the authority of our Letter does not correct them, notify us in your letter who they are so that we may rebuke them, or that they may even be excommunicated by our Letter. And you are not to associate with the excommunicated until they obey and consent to the apostolic precepts; and thus confounded by both parties, that is, by us and by you, may they finally come to their right mind, be corrected, and obey our precepts. In this place the apostle gives a clear sign that we are not to mix with excommunicated persons in action or deliberation or any fellowship.[1]

In the very same people we can simultaneously love our relationship with them and hate their vices. For it is one thing that they are brothers and sisters, another that they are people given to vice. So let us love in them our relationship with them and hate in them their propensity to vice. Let us proceed against the vices in them, and love them once corrected as we do ourselves.[2]

---

[1] No source traced for this passage.
[2] This paragraph is quoted in Smaragdus's Commentary, 65.11; CS 212:505.

That is why blessed Gregory says, "We must show discernment in hatred with regard to our neighbors, such that we love in them their being [human] and hate their being an obstacle on our way to God."[3]

A certain old man said, "A monk must mortify himself from everything evil before departing from the body, and not hurt anyone. . . . And unless he thinks in his heart that he is a sinner, God will not listen to him. What does it mean, to think in the heart that one is a sinner? It means, if one bears his own sins and does not see those of his neighbor. . . . When a person lets go his own will, then God will be reconciled with him, and he receives his prayer.[4] For if we look steadily at our own sins, we do not see those of our neighbor. It is folly for a man who has his own dead to leave him and go off to bewail his neighbor's dead. . . . When the hand of the Lord killed *every firstborn in the land of Egypt . . . there was not a house where someone did not lie dead* [Exod 12:29-30].[5] *For there is no one alive who does not sin* [1 Kgs 8:46; 2 Chr 6:36]. So all must mourn their own dead, that is, their own sin."

The prophet says that "the dead" refers to sin when he says, *One who washes after touching a corpse, and touches it again,* that is, one who mourns sin and then commits it again, *how does the washing bring benefit?* [Sir 34:30].[6]

---

[3] Gregory, Hom ev 37.2; CCSL 141:349; PL 76:1276A; see CS 123:329. *Homines*, "human beings," is supplied by Smaragdus.

[4] PL 73:1014D–15A (2–4); see also PG 65:287 [288]BC; *Sayings*, 119–20 [141–42], 2.3.4. In the Ward translation these apophthegms are identified as from a series of instructions that Abba Moses sent to Abba Poemen, but in PG 65 they are numbered 15 (30), 16 (31) and 17 (32).

[5] PL 73:1015BC (7); PG 65:289 [290]BC (18); *Sayings*, 120–21 [142–43], 7, extracted from Abba Moses' apophthegm and rearranged.

[6] Referred to in Smaragdus, Commentary, 4.17; CS 212:183.

CHAPTER 78

That the Monk Have
the Loins of His Mind Girded

The apostle Peter says, *Therefore have the loins of your mind girded in truth; being perfectly sober, hope in the grace that Jesus Christ will bring when he is revealed* [1 Pet 1:13]. . . . It is as though he were saying to monks: The greater the grace promised you, the greater the care you should take to be worthy so as to be able to receive it. . . . And he rightly says, *hope in the grace that Jesus Christ will bring when he is revealed*; for those who have the loins of their minds girded, that is, who are chaste in mind and body, await the coming of the Lord, and rightly hope for when he is to be revealed.[1]

For this reason too the apostle Paul says, *Stand therefore with your loins girded in truth* [Eph 6:14], that is, stand perfect, with the loins of your mind girded, boldly prepared in every battle and free from all the cares of the world.[2] No one doubts that all the members of the soul are named in the Scriptures equally with the members of the fleshly body. I think that of these members in the present instance there is one, the loins, that Truth orders us to gird up: *Let your loins be girded and your lamps be burning* [Luke 12:35].[3]

---

[1] Bede, In 1 Pt 1:13; CCSL 121:230; PL 93:45D; see CS 82:77. Smaragdus has adapted this for monks.

[2] Pelagius, In Eph 6:14; PLS 1:1307.

[3] Smaragdus, Collect, Heb 22 post Pent; PL 102:493D, quoting Jerome, In Eph 6:14; PL 26:550B.

That is why the prophet also says, *Gird up your loins over your breasts* [Isa 32:11-12].[4] As though to say, Cut off in your hearts sexual desires, lest you fall shamefully into fornication outwardly. For to one who is chaste in body but not in heart no reward is promised, because according to Truth's saying: *Everyone who looks at a woman to lust after her has already committed adultery with her in his heart* [Matt 5:28]. So if thoughts of fornication are first prevented in the heart, they do not burst forth in deed.[5]

Some of the just, girded so as to attain the height of perfection, abandon everything exteriorly in their desire to gain higher things interiorly. They strip themselves of possessions, despoil themselves of glory and honor, and through the constancy of their internal desires become friends of affliction, refusing to receive consolation from exterior things; when with the mind they draw near to internal joys, they utterly destroy in themselves the life of bodily delight. Such as these are told through Paul, *For you have died, and your life is hidden with Christ in God* [Col 3:3]. The psalmist had given expression to their voice when he said, *My soul longs, and faints for the courts of the Lord* [Ps 83(84):3]. . . . Those persons long and faint for the courts of God who, when they desire eternal things, do not dally in love of temporal things. Hence the psalmist again says, *My soul faints for your salvation* [Ps 118(119):81]. [For the just person's soul to faint for God's salvation] means to abandon the good things of the present life by choosing eternity; it means to seek the things that last, and not to put one's trust in temporal things.[6]

---

[4] The words suit Smaragdus's purpose, but a different punctuation and the surrounding context yield quite a different meaning. Smaragdus has *Accingite lumbos vestros super ubera vestra.* The context in Isaiah is that of a prophecy against the women of Jerusalem. The standard Vulgate text reads, *Exuite vos et confundimini; accingite lumbos vestros. Super ubera plangite, super regione desiderabili, super vinea fertili.*

[5] No source traced for this passage.

[6] Paterius, Expositio 11.176; PL 79:870BC, quoting from Gregory, Mor 8.26; CCSL 143:416–17; PL 75:829A–C.

CHAPTER 79

On the Mortification of the Vices

The apostle Paul says, *Put to death your members that are on the earth: fornication, impurity, passion, evil desire,* etc. [Col 3:5].

These vices and sins are said to be our members because through our members they carry out their actions, which the apostle prohibits us from consenting to when he says, *Do not present your members to sin as instruments of iniquity, but present yourselves to God* [Rom 6:13]. For all the sins and vices together make one body, that of the devil, and each of the vices that follow are said to be its members.

That is why it is written in the Letter to the Romans: *We know that our old self was crucified together with him so that the body of sin might be destroyed* [Rom 6:6]—that is, the crimes and sins that he calls one body, which he says is destroyed through a good life and the Catholic faith. For all uncleanness and sexual desire is called by one name, fornication; if it is not[1] first removed from the heart's thinking, it unleashes itself in action. But if it is suckled by delight or consent, it grows into a serpent that kills with its deadly poison the one who suckles it. So let us not suckle it but rather put it to death, lest it put us to death. Let us crucify it, lest it crucify us.[2]

---

[1] Smaragdus's text lacks the *non*, which has to be supplied if the text is to be consistent.

[2] No source traced for this passage.

And so Paul says again, *And those who belong to Christ have crucified their flesh with its vices and concupiscences* [Gal 5:24]. But if all the vices have been crucified together, and the flesh as if hanging on the cross lusts after nothing, why do we have a law given us for restraining the vices? It is to be noted that when he said those belong to Christ who have crucified their flesh with its passions and desires, he was at the same time opposing those who think that faith alone suffices.[3]

There was a certain old man, great among those endowed with foresight, who stated: "The power I have seen standing over baptism I have also seen over the monk's clothing when he receives the spiritual habit."[4]

A certain old man was given the grace to see what was happening, and he said, "I once saw in a coenobium a brother meditating in his cell, and the demon came and stood outside; while the brother was meditating the demon could not enter, but when he ceased meditating, then the demon would enter the cell."[5]

---

[3] Auctor incertus In ep Pauli (ad Gal 5); PL 30:821BC; see also Primasius, In ep Pauli (ad Gal 5); PL 68:601D.

[4] PL 73:994B (9); see *Wisdom*, 63, 234.

[5] PL 73:994B (10); see *Wisdom*, 63, 235.

CHAPTER 80

On the Grace of Tears

I t is written that Achsah the daughter of Caleb said to her father with sighs, *Give me a blessing. You have given me some dry land in the south; give me also some well watered land. And* her father *gave her the upper well watered place and the lower well watered place* [Jos 15:19]. This means that we must with great groaning seek from God, our Creator and Father, the grace of tears. For there are some who have already received other gifts of the Lord, signified by the south land, but have still not received the grace of tears.[1]

The soul that thirsts for God is first pierced by fear, and afterwards by love. It first stirs itself up by tears, because when it recalls the evils it has done it is in great fear of suffering eternal punishments for them. But when fear has spent itself in a long period of anxious grief, a certain security is born from the presumption of pardon, and the mind is inflamed with love of heavenly joys. People who formerly wept lest they be led off to punishment, afterwards begin to weep most bitterly because they are kept away from the kingdom. The mind contemplates who those angelic choirs are, what the society of the holy spirits is like, and what the majesty of the eternal vision of God. And it laments because it is absent from everlasting good things more than it used formerly to weep when it was in fear of eternal evils. And thus it comes about that the perfect compunction

---

[1] Taio, Sent 3.45; PL 80:902C, abbreviating Gregory, Dial 3.34; PL 77:300C. The last sentence is not in Taio. Smaragdus would presumably have known the *Dialogues* more fully than he did Taio's much larger work.

of fear draws the mind to the compunction of love. . . . The soul receives the upper springs when it afflicts itself in tears with desire for the heavenly kingdom. It receives the lower springs when it dreads with weeping the punishments of hell.[2]

They used to say of Abba Arsenius that during his whole life while sitting at manual work, he kept a cloth in his bosom on account of the tears that frequently ran from his eyes.[3]

Saint Syncletica said, "When people are first converted to God it is hard work and a great struggle; but afterwards they have unspeakable joy. For just as those who want to light a fire first of all inhale smoke, and so obtain what they wish, so ought we to light the divine fire in ourselves with tears and toil. For it is written that *our God is a consuming fire* [Heb 12:24; see Deut 4:24; 9:3]."[4]

An old man said, "As we carry around with us everywhere the shadow of our bodies, so must we have the tears of compunction with us wherever we are."[5]

Abba Hyperechius said, "Night and day the monk toils, keeping watch, remaining in prayer; the piercing of his heart produces tears and more speedily arouses the mercy of God."[6]

---

[2] Taio, Sent 3.45; PL 80:902B–D, quoting Gregory, Dial 3.34; PL 77:300AB–301A.

[3] PL 73:860C (1); see also 794B (163c) and 807AB (211c); PG 65:[105] 106BC (41); *Sayings*, 16 [18], 41.

[4] PL 73:862D (16); see also PG 65:[421] 422AB (1); *Sayings*, 193 [230–31], 1.

[5] PL 73:864B (24); see *Wisdom*, 3, 8.

[6] PL 73:862D–63A (17).

CHAPTER 81

That Holy Monks Are Called Children of God

The Lord says, *Blessed are the peacemakers, for they will be called children of God* [Matt 5:9]. Perfection is in peace, which means there is no more fighting. And so peacemakers are called God's children because nothing in them fights against God. Those who regulate all their mind's movements to be a place where God is king are peaceful in themselves.[1]

If we are children of God, we have to be peacemakers. For God's children ought to be peacemakers and humble, meek in mind, simple of heart, pure of speech, innocent of spirit, agreeing in affection, cleaving to one another in oneness of soul.[2]

Hence John the Apostle says, *See what love the Father has given us, that we should be called and should be children of God* [1 John 3:1]. Great is the grace our Creator has given us, of both knowing how to love him and being able to do so; and to love as children love their father, since even this would be a great thing, namely, if we were able to love him as faithful slaves love their masters. . . . Now how we are to become God's children, the same John testifies, *But to as many as received him, who believe in his name, he gave power to*

---

[1] Smaragdus, Collect, In Natali Sanctorum Plurimorum Martyrum; PL 102:546AB.

[2] Smaragdus, Via reg 17; PL 102:957D.

become children of God [John 1:12]. We become God's children, then, through faith and love.[3]

What great kindness, what great mercy: he is the Only Son, and he did not want to remain alone. . . . But God sent into this world his Only Son, the very same whom he had begotten and through whom he had created all things, not so as to be alone but to have adopted brothers [and sisters]. For we are not born of God in the way the only-begotten Son was born, but we are adopted through his grace.[4]

By divine gift we first received the power to be adopted, and afterwards we obtained the merit of being God's children.[5] That is why the same John again says, *Beloved, we are now God's children; and what we will be has not yet been revealed* [1 John 3:2].[6] . . . He says again, *So we have come to know and we believe the love God has for us* [1 John 4:16]. We have come to know that Jesus is the Son of God, and that the Father sent him as Savior of the world: *so we believe the love God has for us* [1 John 4:16]. Because, that is, when he had an Only Son, he did not want him to be alone; but in order for him to have brothers [and sisters] he adopted for him others[7] who might possess eternal life with him.[8]

Abba Pastor said that a certain brother questioned Abba Poemen, saying, "Why is it that in the Gospel the Lord says, *No one has greater love than this, to lay down one's life for a friend* [John 15:13]. How is this done?" The old man replied, "If anyone hears an evil word from his neighbor, and though able to reply in like vein fights in his heart to put up with it, and does violence to himself lest perchance he give

---

[3] Bede, In 1 Jo 3:1; CCSL 121:300; PL 93:98AB; see CS 82:184.

[4] Smaragdus, Collect, In Vigilias Natalis Domini, on Jo 1; PL 102:34AB, quoting Augustine, Tr ev Jo 2.13; CCSL 36:17: PL 35:1394.

[5] Smaragdus, Collect, In Vigilias Natalis Domini, on Jo 1; PL 102:34B, immediately following the passage containing the previous quotation.

[6] Bede, In 1 Jo 3:2; CCSL 121:301; PL 93:98C; see CS 82:185.

[7] *Alios*, "others," is in Smaragdus's text but not in Bede's.

[8] Bede, In 1 Jo 4:16; CCSL 121:316; PL 93:110CD; see CS 82:209.

him an evil answer and sadden him—such a man lays down his life
for his friend."[9]

It happened once that Abba Pambo was making a journey with
the brothers into parts of Egypt, and seeing some layfolk sitting down
he said to them, "Rise, greet and kiss the monks so that you may
be blessed. For they speak frequently with God, and their mouths
are holy."[10]

---

[9] PL 73:805BC (201); see also 974D–75A (10) and 1055A (3); PG 65:351
[352]BC (116); *Sayings*, 154–55 [184], 116. Smaragdus's text distinguishes between
Abba Pastor and Abba Poemen.

[10] PL 73:975A (11); see also 794C (164a); PG 65:[369] 370C (7); *Sayings*, 165
[197], 7.

CHAPTER 82

That Virtues Arise from Virtues, and Vices from Vices

All the virtues are supported in the sight of the Creator by help from one another. So one virtue on its own being no virtue at all or very little, they support each other by being joined. No things are good if they are not approved in the eyes of the hidden judge by the witness of chastity, or if humility forsakes chastity, or chastity abandons humility. In the presence of the Author of humility and purity, proud chastity and polluted humility can be of no benefit.[1]

Thus vice is spawned by vice, and virtue is conceived by virtue. Vice is spawned by vice, as in the case of David, who while he did not avoid adultery, committed murder [2 Sam 11]. Again virtue is conceived by virtue, as through the virtue of Gospel preaching the apostles merited the virtue of martyrdom.[2]

Saint Gregory said that God required three things from every person who has attained to baptism: right faith with all one's soul and might, restraint of the tongue, and chastity of body.[3]

Abba Evagrius said, "Reading and vigils and prayer make firm the wandering or wavering mind. Hunger and toil and solitude cause

---

[1] Taio, Sent 4.12: PL 80:925D–26A, quoting Gregory, Mor 21.3.6; CCSL 141:1068; PL 76:192A.

[2] Isidore, Sent 2.33.2–3; CCSL 111:158–59; PL 83:635B. Also in Taio, Sent 4.12: PL 80:926A.

[3] PL 73:855AB (3); see also PG 65:[145] 146B (1); *Sayings*, 38 [45], 1.

concupiscence to begin to wither. Psalmody and long-suffering and mercy repress anger. But these [are effective] when employed at opportune times and in suitable measures. What is done inopportunely or without due measure helps only for a little while."[4]

---

[4] PL 73:915D–16A (20); PG 40:1225 [1224]AB; *Praktikos* 15.

CHAPTER 83

What Is It to Be Fastened to the Cross of Christ?

When a monk takes up his cross and follows Christ, mortifying his members on the earth, being dead to the world, configured to the death of Jesus Christ and firmly fixed to the wood of the Lord's passion, he is fastened to the cross of Christ.

[One who follows his footsteps] so that he can imitate his way of life, be gentle as he was, and meek and humble of heart, not responding when struck, not answering curse with curse, but overcoming pride with humility, such a person can say with Paul, *[I have been crucified with Christ;] and it is no longer I who live, but it is Christ who lives in me* [Gal 2:19-20].[1]

Blessed and exceedingly happy is one who, with Christ living in him, through every prayer and thought and work can say, *It is Christ who lives in me. And the life I now live in the flesh I live by faith in the Son of God* [Gal 2:20].[2] Christ lives in one in whom live wisdom, righteousness, truth, sanctification, peace and fortitude, and the rest of the virtues. One who does not have them cannot say, *Christ lives in me.* But Christ also lives in those who follow his footsteps and are not captive to any worldly concupiscence, so that living for God they seem dead to the world: *[f]or all that is in the world—the desire of*

---

[1] Smaragdus, Collect, Heb 20 post Pent, on Eph 4; PL 102:480CD, quoting Jerome, In Eph 4:23–24; PL 26:508D.

[2] Smaragdus, Collect, Heb 20 post Pent, on Eph 4; PL 102:480CD, quoting Jerome, In Gal 2:20; PL 26:346B.

the flesh, the desire of the eyes, the pride in riches [1 John 2:16]. Monks who have food and clothing must be content with these, because whatever of this world is lusted after or desired must be quite foreign to monks and is alien to the faith, for it is superfluous.[3]

A certain old man, when asked by a brother what he might do to be saved, stripped himself of his garment, and girding his loins and extending his hands said, "Thus must a monk be naked from all that is of the world, and crucify himself against the temptations and struggles of the world."[4]

Abba Hyperechius said, "A monk's obedience is pleasing to God, and one who possesses it is heard when he prays, and will stand with confidence beside the crucified. For in this way did the Lord come to the cross, that is, *he became obedient even unto death*" [Phil 2:8].[5]

---

[3] No source traced for this passage.

[4] PL 73:891B (16).

[5] PL 73:950AB (11); PG 65:431 [432]A (8); *Sayings*, 200 [239], 8.

CHAPTER 84

That Monks Are to Have a Pure Heart and a Good Conscience

Scripture cries out to us, saying, *But the aim of the precept is love from a pure heart, and a good conscience* [1 Tim 1:5]. When he says "aim" or "end," he is indicating the perfection of the precept and of the whole law.

It is charity, then, that makes us dear to God and to people, despisers of this world and lovers of all things good; it is the source of all good things, the origin of charisms and the perfection of all the virtues. A pure heart is that in which there is no deceit, no evil schemings; where no pretence but complete purity reigns; where there is no holding one thing in the heart and uttering something else with the mouth; where the saying is not realized: *They spoke empty things, each to the neighbor* [Ps 11(12):2]. But, *Blessed are the pure in heart, for they will see God* [Matt 5:8]. *The clean of hand and pure of heart . . . will receive blessing from the Lord* [Ps 23(24):4.5].

A good conscience is one where there are no dead works, but that is cleansed from all the filth of sins. And so the apostle Paul says to the Hebrews, *Through the Holy Spirit he [Christ] offered himself unstained to God, and has cleansed our conscience from dead works* [Heb 9:14], that is, from sins. For dead works are understood to be sins. So a good conscience is one where there is innocence whole and pure, complete simplicity and unfeigned faith. That is doubtless a good conscience where there is no vice to point the accusing finger, no taint of sin to cause remorse or weight of crime to press charges; that hates no one, hurts no one, slanders no one, annoys no

199

one, envies no one, but is agreeable to all, inoffensive to all, meek, peaceful, and kind.[1]

Abba Agathon said, "A monk must not allow his conscience to accuse him of anything."[2]

Monks, then, must understand that as angels stand with fear and trembling before their Creator singing hymns, so must monks stand before God singing psalms with fear and a pure heart at the time of prayer. Therefore the glory of the monk, and his praise in the sight of angels and humans, is humility and simplicity.[3] The glory of the monk is meekness of heart and silence.[4]

---

[1] No source traced for this passage.
[2] PL 73:933B (2, first sentence only); PG 65:[109] 110BC (2); *Sayings*, 17 [20], 2.
[3] No source traced for this saying.
[4] Pseudo-Macarius, Ep ad mon; PL 103:452B; see Dekkers, *Clavis* 313, 1843.

CHAPTER 85

That Monks Are to Be Rich in Good Works, and Store Up for Themselves a Solid Foundation

Monks, who are not rich in earthly things, must be rich in holy virtues and good works, because it is not fleshly but spiritual riches that free the soul on the day of chastisement and vengeance. Hence Solomon says, *Riches will not profit in the day of vengeance, but righteousness will deliver from death* [Prov 11:4].

The foundation he calls solid signifies either Christ or the reward of good works that every monk by living well and righteously is storing up in heaven, that he may there be well established *like Mount Zion, which cannot be moved forever* [Ps 124(125):1]. For our eternal home not made by hand [see 2 Cor 5:1] is being built in heaven with good works if it is established on the rock [see Matt 7:24], that is, on Christ; it will not suffer ruin from the onset of anything that comes upon it. It has Christ as its foundation, and so will not fear the assault of anyone. Earthly treasure is broken into and stolen by robbers because it does not have Christ in its foundation. But the treasure that is being stored up in heaven by holy monks, because it has Christ in its foundation, is not broken into or stolen by robbers. The Lord himself orders us to lay up treasure there when he says, *Store up for yourselves treasures in heaven, where neither moth nor rust drives out, nor do thieves break in and steal* [Matt 6:20].

The apostle declares that we take hold of true life there if we carefully keep the Lord's precepts while we live in the present life.

Without doubt they take hold of true life in the future age who, while still living in the world, daily store up for themselves the treasure of their good works. And so elsewhere it is written: *Place your treasure in the precepts of the Most High, and it will profit you more than gold* [Sir 29:14]. For earthly treasure holds deceitful riches; but heavenly treasure prepares life that is both true and eternal. In comparison with this transitory life, that is called true life in which monks rich in virtues reign happily with Christ forever.[1]

Zachary once went to his Abba Silvanus and found him in ecstasy, with his hands stretched out to heaven. When he saw this he closed the door and went out. And entering around the sixth and the ninth hour he found him in the same attitude. About the eleventh hour he knocked, went in and found him resting, and he said to him, "What was wrong today, Father?" And he told him, "I was sick today, my son." He grasped his feet and said, "I will not let you go unless you tell me what you saw." The old man answered him, "I was caught up to heaven, and I saw the glory of God, and I stood there until just now, and now I have been dismissed."[2]

---

[1] No source traced for this passage.
[2] PL 73:993A (1); PG 65:409 [410]A (3); *Sayings*, 186–87 [222–23], 3.

CHAPTER 86

On the Eternal Dwelling That God Has Prepared for the Saints

L et us guard our heart with all care [see Prov 4:23], brothers, as we wait for the father of the family, Christ our Lord and God, who though he was rich became poor for our salvation [see 1 Cor 8:9], so that he might make us partners in his riches and display us as sharers in ineffable future glory. Therefore we must love him without ceasing so that we may also deserve to be loved by him and with him enter that dwelling which has been prepared with the Father for the saints. There we shall contemplate the whole nature of angels and archangels, virtues and powers, and that of all the saints. There we shall be called children of God, there the gates of the kingdom will be opened for us, and we shall enter the inner chambers of the Father; there the Sun of justice, Christ, will appear to us. There God *will transform the body of our lowliness, now conformed to the body of his [Christ's] glory* [Phil 3:21]. There our *youth will be renewed like the eagle's* [Ps 102(103):5]; there we shall receive a crown of beauty and a garment of delight from the hand of the Lord, and we shall say on that day, Let our soul rejoice in the Lord, because he has clothed us with the garment of salvation and righteousness, and has surrounded us with the raiment of joy. As on a bridegroom he will place on us a turban, and as a bride he will adorn us with jewels [see Isa 61:10]. There we shall shine like the sun in the kingdom of our Father [see Matt 13:43], there we shall find immortal and abiding ages. There we shall be given length of days without disturbances and fluctuations, and there will always be the voice of those who rejoice and exult. There a place has been prepared for us, and an eternal dwelling in the Lord's house and in his walls, and an everlasting name that will not be blotted out.

Let us pray, then, dearly beloved, that the kind and loving Lord may bring us into that blessed hope and unutterable joy and eternal dwelling, where there is always praise and exultation and eternal delight. If you desire to belong to heaven, always abhor and despise what is earthly; follow the example of the perfect and imitate them. Do not think and say within yourself, There is much hard work involved in undertaking and pursuing our monastic life; but I am small and weak, and am not able to stand firm in this purpose. Dearly beloved, understand what I say. If you wish to set out for a distant region, you will not be able to run the whole journey in the space of one hour; but step by step and day by day you complete each stage, and after much time and labor you will reach the homeland you desire. That is what the kingdom of heaven and the paradise of delight and the desirable homeland of monks is like; it is reached by means of prayers, vigils, fasts and self-restraint, through tears and obedience, through charity and perseverance, through humility and righteousness and any other possible virtues. These are the stages through which we believe we shall come to the heavenly kingdom and to God our Father. Observe these; do not be afraid to undertake the beginning of the good path that will lead you to eternal life.[1]

---

[1] *Mansio* means a dwelling and a halting place or stage. There is a kind of play on words in this chapter with the word *mansio*. No source traced for this passage.

CHAPTER 87

How Humans Become Blessed

B lessed is the one who hates this world and whose meditation is only on God. Blessed is the one who abhors sin and malice, who loves God as the only kind and loving Redeemer, and constantly has chaste and holy thoughts. Blessed is the one who has been cleansed of all polluted thoughts, and is not involved in the actions of this world, but being totally free in the Lord has been delivered from all the exceedingly vain affairs of this world. Blessed is the one who has always kept in mind that fearful day, who has hastened to wash with fountains of tears and always to attend to the soul's wounds. Blessed is the one who has become like the clouds so as to produce the rain of tears with which to be able to extinguish the flames of all the vices.

Blessed are those who walk in the way of the Lord's commandments [see Ps 118(119):1.3], and living continually in holy works have kept their soul spotless. Blessed are those who have grown daily in good works through holy discipline, having in the Lord a sure hope of seeing him in his brightness, his kingdom and his glory. Blessed are those who have been mindful of the Lord's precept and carefully kept his commandments so as to work and live in them. Blessed are those who have placed a guard over their mouth and a sentry at the door of their lips, so as not to turn aside to malicious words [see Ps 140(141):3-4].

Many are the ways by which people become blessed, as the Lord says in the Gospel, *Blessed are the poor in spirit, for theirs is the kingdom of heaven. Blessed are the meek, for they will inherit the earth. Blessed are*

*those who mourn, for they will be comforted. Blessed are those who hunger
and thirst for righteousness, for they will be filled. Blessed are the merciful,
for they will obtain mercy. Blessed are the pure in heart, for they will see
God. Blessed are the peacemakers, for they will be called children of God.
Blessed are those who suffer persecution for righteousness' sake, for theirs is
the kingdom of heaven* [Matt 5:3–10].[1]

---

[1] Ephrem, *De beatitudine animae*; the second and third beatitudes are reversed
in order. For reference see D. Hemmerdinger Iliadou, "Éphrem (Versions)," *DSp.*
4:819 in paragraph 3.

CHAPTER 88

On the Hour of Death and the Separation of Soul from Body

Blessed are those who always have the day of their death before their eyes, and hasten to be found ready at that hour, without any fear coming from sin or from a bad conscience. Blessed are those who find assurance in that hour of their death, when the soul will be separated from the body; for the separation takes place with great fear and great sorrows. The angels will come to take up the soul and will separate it from the body and lead it to the tribunal of the immortal and dread judge. But when it remembers its works it begins to tremble, and seeing and considering what it has done, it becomes very afraid to leave, out of the fear and great dread it feels. But in fear and dread it advances to the eternal judgment.[1]

So everyone must live with solicitude . . . [lest the soul be snatched amid its iniquities and its life finish with sin]. We are ignorant and uncertain of our coming death, and while people are not thinking of dying they are taken away. . . . For the devil inflames people to vices while they are living, and suddenly when they are dying tries to drag them away to torments. . . . Suddenly, at an hour they know not, they are snatched away by a death unforeseen; swallowed up by the deep, they are handed over to be tortured by

---

[1] Ephrem, *De beatitudine animae*; for reference see D. Hemmerdinger Iliadou, "Éphrem (Versions)," *DSp.* 4:819 in paragraph 3.

the eternal fires of Gehenna. It is written of them,[2] *They spend their days among good things, and in a moment they go down to the lower world* [Job 21:13]. For the apostate angels take the souls of the wicked as they depart the body, to be themselves their torturers in punishments who were their counselors in vices.

[Sometimes] the peaceful summoning of the just commends their most virtuous end, so that it may be understood that they belong to the company of the holy angels from their being taken away from this body without severe distress. And so although human feeling ordains that we weep for such people, faith forbids us to mourn. For those are to be lamented who are swallowed up in the depths of hell, not those who are received rejoicing into the court of paradise.[3]

We read that when a certain old man was dying in Scetis, the brothers surrounded his bed and dressed him and began to weep. But he opened his eyes and laughed. And he laughed a second time. And a third. When the brothers saw this, they asked him, "Tell us, Abba, why do you laugh while we are weeping?" And he said to them, "I laughed a first time because you are afraid of death. I laughed a second time because you are not prepared. But I laughed a third time because I am going from labor to rest." When he said this, the old man at once closed his eyes in death.[4]

They used to say of Abba Sisoes that on the day of his falling asleep, while the brothers were seated around him, his face shone like the sun, and he said to them, "See, Abba Anthony is coming." And after a little while he again said to them, "See, the choir of prophets is coming." And again his face shone and he said, "See, the choir of apostles is coming." And his face shone twice as brightly still, and he was speaking with some persons. They asked the old man, saying, "Father, with whom are you speaking?" He said to them, "See, angels have come to receive me, and I am asking to be allowed a little time to repent." The seniors said to him, "You do not need

---

[2] Isidore, has *De quibus bene per prophetam dicitur,* "Of whom it is well said through the prophet."

[3] Isidore, Sent 3.62.3a, 4ac, 5b, 11, 10, 12 (in that order); CCSL 111:328–30; PL 83:736C–47A.738AB.

[4] PL 73:940C (52); see also 793AB (159); *Wisdom,* 41, 147.

repentance, Father." But he told them, "I do not really know that I have begun to repent." And they all knew that he was perfect. And again suddenly his face became like the sun and all were afraid. And he said to them, "See, see the Lord is coming and saying, 'I will take away my chosen vessel of the desert.'" And immediately he gave up his spirit. There was a flash of lightning, and the whole place was filled with a sweet odor.[5]

---

[5] PL 73:1007CD (6); see also 793CD–94A (162); PG 65:395 [396]BC (14); *Sayings*, 180 [214–15], 14. And see chapter 50 of the present work.

CHAPTER 89

On Innocence

Those are truly innocent who do not harm themselves or anyone else.[1] But those who harm themselves, even though they do not harm others, are not innocent.[2] Trusting in God about his own innocence, David used to say, *Judge me, O Lord, for I have walked in my innocence, and trusting in the Lord I shall not be weakened* [Ps 25(26):1]. And again: *But as for me, I entered in my innocence; redeem me, and have mercy on me* [Ps 25(26):11]. And when he asked the Lord who should dwell in his tent, or who should rest on his holy mountain [see Ps 14(15):1], he heard the divine response saying, *The clean of hands and pure of heart, who have not received their life in vain, and have not sworn deceitfully to their neighbor. They will receive blessing from the Lord, and mercy from God their salvation* [Ps 23(24):4-5].[3]

Rejoice, innocence, and exult. Rejoice, I say, because you are everywhere unharmed, everywhere secure. If you are tempted you make progress; if you are humbled you are raised up; if you fight you win; if you are put to death you are crowned. You are free in slavery, safe in dangers, joyful in imprisonment. Every kind of accusation is leveled at you, every kind of malice is subjected to you. The powerful honor you, rulers support you, great ones seek you, and even those who attack you sometimes desire you. The good obey you, the evil envy you. Your rivals are jealous of you, your enemies succumb, and

---

[1] See Augustine, En in ps 100; PL 37:1286.

[2] Sirmondus, *Index in opera Prosperi*; PL 51:977.

[3] No source traced for this passage.

you can never fail to be victorious, even if in the midst of people you do not have a just judge.[4]

They used to say of Abba Paul that he would take in his hands horned snakes, serpents, asps, and scorpions, and he would split them through the middle. When the brothers saw this they excused themselves and asked him, "Tell us what you did to receive this grace?" He said to them, "Forgive me, Fathers. If anyone possesses purity and innocence, all things are subject to him, as they were to Adam when he was in paradise before he transgressed the divine commandment."[5]

[4] Joannes Chrysostomus, Hom 7, On Joseph sold by his brothers; PLS 4:680 (and with variant readings at 684).

[5] PL 73:1002D (11); see also PG 65:379 [380]D–[381] 382A; *Sayings*, 171 [204], 1.

CHAPTER 90

What It Means to Sanctify a Fast

When we ponder the victories the Lord won when he was fasting, we recognize the triumph of our salvation; let us accordingly sanctify our fasts with religious observances. What else is it, to sanctify a fast [see Joel 1:14], than in view of a fast to will what is holy, do what is just, avoid what is sinful? . . . That person sanctifies a fast who quenches the flames of raging anger with the mildness of a meek mind. That person sanctifies a fast who averts wanton eyes from gazing on what is shameful, using the reins of chastity.

Those persons sanctify a fast who scatter the invectives hurled at them, knocking them back with the shield of patience. Those persons sanctify a fast who curb the uproar of litigants with the art of peaceful speech and language adopting the more prudent approach. Those persons sanctify a fast who root out the thorns of vain thoughts rising up in them, using the furrow of the gospel ploughshare, like one who ploughs his own heart. Those persons sanctify a fast who relieve the needs of the destitute according to their means, with the kindness of a merciful hand. Those persons above all sanctify a fast who, intent on the precepts of the divine law in all circumstances, spit out from their heart the temptations of the devil.

And so, beloved, if we want to offer God pleasing fasts, let us be strong in faith, just in judgments, faithful in friendship, patient in wrongs, moderate in disputes, shrinking from shameful speech, steadfast against unfairness, sober in feasting, self-restrained in pleasures, simple in charity, cautious amid the crafty, sorrowing with the

212

sad, resisting the obstinate, not given to suspicion, silent among those who speak evil, and of like mind with the humble. If we wish to sanctify our fasts with such virtues, we shall by the Lord's gift with unwavering trust and a joyful conscience reach the festivity of the Pasch and the joys of the heavenly promises.[1]

[1] Pseudo-Maximus, Hom 1 On the Fast of Lent; PL 57:307AB–8AB. This homily and those quoted in the next chapter are not found in Maximus Taurinensis, *Sermonum collectio antiqua, nonnullis sermonibus extravagantibus adiectis*, ed. Almut Mutzenbecher, CCSL 23 (Tournhout: Brepols, 1962). They appear under the name of Maximus of Turin in Migne's *Patrologia Latina*.

CHAPTER 91

What It Means to Fast Well

Those people fast well who sustain their hunger by satisfying and refreshing the poor. Those people fast well who, curbing themselves by the memory of the divine judgment, withhold themselves from enjoying any allurements. Those people fast well who chastise their flesh [sprouting as it is with the seeds of the vices] by meditation on holy virtues and love of sobriety. Those people fast well who forgive the injuries a neighbor inflicts with the gentleness of a peaceful heart. Those people offer a most pleasing fast to God who guard their mind from wrongful thoughts, their eyes from lust, and their tongue and hands from contention.[1]

And so let chastity sanctify our fast, patience adorn it, kindness foster it, mercy make it joyful, and humility commend it, in such manner that we may always commend ourselves to divine grace with a twofold fast, that is, of body and of mind.[2]

[1] Pseudo-Maximus, Hom 7 On the Fast of Lent; PL 57:325A–26A. Also, see chapter 90, footnote 1, of the present book.

[2] Pseudo-Maximus, Hom 8 On the Fast of Lent; PL 57:328AB. Also, see chapter 90, footnote 1, of the present book.

CHAPTER 92

On What Is Written:
Many Will Come from East and West and Will Recline with Abraham, Isaac and Jacob in the Kingdom of Heaven [Matt 8:11]

Many will come from east and west and recline at table, not lying down bodily but resting spiritually, not drinking in time but feasting eternally. They will recline at table in the kingdom of God, where there is light and beauty, joy and exultation, glory and blessing, where there is the light of the eyes and the longevity of eternal life; where all find their pleasure, all rejoice, where those blessed Fathers recline at table and all the prophets rest, where the apostles and evangelists are seated on glorious thrones, where the multitude of martyrs is glorified in eternal glory, where the great crowd of virgins exults forever, wearing the crown of immaculate virginity.

O dearly beloved, unanimous assembly, cheerful gathering, brilliant society! Such is the well-pleasing exultation announced ages ago, such is the rest spoken of from the beginning. All who love the Lord have hastened to it; all from among the nations who believe in the Lord and observe the practice of religion are gathered to it. Let all of us as well make our way to it. O religious children of God, let us hasten to it with all our strength! Let nothing call us back, nothing delay us, nothing hinder us from hurrying to this desirable banquet. Let us banish from ourselves all negligence, and from our mind all sloth; let us cast far from us the body's impediments so that we may become family members of this beatitude and rest, and be found worthy of this holy feasting, as has been said.[1]

---

[1] Paulus Diaconus, (ex Origine) Hom 54; PL 95:1195D–96A.

CHAPTER 93

That Every Chosen and Perfect Monk Is Figuratively Both Human and Calf and Lion and Eagle

E very person chosen and perfect in the way of the Lord is both a human and a calf, and at the same time a lion and an eagle. For the human being is a rational animal. It is customary for a calf to be slain in sacrifice. The lion is a brave beast, as it is written: *The lion is the strongest of beasts and will not fear a meeting with anyone* [Prov 30:30]. The eagle soars to the heights and gazes intently upon the sun's rays with eyes that are not beaten back. So all who are perfect in reason are human beings. And because they mortify themselves from this world's pleasures they are represented by a calf. And because by their spontaneous mortification they have the courage of security against all adversity, they are a lion. Hence it is written: *The righteous are bold as a lion and are without dread* [Prov 28:1]. But because in a sublime way they contemplate things heavenly and eternal, the eagle represents them.

Therefore because the just person is human through reason, a calf through the sacrifice of mortification, a lion through the courage of security, and an eagle through contemplation, every perfect person can rightly be designated through these holy animals. . . . The whole intention and contemplation of the saints aims beyond itself, so that it can attain the heavenly things it desires. Whether one is intent on a good work or on heavenly contemplation, what we do is truly good when we long to please him from whom we receive existence. . . . In this matter we must think of how every good thing we do is always to be lifted up to heaven through the intention. . . . Because the elect seek both to please almighty God in good works, and through the grace of contemplation earnestly desire to taste eternal beatitude already, they extend their faces and wings from above [see Ezek 1:11].[1]

[1] Gregory, In Hiez 1.4.2, 4; CCSL 142:48–50; PL 76:815CD–16A.817A.B.C.

CHAPTER 94

On What the Apostle Says: The Flesh Lusts, etc. [Gal 5:17]

The lust of the flesh is a shameful movement of the soul to a state of sordid pleasure. But the lust of the spirit is an ardent intention of the mind to desires for holy virtue. The latter escorts those consenting to it to the kingdom; the former to everlasting punishment. For lust of the flesh first begets the enticements of the vices in the thoughts. But the lust of the spirit on the contrary unceasingly sets holy thoughts before it. The former is delighted with empty fables and words, the latter with meditations on the Scriptures and with the precepts. The former rejoices in displays of earthly things, the latter in the contemplation of heavenly joys. The former seeks earthly joys; the latter prolongs its groans and sighs. The former relaxes the body into sleep and laziness; the latter works in vigils and timely prayers. The former through gluttony boils in the enticements of the stomach and the desire of the gullet; the latter weakens itself with fasts and the torments of abstinence. The former, being subject to impurity, aims to carry out fully and deliberately its longings for the shameful actions it ponders intently; the latter loves the decency of chastity and modesty. The former, aflame with avarice, longs for gain and flees the loss of temporal things; the latter despises the world and claims only Christ for itself. The former, full of envy, allows no one to be its superior or even its equal, but pines away from the wound of inner spite at everyone else's progress; the latter rejoices at the virtues of everyone, and in charity puts before itself those of less importance. The former, continually on the boil,

219

bears nothing with equanimity, but with its mind all upset raises an uproar even unto words; the latter is not moved by any upset, but patiently bears it with tranquil meekness. The former is infected with sadness when it gets a whiff of any adversity whatsoever; the latter is not broken by any grief, but even when it bears evils from its neighbors it is not moved from its interior joy. The former is infected with ambition for honors, and is captivated by human praises and the allurements of vain glory; the latter loves humility, and delights to please its God alone, the observer of the mind. The former, inflated with the arrogance of pride, lifts up a miserable heart; the latter, so as not to be cast down from its high place, humbles itself to the lowest.

But why say more? The lust of the flesh casts down those who consent to it into the multitude of all the vices. But the lust of the spirit strengthens the weary mind[1] with the hope of future glory, in case it should fail.[2]

---

[1] Isidore (Diff 2.31.113a) has *mentem lapsam*, "fallen mind," while Smaragdus has *mentem lassam*.

[2] Isidore, Diff 2.31.109a, 110–13a; PL 83:86B–87B.

CHAPTER 95

What Is the Impulse of the Spirit, and What Is the Impulse of the Flesh

In the elect and the reprobate there are different impulses. In the elect the impulse is of the spirit, and in the reprobate the impulse is of the flesh. The impulse of the flesh urges the mind to hatred, to conceit, to uncleanness, to robbery, to outward glory, to cruelty, to treachery, to despair, to anger, to quarrels, and to sensual gratifications. The impulse of the spirit strongly draws the mind to charity, to humility, to self-restraint, to the largesse of mercy, to interior progress, to works of piety, to faith in eternal things, to the hope of joy to follow, to patience, to peace, to the consideration of immortal life, and to tears. And so it is necessary for us always to consider with great care in all we do where our impulse is leading us: whether our thought is driven by the impulse of the flesh or by the impulse of the spirit. To love earthly things, to prefer temporal things to eternal, to have exterior goods that are not necessary for our use but to thirst after them for pleasure, to seek revenge on an enemy, to rejoice in the fall of a rival—this is the impulse of the flesh. On the contrary, to love heavenly things, to despise what is transitory, to seek what is passing only for necessary use and not simply for pleasure, to be saddened at the death of an enemy—this is the impulse of the spirit. And because those who are perfect always exercise themselves in these virtues, it is now rightly said of the holy animals, *Where the impulse of the spirit was, there they would walk* [Ezek 1:12].[1]

[1] Gregory, In Hiez 1.5.2; CCSL 142:57–58; PL 76:821C–22A.

CHAPTER 96

That All the Righteous Walk Before Their Own Face and in the Presence of Their Face

The righteous walk before their own face because they do not look with any longing at what they have left behind; under the gaze of their contemplation they place the foot of a good work in the eternal things they long for.[1]

To walk before one's face is to seek what lies ahead. But in the present, to walk means not to be absent from oneself. All the just who look carefully at their life and diligently consider how much they increase each day in good, or perhaps decrease in it, because they place themselves before themselves, walk before themselves, and keep watch to see whether they are rising or falling. But all who neglect to keep guard over their life, or fail to examine what they do, what they say, what they think or despise or do not know, such as these do not walk before themselves because they are ignorant of the kind of persons they are in their behavior and their actions. And those who are not careful to examine themselves and get to know themselves each day are not present to themselves. But they really place themselves before themselves and are present to themselves who attend to themselves in their acts as if to someone else.[2]

So we must carefully see ourselves as we see others, and put ourselves, as has been said, before ourselves, . . . and in all that we do we must keep diligent guard over ourselves within and without.[3]

---

[1] See Gregory, In Hiez 1.3.17; CCSL 142:43; PL 76:813B.
[2] Gregory, In Hiez 1.4.8; CCSL 142:53; PL 76:819BC.
[3] Gregory, In Hiez 1.4.9, 10; CCSL 142:54–55; PL 76:820B.821A.

CHAPTER 97

On the Fact That It Is Written: Keep Your Heart with All Care [Prov 4:23]

Perhaps you say, "How can I keep my heart so that it does not think evil?" Listen briefly to the explanation. Clearly you can if you meditate on divine and heavenly things. But there are three things that can free the soul from evil thoughts: holy vigils, prayer, and meditation. Assiduous practice of these confers stability on the soul so that it is occupied in good thoughts and not evil ones. If you wish to have a clean heart in the world, say with David, *At night I meditated with my heart, and I fanned my spirit in me* [Ps 76(77):6]. To the extent that you tame your heart by meditating you will gain a more sublime reward, and you will shine with a brighter light of wisdom and knowledge. If you wish, as was said above, to have a clean heart, never busy yourself with empty stories. Never do and never take pleasure in hearing anything shameful and contrary to holiness. You have already laid aside the things of the world. You have put on Christ the Lord [see Rom 13:14; Gal 3:27].

See that you do not come down from the roof of virtues to look for your former clothing, and do not return from the field to the house [see Matt 24:17–18] so as not to let go at any time of the hem of the Savior's garment [see Matt 9:20; 14:36] or the curled hair moistened by the dew of the night [see Song 5:2], which once you began to take hold of.[1]

Be like a house founded on rock [see Matt 7:24]; let no breath of this world shake you, no wind of wrongful desire scorch you. Be a most prudent bee; let your works form a honeycomb full of

[1] See Jerome, Ep 71; PL 22:669.

223

honey so that you may completely satisfy Christ with your sweetness. Soar above the vices and you will touch him who says to you,
I am a flower of the field [Song 2:1] and a flower of the plain [see
Isa 40:6]. Pluck flowers throughout the Sacred Scriptures, that you
may say with the prophet, *My heart belched forth a good word; I ad-
dress my works to the king; my tongue is like the pen of a scribe writing
swiftly* [Ps 44(45):1]. Therefore, imitate and follow those who have
merited to hear these words, whose character, speech, manner, and
way of life offer a model to those who look attentively at them. For
those whom you see modeling their style of walking on that of the
turtledove—curious, wordy, ready in laughter, without modesty or
shame, telling old wives' and idle tales, ambling along, ready for the
table, unhappy at fasting, whose eyes like burning torches, blown
hither and thither by the changing wind of the mind, scatter sparks
of lust and roll around like a wheel, who in the frying pan of their
own mind are tormented by their own fire—these people, as I said,
avoid, because you read what is written: *With the holy you will be holy,
and with the perverse you will be perverse* [Ps 17(18):26-27].

But love the humble and obedient, those who love *lectio* and are
earnest in prayer, and esteem them highly as members of Christ.
Pay no attention to those I have warned you to avoid; I wish rather
that the evil may fear and envy you, and the good may esteem and
accept you.[2]

---

[2] No source traced for this passage.

CHAPTER 98

What It Means That God Said to Abraham: Go out from Your Country and Your Kindred, and Come to the Land That I Will Show You [Gen 12:1]

Dearly beloved, as we come to the example of blessed Abraham, let us go out from our country and our kindred, and let us come to the land that the Lord is going to give us [see Gen 12:1] after this life. What is our country from which we are commanded to go out, if not our flesh?

Those who despise carnal lusts spit out self-will like devil's poison, and apply themselves frequently to *lectio* and prayer, truly go out from their country; those who scorn cupidity and love mercy, who flee impurity and embrace chastity, truly go out from their country. Those who forsake malice so as to hold fast to charity, who spurn pride and eagerly pursue humility, truly go out from their country. So what does going out of one's country mean, if not to relinquish all sins and fleshly vices?

And come, says the Lord, *to the land that I will show you* [Gen 12:1]. So if we leave our country we shall come to the land the Lord shows us. But what is this land the Lord deigns to show? Let us believe without any doubt that it is the land of which the prophet said, *I believe that I shall see the good things of the Lord in the land of the living* [Ps 26(27):13]. Therefore the country of our body is known to be the country of the dying when it is put at the service of great crimes. But if it has worked hard at the virtues, it passes over by a most happy change to the land of the living.[1]

Now, dearly beloved, we can by God's grace do this, not outside us but within us, if we wish. For if we leave sin behind and devote our attention to the virtues, we have happily gone out of the country of the dying and shall happily come into the land of the living.

And so let the one who was accustomed to curse bless; let the one who was accustomed to slander always aim to utter what is good. Let the one who was accustomed to store up anger in the heart hold fast to patience. Let the one who was accustomed to practice fraud in business, and to seek the world's gain through false balances and measures, strive to raise the mind from all fraud and from all iniquity through repentance and mercy.

Therefore do this, beloved, *and the God of love and peace will be with you* [2 Cor 13:11].[2]

[1] See Augustine, Serm 2 inter App.; PL 39:1741–1742:1.2.
[2] No source traced for this passage.

CHAPTER 99

On the Martyrdom That Takes Place in the Church's Peace

eloved, let no one say that the contests of the martyrs cannot happen in our times. Our peace also has its martyrs. For as we have frequently suggested, to mitigate anger, to flee lustful desire, to safeguard justice, to despise avarice . . . all these form a large part of martyrdom. It is not inappropriately said: to despise avarice, to mitigate anger, to flee lustful desire; for avarice is to be despised, since it procures for us unjust gains, thus gaining possession of us. We would in fact possess ourselves if it did not possess us. Avarice is discontented; like fire, the more it gets the more it seeks to obtain. But anger is to be mitigated; it harms those intending to harm before it harms those it wants to harm.

We join to this that we must flee lustful desire, and the apostle Paul evidently shows this. He preached that all vices are to be resisted, but when he was speaking against lustful desire he did not say "resist" but *flee fornication* [1 Cor 6:18]. If with God's help we must resist the other vices in the present life, we must conquer lustful desire by fleeing from it. . . . Therefore, against lustful desire take flight, if you wish to gain the victory. And do not let flight be a source of shame for you, if you wish to gain the palm of chastity.

Hence, beloved, all Christians, but especially clerics and monks, must flee unworthy and dishonorable familiarity, because without any doubt one who refuses to avoid suspect familiarity quickly sinks into ruin. . . . Among all the contests of Christians none are harder than the battles of chastity, where the fight is on every day, and victory is rare. Chastity was assigned a serious enemy, who is every day conquered and every day feared. And so, as has already been said, let none deceive themselves by a false security, nor dangerously presume on their own virtues, but let them hear the apostle saying, *Flee fornication* [1 Cor 6:18]. . . . And therefore, beloved, against the devil's deadly blandishments and against his helpers, that is, those who do not fear and do not blush to maintain suspect familiarity, so that they may not deceive us by their example, let us continually implore God's help, that he may deign to deliver us *from the snare of the fowler* [Ps 90(91):3]. We know that in the evils we have mentioned above all Christians can find occasions of daily martyrdom.

For if Christ is chastity and truth and righteousness, just as those who lay the snare are persecutors, so also those wishing to defend these virtues in others and guard them in themselves will be martyrs. And therefore if people esteem these with all the power of their mind and show them by word and example so that others may esteem them; if people of their own accord involve themselves as much as possible, and according to their strength strive to defend peace, truth, righteousness, and chastity wherever they are at work, they will receive as recompense from the Lord the crown of martyrdom.

But some will say, "I am young, I will do what delights me now, and afterwards I will do penance." This is like saying, "I will strike myself with a cruel sword, and afterwards go to the doctor." And they do not know that one short hour is enough to produce the wound, but a long period of time is scarcely enough to bring them back to their former health. Someone commits adultery, saying that he will do penance afterwards. Why is he not afraid that a sudden slight fever may come upon him and snatch him away, and that putting off may peter out for him and eternal damnation take its place?[1]

---

[1] Caesarius, Serm 41, parts of 1, 2, 3, 4; CCSL 103:180–83. Formerly attributed to Saint Augustine. For an enlightening account of the painstaking work of Dom Germain Morin in reclaiming numerous sermons for Caesarius, including this sermon and the one quoted in the next chapter, see the introduction to *Saint Caesarius of Arles: Sermons*, trans. Mary Magdeleine Mueller, FCh 31 (Washington, DC: Catholic University of America, 1956), v–xxv, especially xxiv–xxv.

CHAPTER 100

On the Two Altars in the Human Being, of Which One Is in the Body, and the Other in the Heart

Two altars are set up in us, that of our body and that of our heart. Again, God seeks from us a twofold sacrifice: the one, that we be chaste of body, the other, that we be clean of heart. Therefore in the exterior, that is, in our body, let good works be offered; in the heart, let a holy way of thinking yield sweet odors. On the altar of our heart let us always think good thoughts; on the altar of our body let us continually do what is well-pleasing to God.

For we celebrate in lawful order and with joy the consecration of the altar when we offer the altars of our heart and body with a clean and pure conscience[1] in the sight of the Divine Majesty. I cannot grasp what boldness or what state of mind makes one want to rejoice in the consecration of an altar when one does not take pains to guard cleanness on the altar of the heart. As for us, dearly beloved, let us take pains to act in such a way that we may always merit to celebrate a twofold festivity. And as we rejoice in the visible consecration of the altar of a temple, so may we merit to have an invisible spiritual joy by our chastity of body and purity of mind.[2]

[1] Smaragdus's text omits *conscientia* here, turning *munda et pura* from ablative singular feminine agreeing with *conscientia* into neuter plural accusative agreeing with *altaria*. The translation follows Caesarius's text.

[2] Caesarius, Serm 228.2; CCSL 104:902. Olim Augustine, Serm [255 de temp or] 230 inter append; PL 39:2169–70.4.

Bibliography

Augustinus. *Enarrationes in Psalmos.* Edited by Eligius Dekkers and Johannes Fraipont. 3 vols. CCSL 38, 39 and 40. Tournhout: Brepols, 1990.

Augustinus. *In Johannis evangelium tractatus CXXIV.* Edited by R. Willems. CCSL 36. Tournhout: Brepols, 1954.

Augustine, Saint. *Tractates on Saint John's Gospel.* Translated by John W. Rettig. FCh 78, 79, 88, 90, 92. Washington, DC: Catholic University of America, 1988–1995.

Basil, Saint. *The Ascetical Works of Saint Basil.* Translated by William K.L. Clarke. London: SPCK, 1925.

Basil, Saint. *Ascetical Works.* Translated by Monica Wagner. FCh 9. Washington, DC: Catholic University of America, 1950.

Beda Venerabilis. *Opera exegetica: In Lucae evangelium expositio. In Marci evangelium expositio.* Edited by David Hurst. CCSL 120. Tournhout: Brepols, 1960.

Beda Venerabilis. *Opera exegetica: Expositio actuum apostolorum. Retractatio in actus apostolorum. Nomina regionum atque locorum de actibus apostolorum. In epistulas VII catholicas.* Edited by Max L.W. Laistner and David Hurst. CCSL 121. Tournhout: Brepols, 1983.

Bede the Venerable. *Commentary on the Seven Catholic Epistles.* Translated by David Hurst. CS 82. Kalamazoo, MI: Cistercian Publications, 1985.

Caesarius Arelatensis. *Sermones.* Edited by Germain Morin. 2 vols. CCSL 103, 104. Tournhout: Brepols, 1953.

Saint Caesarius of Arles: Sermons. Translated by Mary Magdeleine Mueller. 3 vols. FCh 31, 47, 66. Washington, DC: Catholic University of America, 1956–1973.

Cassian, John. *The Institutes.* Translated by Boniface Ramsey. ACW 58. New York: Newman, 2000.

Cassiodorus. *Expositio psalmorum. I-CL.* 2 vols. Edited by Marcus Adriaen. CCSL 97, 98. Tournhout: Brepols, 1958.

Cassiodorus. *Explanation of the Psalms*: Psalms 1–150. 3 vols. Translated by Patrick G. Walsh. ACW 51, 52, 53. New York: Newman, 1990, 1991.

Evagrius Ponticus. *Praktikos and Chapters on Prayer.* Translated by John Eudes Bamberger. CS 4. Kalamazoo, MI: Cistercian Publications, 1979.

Gregory the Great. *Dialogues*. Translated by Odo J. Zimmerman. FCh 39. Washington, DC: Catholic University of America, 1977.

Gregorius Magnus. *Homiliae in evangelia*. Edited by Raymond Étaix. CCSL 141. Tournhout: Brepols, 1999.

Gregory the Great. *Forty Gospel Homilies*. Translated by David Hurst. CS 123. Kalamazoo, MI: Cistercian Publications, 1990.

Gregorius Magnus. *Homiliae in Hiezechihelem prophetam*. Edited by Marcus Adriaen. CCSL 142. Tournhout: Brepols, 1971.

Gregorius Magnus. *Moralia in Iob: libri I–XVI*. Edited by Marcus Adriaen. CCSL 143. Tournhout: Brepols, 1971.

Gregorius Magnus. *Moralia in Iob: libri XVII–XXII*. Edited by Marcus Adriaen. CCSL 143A. Tournhout: Brepols, 1971.

Gregorius Magnus. *Moralia in Iob: libri XXIII–XXXV*. Edited by Marcus Adriaen. CCSL 143B. Tournhout: Brepols, 1985.

Gregory the Great. *St. Gregory the Great: Pastoral Care*. Translated by Henry Davis. ACW 11. Westminster, MD: Newman Press, 1950.

Isidori Hispalensis Episcopi: *Etymologiarum sive originum: libri XX*. 2 vol. Edited by Wallace M. Lindsay. Clarendon Press: Oxford, 1911. Reprinted 1957, 1962.

Isidorus Hispalensis. *Sententiae*. Edited by P. Cazier. CCSL 111. Tournhout: Brepols, 1998.

Julianus Pomerius. *The Contemplative Life*. Translated by Mary Suelzer. ACW 4. Westminster, Maryland: Newman Press, 1947.

Rotelle, John. Gen. ed. *The Works of Saint Augustine: A Translation for the 21st Century. Expositions of the Psalms 1–150*. 6 vols. Translated by Maria Boulding. Part III, vols. 15–20. New York: New City Press, 1990–2004.

Silvas, Anna M. *The Asketikon of St Basil the Great*. Oxford: Oxford University Press, 2005.

Smaragdus of Saint-Mihiel. *Commentary on the Rule of Saint Benedict*. Translated by David Barry. CS 212. Kalamazoo, Michigan: Cistercian Publications, 2007.

Ward, Benedicta, trans. and ed. *The Sayings of the Desert Fathers: The Alphabetical Collection*. London: Mowbray, 1975. CS 59. Revised ed. Oxford: Mowbray, 1981. Also CS 59.

Ward, Benedicta, trans. and ed. *The Wisdom of the Desert Fathers: Systematic Sayings from the Anonymous Series of the Apophthegmata patrum*. Oxford: SLG Press, 1975.

Scripture Index

Index of Authors and Works

13	54	42	41, 42, 109	12	195
14	63, 64	43	94, 95	13	90, 91
16	80	45	47, 190, 191	22	102
19	111, 112	46	48, 49	25	182, 183
21	62	48	45	26	97
22	5	49	122	33	141
28	138	53	76	37	51, 67
31	36, 37				
37	63	Book 4		Book 5	
40	11	3	87, 88	35	48